W9-AAG-331

the Unofficial Guide® to Making Money on eBay®

Lynn Dralle

WILEY

Wiley Publishing, Inc.

This book is dedicated to Houston and Indiana
The Best Kids Ever!
(And I am not just saying this because I am their Mom.)

I love you guys!
—Lynn Dralle

Acknowledgements

Thank you to my rebel housewife buddy Sherri Caldwell (www.rebelhousewife.com) for introducing me to her agent, Marilyn Allen. My thanks go to Marilyn for giving me the opportunity to write this book.

It was great working with all the folks at Wiley. They are very professional and a pleasure to write a book with. My thanks go to Pam Mourouzis the acquisitions editor and to Suzanne Snyder the project editor. You are both awesome! I also want to thank Susan Thornberg for her excellent job of tech editing. Tere Stouffer did a great job of editing and rearranging text.

I am so grateful for my family and circle of friends who all rallied to make this book happen. I want to thank my dad and stepmom, Wayne and Sue Dralle, who took my kids for most of the summer in Washington so that I could write. Also, a big thank you goes to my mom, Schaara Chase, for always being happy to help (or fly to Mexico) at the drop of a hat. I am also indebted to my sister, Kristin Dralle, for spending two months in 120 degree weather taking care of my kids so that I could finish this book! I also want to acknowledge my brother, Lee Dralle, who always does a fantastic job on graphics and photography. I want to thank my two children for being so wonderful and putting up with a mommy who always has a book to finish. Their independence, sense of humor and intelligence continues to amaze and inspire me. I want to thank my friend Melanie Souve for her positive support and cheerful phone calls. I am indebted to Peter Gineris for helping me to see the big picture and for always encouraging me. I am grateful for Maureen Arcand, who is such a great assistant and friend, and who makes my job easy!

Finally, I want to tell all my fellow eBayers, students and readers of my books that I appreciate you all! I enjoy hearing from you—keep me posted at Lynn@TheQueenofAuctions.com. God Bless.

—Lynn

Contents

M y name is Lynn Dralle, and I've been buying and selling on eBay since 1998. I was fortunate to grow up in an entrepreneurial environment with an amazing grandmother to teach me. My grandmother was Cheryl Leaf, and she owned and operated an antiques and gift store in Bellingham, Washington, for over 50 years.

From the age of three, I was allowed in the store and was trained early on in the art of selling. I started accompanying my grandmother to antiques shows when I was about seven years old. I loved learning about antiques and collectibles from this awesome woman.

In 1993 my grandmother fell and broke her hip, so I moved back home to run the store. For seven years, I got to go to work every day with my best friend, my grandma. We would laugh so hard. It wasn't a job, it was an adventure. My grandmother passed away on August 2, 2000, and I miss her every day. We shut the store on August 2, 2002, two years to the day after she died.

How I got started on eBay

eBay played a huge part in the story of my grandmother and her shop. In 1998, we found that we needed to raise a lot of money quickly for her nursing-home care. Friends had been telling me about eBay for a few years, but I was hesitant to try it until my grandmother got sick.

The set-up to get me selling on eBay took almost a month. During this time, I realized that I needed a way to keep track of my eBay purchases and my eBay sales, so I created two tracking systems, I Buy on eBay and I Sell on eBay. These recordkeeping notebooks were and are a lifesaver, and eBay liked them so much that they carried them for three years in their online store from 1999 to 2002 and they are now for sale in the eBay online shop again! I include blank copies of both tracking sheets in the Appendix for you to use. The notebooks that are sold in the eBay store come with a three ring binder, tab dividers, instructions and 200 double sided tracking sheets.

From 1998 until 2000, my family and I used eBay to pay for my grandmother's nursing care. I was selling $20,000 during the best months. Things that had sat in the store for years gathering dust were now bringing in 10 to 100 times what they were priced. It was incredible!

Why I should be writing about eBay

It was about this time that the Learning Annex in Los Angeles contacted me to teach classes on eBay for them. I taught for them in Los Angeles, San Diego, and San Francisco for about three years. We also decided that a DVD series explaining how to sell on eBay was definitely needed in the marketplace. In 2001, we produced the *Trash to Cash* video/DVD series, and it has been a huge hit.

After we closed the doors of the shop in August of 2002, I realized that I could continue having a retail business without the overhead and headache of owning an open store. What a concept. I also realized that I didn't have to live in Washington state anymore. I could move back to beautiful sunny California.

It was a great experience for me to write this book, because I tried many tools for the first time. There is no doubt in my mind that the things I learned and share with you here in this book will help to increase both of our businesses. I am pleased to introduce you to the wonderful world of eBay and teach you all the tips, tricks, and secrets I have learned in my journey. Please e-mail me and let me know how you are doing at allaboard@mail.com. I love to hear from my readers. Thanks for taking the time to read this book. I appreciate it!

Fortune magazine calls eBay the world's largest online marketplace, the world's most valuable Internet brand, and the fastest growing company in history. Wow! I just call it the best place to make a living as an entrepreneur. There are over 430,000 people just like me who are making their full-time living selling on eBay. I want to teach you how to become one of them.

On any given day, more than 29 million items are for sale on eBay, and eBay says that in 2005 they sold 90,000 items a day. eBay has changed the way the world does business and the company is such a force that *USA Today* does an article every January 1 entitled "The Year According to eBay." eBay is a huge gold mine of opportunity for any person who wants to be his or her own boss or even for any person who just wants to sell a few items for fun and profit!

The only thing constant about eBay is change. eBay is one smart company, and it knows how to stay one step ahead of the competition at all times. For this reason, eBay is always making tiny changes. A tweak with the way a page looks here and the way a page looks there.

If you go to a page and the button that I've described happens to be in a little different position, don't worry. If you ever get stuck, click on the "Live help" link next to the yellow question mark icon that is on every single one of eBay's sell pages and an operator will be there by e-mail to help you within minutes.

Also, if there have been any major changes to eBay, you can check my Web site at www.thequeenof auctions.com/guidechanges.html, and I will post anything that you must know about. My goal is for you to be as successful on eBay as I am and to do this, I want to keep you updated and motivated.

One of the differences between this book and many of the other eBay how-to books out there is that I still sell on eBay every day! I can't stop. I am addicted to making money on eBay. I sell about 400 items a month and have no desire to cut back. It is such a fun way to make a living and I can't wait to let you in on all my secrets and the strategies that have been so successful for me.

Special Features

Every book in the Unofficial Guide series offers the following four special sidebars that are devised to help you get things done cheaply, efficiently, and smartly.

1. **Moneysaver:** Tips and shortcuts that will help you save money.

2. **Watch Out!:** Cautions and warnings to help you avoid common pitfalls.

3. **Bright Idea:** Smart or innovative ways to do something; in many cases, the ideas listed here will help you save time or hassle.

4. **Quote:** Anecdotes from real people who are willing to share their experiences and insights.

We also recognize your need to have quick information at your fingertips, and have provided the following comprehensive sections at the back of the book:

1. **Appendix:** Shows Lynn's I Buy and I Sell sheets that you can use to create similar sheets for yourself.

2. **Index**

Laying the Foundation
for Selling on eBay

GET THE SCOOP ON...
Looking at an overview of eBay ▪ Understanding
basic auctions and terminology ▪ Selling on eBay
versus using an auction drop

eBay Basics

In this chapter, you can get a feel for eBay's humble beginnings and see what happened along the way to make it such a market leader. You will also learn some basic auction terminology (for instance, what a regular auction is as opposed to a reserve price auction) that will make reading this book and going on eBay much easier to understand. Finally, you'll read about the new phenomenon that is sweeping the on-line auction world, the eBay drop-off stores, which are in no way affiliated with eBay. These stores take in your items, much like a consignment store would, and then sell them on eBay. I examine the pros and cons of these chains and stand-alone stores.

A brief history of eBay

eBay began in San Jose, California, in September of 1995 as the brainchild of Pierre Omidyar. With a background in technology, Omidyar developed an interest in computing while still in high school in Washington, D.C. He received a computer science degree from Tufts University and went to work for Claris, an Apple subsidiary, where he helped write MacDraw.

Rumor has it that Omidyar was just messing around when the eBay concept came to him, trying to come up with a site where his girlfriend (now wife—lucky girl) could buy and sell her Pez dispensers. His dream was to have a Web site run much like the stock market for people to buy and sell consumer goods. What a concept! He shopped it around to Silicon Valley's venture capital firms in the 1990s, and no one was interested. They believed that no one would buy merchandise from an unknown seller.

Omidyar's original site was called AuctionWeb. A section of that site was called Echo Bay Technology Group, and when Omidyar went to register that name, echobay.com was taken. He decided to abbreviate it. "What about eBay?" he thought, and history was made!

In the beginning, Omidyar ran the company on his own from his apartment. Because he didn't have time to answer questions by phone, he created message boards that buyers and sellers could use to communicate with one another and establish their reputations. These simple message boards grew into an elaborate way for collectors to connect, and they also established trust. Omidyar took this concept and turned it into the current feedback system that self-regulates how business is done on eBay (see "Feedback" later in this chapter).

eBay grew so quickly that Omidyar and his business partner, Jeff Skoll felt that it was spinning out of control. So, in 1997, they lured Meg Whitman away from her position at Hasbro's Preschool Division, where she was general manager. Whitman was the perfect choice to be this growing company's CEO and, in fact, much of eBay's success has been attributed to her.

Also in 1997, eBay finally got the venture capital it had been looking for, and officially changed its name from AuctionWeb to eBay and considered an IPO (Initial Public Offering). By 1998 eBay had gone public, which made Omidyar a billionaire. Omidyar and his wife Pam are now well-known philanthropists.

eBay has experienced growing pains, most notably during the summer of 1999 when the eBay site crashed for 22 hours. I remember when this happened—it was something that affected many buyers and sellers. eBay took the event as a wake-up call and the technical aspect of the site was overhauled and beefed up.

eBay has done a great job since 1999 in keeping the Disneys and Sun Microsystems of the world selling on the site, while still endeavoring to keep the moms and pops happy. Recently, however, eBay raised listing fees in 2005 and faced an outcry from sellers, me included. Despite this, eBay continues to be the market leader and strives to please both its buyers and sellers.

One of the reasons eBay works so well is that buyers don't have to spend hours surfing the Internet to find items to purchase. eBay has taken the time and work out of buying online. On one site, you can find millions of items for sale. The search is quick, and the results are fantastic. In my opinion, eBay has been successful because it is the perfect economic model of supply meeting demand in the real world.

Over the years, other auction sites have sprung up to compete with eBay. Yahoo!, Amazon.com, and others have all tried to knock down the giant. Despite their efforts, eBay continues to have the lion's share of the market, although auction sites like ubid, Overstock and Yahoo! are still trying to grow market share.

Sellers like myself continue to sell on eBay because that is where the buyers are. As a result, eBay continues to dominate the marketplace, and people spend more time on eBay than any other online site, making it the most popular shopping destination on the Internet.

Business potential on eBay

eBay has nearly 150 million registered users who bought and sold $24 billion worth of merchandise in 2004. There are 430,000 eBay sellers who make their full-time living by selling on eBay. The potential is staggering.

Of the registered users, more than 60 million are active. An *active user* is someone who has bid, bought, or listed an item on eBay within the previous 12 months. That is a lot of people using this site!

eBay estimates that gross merchandise volume (GMV), or the total value of all successfully closed listings on eBay, will be $40 billion in 2005, and that 12 categories will deliver over $1 billion in sales for 2005. Take note of these categories, because there is a huge dollar volume potential in selling these items.

- eBay Motors at $12.9 billion (this is the world's largest car dealership)
- Consumer electronics at $3.4 billion
- Computers and networking at $3.2 billion
- Clothing, shoes, and accessories at $3.1 billion
- Books, movies, and music combined at $2.7 billion
- Home and garden at $2.2 billion
- Collectibles at $2.2 billion
- Sports at $1.9 billion
- Toys and hobbies at $1.7 billion
- Jewelry and watches at $1.6 billion
- Business and industrial at $1.4 billion
- Cameras and photo at $1.3 billion

Moneysaver

A few years ago, eBay began offering company-subsidized health care for PowerSellers (and their employees) who sell more than $24,000 worth of goods yearly. When you get to that level go to pages.ebay.com/services/buyandsell/powerseller/healthcare.html to apply. The rates are great.

On an average day, sellers list millions of items on eBay. The site's thousands of categories range from toys, antiques, furniture, and clothing to big-ticket items like cars and houses. Yes, I did say houses!

eBay is global, too. People from all over the world buy and sell on eBay. I ship about 20 percent of the items I sell to foreign countries. eBay has local sites in Australia, Austria, Belgium, Canada, China, France, Germany, Hong Kong, India, Ireland, Italy, Malaysia, the Netherlands, New Zealand, the Philippines, Singapore, South Korea, Spain, Sweden, Switzerland, Taiwan, the United Kingdom, and of course the United States.

All this can make doing business on eBay sound a bit overwhelming. However, the good news is that small mom-and-pop sellers, people just like you and me, still make up over 90 percent of all transactions on eBay. eBay works hard to keep the small sellers happy.

Understanding auction terms

Before I talk about how an auction works, I need to define some of the more common terms. Knowing the meanings of these words will make it much easier for you to understand the concepts throughout the book.

Bid increment

Bid increment is the amount by which a bid must be increased in order for it to be accepted. For example, if the bidding for an item is currently at $10 and the next bid must be at least $10.50, the bid increment is 50¢. Bid increments are set by eBay. Table 1.1 lists the current bid increments.

 Bright Idea

For an in-depth eBay glossary, visit pages.ebay.com/help/newtoebay/glossary.html.

Table 1.1. Bid Increments

Current Price	Bid Increment
$0.01–$0.99	$0.05
$1.00–$4.99	$0.25
$5.00–$24.99	$0.50
$25.00–$99.99	$1.00
$100.00–$249.99	$2.50
$250.00–$499.99	$5.00
$500.00–$999.99	$10.00
$1,000.00–$2,499.99	$25.00
$2,500.00–$4,999.99	$50.00
$5,000.00 and up	$100.00

Buy It Now

Buy It Now is a feature that enables a buyer to click on the Buy It Now icon and pay the asked price. You can select this option (for an extra 5¢) when you list your item. Buy It Now is much like a set price, but it's often used in an auction format. If there is also a starting bid, once that starting bid has been placed by a buyer, the Buy It Now icon disappears and is no longer an option.

Category

eBay has organized sales on its site into thousands of categories. When you sell on eBay, you must pick a *category* and list your item using that category's number. eBay says that these categories are like the aisles and shelves in a vast store. As a buyer, you can browse the categories and look at lists of items until you find something you're interested in. This is an alternative to a keyword search. (See *keyword search* later in this chapter.) Examples of categories are:

☼ **Bright Idea**

If you find that you use the same categories over and over again, make yourself a little cheat sheet with those numbers. If you keep it handy by your computer, you'll save a lot of time. Some of my favorites are 453 Majolica, 25 Dinnerware-Other, and 38242 Stainless Flatware.

- #453 Pottery & Glass→Pottery & China→Art Pottery→Majolica
- #57886 Clothing, Shoes & Accessories→Infants & Toddlers→Boys' Clothing→12–24 Months→Outfits & Sets

There are quite a few levels to the categories, and some get quite specific. The category numbers serve as quick shortcuts when you're listing your item. Instead of having to search by the different top categories and follow numerous threads, you can just type in the number. As an example, I list a lot of items in category #25:

> Pottery & Glass→Pottery & China→China, Dinnerware→Other

You see, I would have had to go through four steps to get to this category the traditional way.

Dutch auction

Also known as a multiple item auction, a *Dutch auction* involves a seller offering multiple identical items. Dutch auctions can have many winners. A bid is placed when the bidder decides how many of the items he wants and at what price. The winning bids are determined by the total overall value (items × price).

As an example, I could put up 10 glass prisms at 99¢ each. If someone comes in and bids $1.10 each for all 10 of them, and no one else bids, this bidder would get 10 prisms for 99¢ each, or a total of $9.90. If, however, someone else comes in and bids for 8 of them at $1.50 each, who do you think will win? It'll be the person who bid for 8 at $1.50 each, because that total is

$12.00, which yields more money to the seller than the bidder who bid $11.00 for all 10.

The main advantages to a Dutch auction are that you can move a lot of merchandise in one listing, and it can attract buyers who need more than one item and don't want to risk bidding on several different auctions. The disadvantage is that it makes your items appear less special and unique. For this reason, I rarely use Dutch auctions.

eBay store

An *eBay store* is basically a set of special pages on eBay that show all the items a seller has for sale, including buy-it-now items that don't show up in an auction search. If you have an eBay store, a red price tag icon appears next to your user ID. Please see Figure 1.1 for what this looks like. Potential buyers can click on this icon and go directly to your eBay store.

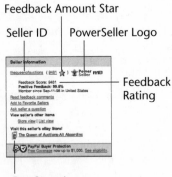

Figure 1.1. This is what my user ID looks like on eBay. It has my user name, "TheQueenofAuctions," my PowerSeller icon, my eBay store logo, and my feedback rating.

Listing items in a store is cheaper than listing them at auction, although you pay a flat monthly rate to have the store. A basic store costs $15.95 per month. The process of listing items in a store is the same as it is to list at auction, except that you choose a different selling format and click the **store with a fixed price** radio button. Items can stay in your store for 30 days, 60 days, 90 days, or GUC (good until cancelled).

When a buyer does a title search, your auction item matching that title will come up for the buyer to view. That same search, however, will not bring up store items unless there are less than an eBay-specified number (this number changes) up for sale at auction.

I have been very successful with my eBay store—see Chapter 18 for more information.

Escrow

Escrow is a great feature if you're selling or buying expensive items. eBay recommends escrow for items that sell for more than $500. In addition to the buyer and seller, a third-party escrow company is involved in an escrow transaction. This is how it works:

1. Once the auction has ended, the buyer sends his payment to the escrow company.

2. After verifying the funds, the escrow company tells the seller to go ahead and ship the item.

3. Once the buyer has received the item and is satisfied, the buyer tells the escrow company to release the funds to the seller.

Escrow is a great feature to use for auctions paid for with cash, money orders, and checks.

  Watch Out!

Unscrupulous sellers set up scams in which the seller sends you a link to a fake escrow company to use. Be very careful, because some of these companies are not real, and they are out to steal your money. Only use escrow companies that are bonded and licensed, and do your research first. eBay recommends Escrow.com, which is eBay's approved escrow service.

Feedback

Feedback is the system that eBay uses to regulate itself. This is one of the ways in which eBay remains a safe place to buy and sell. A user's feedback rating, which is a number, can be found in parentheses next to his or her user ID. Once a transaction is completed, both the buyer and seller can leave feedback for one another.

> +1 point for a positive
>
> 0 for a neutral
>
> −1 point for a negative

The feedback score is the total of all the ratings that a member has received from unique users. This means that if I sell 20 items to one buyer and that buyer is very happy and leaves me 20 positive feedback comments, it will count as only one point.

As a seller, I work very hard to keep all my feedback positive. My rating is now at over 9,000, even though I have completed many more transactions. (Not everyone leaves feedback.) However, once in a while, you do get someone who leaves you a negative comment. I was so upset when I got my first negative feedback, but now I know it's just a part of doing business. I talk more about feedback in chapters 6, 10, and 15.

 Watch Out!

It's a good idea to buy from a seller with a feedback score of at least ten and a high percentage of positive feedback. You can read a seller's feedback comments by clicking on the feedback number in parentheses next to his or her name. Do your research, and don't buy from someone who just signed up to sell on eBay yesterday, has a big zero next to his or her name, and will only accept cash. Be smart! As a new seller on eBay, I highly encourage you to begin building your feedback rating by buying a few inexpensive items. I show you how to do this in Chapter 7.

Final value fee

Also known as a selling fee, the *final value fee* is the fee that eBay charges you when your auction ends. This fee is based on the final sales price of the item. If there are no bids, or if the high bid does not meet a reserve that you set, no fee is charged. Table 1.2 lists the current fee structure.

Table 1.2. Final Value Fees

Closing Price	Final Value Fee
Item not sold	No fee
$0.01–$25.00	5.25% of the closing value
$25.01–$1,000.00	5.25% of the initial $25.00 ($1.31), plus 2.75% of the remaining closing value balance ($25.01 to $1,000.00)
Over $1,000.01	5.25% of the initial $25.00 ($1.31), plus 2.75% of the initial $25.00 – $1,000.00 ($26.81), plus 1.50% of the remaining closing value balance ($1,000.01 – closing value)

For example, if your item sells for $10, you pay 53¢ in final value fees (5.25 percent). If your item sells for $500, you pay $1.31 for the first $25, and then an additional $13.06 for the next $475, for a total of $14.37 (this works out to 2.87 percent in selling fees). If it sells for $2,000, you pay $1.31 for the first $25.00, $26.81 for the next $975, and $15 for the final $1000, for a total of $43.12 (this works out to 2.15 percent). As you can see: the higher the price, the cheaper the overall selling fee.

Keyword search

A *keyword search* is what most shoppers use to find items to bid on. There is a search field on every eBay page; you simply type your keywords into that field and hit the **Search** button located next to or underneath it in order to perform a search. For example, if you're looking for a digital camera, you can type "Canon digital camera" to limit the results to Canon brand digital cameras.

eBay has two different options for bidders to use when they are searching to purchase:

- Title-only search
- Title and description search

When a bidder does a search by both title and description, it typically brings back way too many unrelated auctions. For this reason, most buyers only do a title search. This keyword title search checks only titles, not subtitles. This means that you have to choose the most important keywords to describe your items when you write your titles (see Chapter 12).

The default option (that is, the search option that eBay will assume you want unless you indicate otherwise by checking a special box) is a title-only search. The eBay search engine will look through all current auction listings for auction titles with the keywords you entered and return information about all matches. As an example, I was looking for a Burberry backpack. So I typed in "Burberry backpack" and "Burberry back pack" and found what I was looking for by just using a title-only search.

As I mentioned, most buyers stick to title searches for the majority of their searches, but sometimes it's useful to search by both title and description. You might choose to try this if you do not expect an important search term to appear in the auction title—if, for example, you are looking for all movies featuring a given actor, or all CDs featuring a given musician. The **Search by title and description** checkbox is displayed below the keyword search field.

Insertion fee

eBay charges sellers a fee at the beginning of an auction (the *insertion fee* or listing fee) and at the end of the auction (the final value or selling fee). The insertion or listing fee is based on your starting price. Table 1.3 lists the current listing-fee structure.

Table 1.3. Insertion Fees

Starting or Reserve Price	Insertion Fee
$0.01–$0.99	$0.25
$1.00–$9.99	$0.35
$10.00–$24.99	$0.60
$25.00–$49.99	$1.20
$50.00–$199.99	$2.40
$200.00–$499.99	$3.60
$500.00 or more	$4.80

I try to list items at starting prices that fall at the high end of these ranges. I list almost all of my items at $9.99, but sometimes go to $24.99, $49.99—or even $199. The reason that I do this is to get all the benefit of being at the top of the range. Why list something at $10 when it will cost you 25¢ more than if you listed it at $9.99? That 25¢ may not sound like much to you, but I list 400 new items each month, so it would cost me $100 extra just for that penny difference!

PowerSeller

A *PowerSeller* is an eBay seller who has at least 100 feedback points, of which at least 98 percent are positive, and who sells at least $1,000 worth of merchandise per month. PowerSellers must provide a high level of customer service and sustain their 98 percent positive feedback rating. (Check the eBay site for details.) A PowerSeller gets an icon next to his or her name that has become a status symbol. Buyers also tend to be more comfortable purchasing from PowerSellers.

There are five levels of PowerSellers on eBay. The bronze sells an average of $1,000 per month, the silver $3,000, the gold $10,000, the platinum $25,000, and the titanium $150,000. FYI:

PowerSeller levels are considered private information and not viewable/accessible to anyone but the individual PowerSeller.

Proxy bidding

All bidding on eBay is done by *proxy*. As a buyer, you can enter your maximum bid price, and eBay will bid on your behalf up to your maximum. This feature is very handy, because you don't always have to be checking your computer. eBay will bid the increment required to outbid the other buyers or bid until the bidding reaches your maximum.

Reserve price

The *reserve price* is the lowest price that a seller is willing to let his item go for in an auction-style listing. This feature costs extra money, but if your auction reaches the reserve price, that extra charge is refunded. This is a nice option, because it allows you to set a low starting price to get the bidding going, yet protects you from selling your item at too low a price. Current extra fees for reserve auctions are listed in Table 1.4.

Table 1.4. Reserve Fees (Fully Refunded if the Item Sells)

Reserve Price	Fee
$0.01–$49.99	$1.00
$50.00–$199.99	$2.00
$200.00 and up	1% of reserve price (up to $100)

Watch Out!

The amount of money a bidder is willing to spend on an item is the *proxy bid* and this is always confidential. The final actual bid or selling price may be less than the winner's proxy bid (if other bidders do not drive the price up).

Second chance offer

The *second chance offer* is a neat feature that allows you to make an offer to the second-place bidder if, for some reason, your first-place buyer doesn't pay or you have a duplicate item. You do not pay another insertion fee, but if the second bidder accepts your offer, you do pay another final value fee. You click on a button on the auction page to send this offer.

Shill bidding

This is illegal. *Shill bidding* is when someone places bids on your item to artificially raise the price with no intention of purchasing it. This is a serious offense. To protect yourself, family members, friends, and people sharing computers should not bid on one another's auctions.

Sniping

Sniping is the practice of coming in at the last second to place the winning bid. A lot of software programs will do this for you. My favorite is a Web-based program at www.auctionsniper.com. It costs a small percentage to use but is very inexpensive, and it has won me a lot of auctions.

 Watch Out!

Don't get discouraged if your auction has no bids during most of the time that it's up for sale. Most buyers now bid in the last few seconds—this is called *sniping*. Also, never offer to sell an item early. Many buyers prey on unsuspecting new sellers and ask them to "Please, please end this auction early and add a buy-it-now price. It's my dad's birthday, and I must have this item by Friday." This is just one of the excuses I've heard. More often than not, these bidders are trying to get you to sell your item too cheaply. Let the auction format play itself out. If the item doesn't sell, you can do a Buy It Now for the eager buyer.

Sniping is an important feature to win auctions because you are not showing your hand early to other bidders. The other bidders will not know that anyone else is interested in that item and may become complacent with their bid. They won't feel that it is necessary to be watching the end of the auction because they are confident that they are winning. Then you come out of nowhere in the final seconds with the winning bid.

User ID

The name by which you will be known on eBay as both a buyer and a seller is your *user ID*. eBay calls it your *nickname*. You want to choose a user ID that's easy to remember and is not being used by anyone else on eBay. I sell as "TheQueenofAuctions."

Understanding auctions

You've probably been to a live auction or seen one on television. The auctioneer speaks rapidly, and if you aren't careful when scratching your ear, you may be the buyer of something you don't really want. eBay has taken this concept and changed it for the better, making it easy for both buyers and sellers. You can bid from the comfort of your own home. You don't have to be pressured into making quick decisions. You can take your time and carefully check out the seller and the item being sold, and strategize how much and when you're going to bid.

The definitions in the preceding section should have given you an initial idea about eBay and auctions in general. In this section, I take it a step further and talk about how eBay works.

When you put up an item to sell on eBay you will need to choose the starting price, decide on the duration, and set your terms. You will also need to decide what kind of auction you want to sell your item in. There are two types of auctions: a reserve price auction and a regular auction.

Regular auctions

A regular auction has a starting bid price with no reserve. What this means is that if you start the auction at 99¢ and someone bids 99¢, you're obligated to sell at that price. If you decide that your item is worth $99, in a regular auction, you simply start your auction at $99. If no one bids, you will probably realize that you had set the price too high, and you will relist the item at a lower price.

Here's an example of one of my recent auctions. I bought a broken vase at an estate sale a few weeks ago. It was signed "Royal Preussen" (Preussen is German for Prussia, by the way) and "Germany." It was beautiful, but it had been badly damaged and had been repaired. It was marked $10, and I bought it because it reminded me of all the antiques my grandmother used to sell in her store. I got it home and put it on eBay with a $24.99 starting price and no reserve. I figured if I doubled my money, I would be happy and had nothing to lose by starting it so low.

See Figure 1.2, which shows the vase, and Figure 1.3, which shows the bidding history. The bidding history for any item on eBay is public record and can be found by clicking on the blue **History** button that says how many bids an item has received. The auction for this vase started at 6:35 p.m. on a Saturday. By 7:17 p.m., it already had a bid of $31.68. By 7:39 p.m., it was up to $50, and the user ID of the bidder was prussia-prince. (When I did my research for this piece I found that it was RS Prussia–type and it is very collectible.) This piece steadily climbed in value and on Monday, a bidder with a user ID of theron607 took it up to $175.99. When you look at the bid history, it can be confusing because only actual bids, not the proxy bids, are shown. A *proxy bid*, remember, is a bidder's maximum as opposed to an actual bid, and eBay will never reveal the bidder's maximum (see "Proxy bidding," earlier in this chapter).

☼ **Bright Idea**

To get to your item's auction page, just type the eBay item number into any search box on any of the pages. eBay will then return your auction listing.

So a lower bid was placed for this item on Monday at 6:56 p.m. by bchinacloset. A proxy bid had been placed by theron607 at some point, but we don't know when. We see just the actual bids. By Friday at 5:38 p.m., some bidder (we don't know who) had inched him up to his maximum of $500.99. The winner bgbg had placed a higher proxy bid at 3:20 p.m. on Friday, and that is the bid that took the vase at $501.99 about an hour before the auction ended. Boy, was I happy with that price!

It is really interesting to follow the bidding of your item, and then to go back and see the history when it is finished. You can learn a lot from taking the time to analyze what happens during an auction frenzy.

Figure 1.2. RS Prussia–type vase that sold for $501.99.

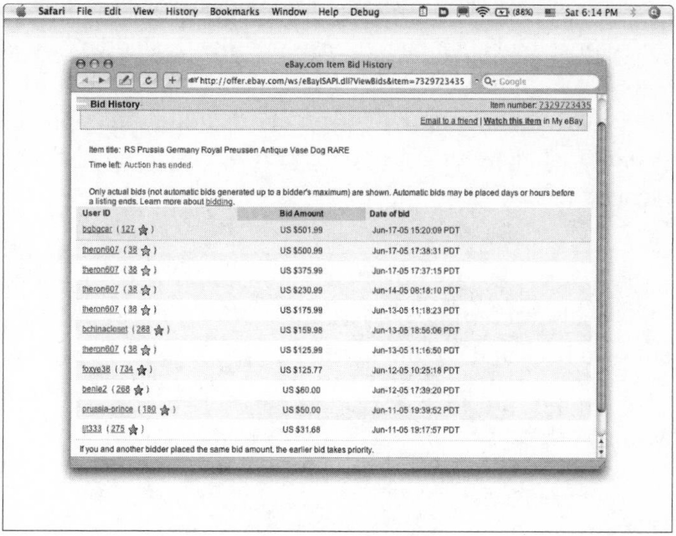

Figure 1.3. Bidding history for RS Prussia–type vase.

Reserve price auctions

Now I take a look at a reserve price auction. I had a little carved wooden bird that I knew was valuable because it was signed by a famous maker. I didn't want to risk selling it for $9.99, so I used a hidden reserve of $1,999 and started the bidding at $99. The $1,999 was the minimum amount for which I was willing to sell the bird. Of course, I hoped bidders would be competing to drive the price higher than that! Over the course of seven days, the price went up steadily. As more and more people joined in the bidding, the price went up to $1,676. Up until this point, eBay placed a note on the page that said, "Reserve price not yet met." Finally, on the last day, the bidding reached $2,051. When it passed $1,999, eBay placed a note on the page that said, "Reserve price has been met." Please see Figure 1.4 to see what this darling bird looked like and the auction page that says "Reserve met."

I was obligated to sell the bird for $2,051, because my reserve price had been met. It turns out that the bidders did get into a frenzy and drove the price up over my reserve price of $1,999. This is something that you always hope will happen. If the bidding had never gone above $1,676, I wouldn't have been obligated to sell.

Figure 1.4. Bird and auction results of the winning bid.

Selling direct versus using eBay drop-off stores

Auction drop stores have been springing up faster than drive-through coffeehouses. I was just at eBay Live (an annual conference for eBay sellers), and there were over 20 companies competing for the eBay drop-off franchise business.

In January 2005, David Steiner at Auctionbytes.com did a survey of 100 eBay drop-off stores, and here is what he found: "It was apparent how labor-intensive this business is, with an average in excess of 20 minutes to research, caption, photograph, and list one item on eBay. This did not take into account the amount of time spent packing, shipping, and answering e-mails about the items. Looking at the results of this survey, it is obvious this is not a get-rich-quick business, but rather a challenging, labor-intensive one."

> **Moneysaver**
>
> As a funny side note, I had an idea for an eBay drop-off store about three years ago and, after running the numbers, decided that I could make much more money selling my own items. I also realized that the overhead (labor especially) would not allow these businesses to make money easily. My personal opinion is that these franchises are not going to make a whole lot of money, and most will not last.

You can make a lot more money selling your own items for yourself. Who is going to do the most in-depth research and really care about your item? Of course, the answer is *you*, not a drop-off store employee working for minimum wage!

eBay is a labor-intensive undertaking, and the money you pay someone else to list and sell your item could be going right into your own pocket. That is, of course, if you have the free time.

Pros of using a drop-off store

If you meet any of the following criteria, an auction drop-off store may be right for you:

- You have absolutely no free time.
- You don't own a computer or digital camera and have no desire to buy one.
- You have dial-up Internet access and cannot upgrade to DSL or cable.

An auction drop-off store will take the mess, the stress, and the learning curve out of the equation and do it all for you.

To wrap it up, the pros to an auction drop-off store are:

- They save you from having to learn the ropes.
- They do everything for you, from photographing and listing the item to shipping it to the winning bidder.
- All you have to do is drop off your item and wait for a check.

Cons of using a drop-off store

If you intend to use eBay as an ongoing concern (as opposed to someone who just wants to get rid of one or two items), there are many more cons to auction drops than there are pros:

- They take a huge chunk out of your sales price. Not only do they charge a percentage for selling, but they charge you the actual eBay listing and selling fees. For example, I Sold It for You charges 30 percent plus the listing, selling, and PayPal fees (see Chapter 7). On average, they charge 37 percent per sale. If you had $2,000 worth of great items to sell on eBay, this company would take $740. Yikes!

- Most auction drops don't take any item that is worth less than $30. Yet, I couldn't tell you what is or isn't worth less than $30, and I've been in the antiques and collectibles business for almost my whole life. Things that I think won't sell for anything sometimes sell for hundreds of dollars, and things that I think will sell for big bucks never sell. It's a whole new marketplace, and auction drop-off stores take the cream of the crop and leave you with the challenging items. They do their research, and if something has not sold for $30 or more, they turn you down.

  One of the nation's largest sites, AuctionDrop.com, goes even further and won't take an item if it's not worth more than $75. I have sold 50,000 items on eBay in the past seven years, and my average sales price is $14. What does that tell you? It tells you that the majority of items being sold on eBay are not in the $75 range.

  Most of the time, when I do my research, I still don't know if something is going to sell or for how much. eBay gives you only two weeks of completed auction research—it is just a small snapshot, and not the big picture that a year's worth of data would yield. The selling price also depends on how well you do with your title, description, photo, and research. And success also has to do with who is watching the auctions that week.

If you go to some of the eBay drop-off Web sites, you see that they often take only easily identifiable items that are signed with the maker's marks, such as Lladro and Wedgwood. They often don't do the intense research required to find out what you have and what it could be worth.

- Auction drop-off stores restrict weight and dimensions so that they do not have to ship anything oversized. WeSellit takes items that weigh up to 150 pounds, but AuctionDrop accepts items only up to 25 pounds. This really limits you if you have furniture or other large items to sell, like a car.

- You take on plenty of risks when you use an auction drop-off store. First, what if your item is lost, stolen, or broken? Most of the eBay drop-off stores have you assume this risk. Second, what if the item doesn't sell, and you forget to pick it up? Most of the eBay drop-off stores donate your item to charity or give it away. What if the company is a fly-by-night operation and neglects to pay you? My very good friends, the Scalises, took some items to a consignment store here in Palm Desert. Their items sold, but they were never paid, and the man who owned the store went bankrupt and closed his doors.

Moneysaver

Here is a great Web page from Ina and David Steiner at Auctionbytes.com. They have done an intensive look at the costs, locations, and terms from over 50 different auction drop-off stores. Check it out at www.auctionbytes.com/cab/pages/consign.

Do your research before you let someone sell your items for you. In fact, you may want to test the auction drop-off store with some cheaper items before you bring in more expensive things.

Auction drop-off stores are very careful to limit their liability. My grandmother always told me never to take items to sell on consignment. It is a huge headache. She asked me, "Who is responsible if it is stolen or broken?" Do your research and make sure that the place you are considering using is responsible. Most of the eBay drop-off stores have you sign a waiver limiting their liability.

Just the facts

- Know that there is a huge business potential awaiting all of us on eBay.
- Take some time to become acquainted with the useful auction terms listed in this chapter.
- Spend some time on eBay figuring out how the eBay auction works.
- Learn what the pros and cons are for using an eBay drop store.

GET THE SCOOP ON...
Finding out about the business and economic
advantages to eBay ▪ Letting eBay save
you from a life of garage sales ▪ Using
eBay to fit your needs

The eBay Advantage

Chapter 2

Bay is an incredible tool that everyone in the world should try at least once, for either buying or selling. Before eBay, if you wanted to make a living buying and selling goods of any kind, you had to invest in a shop or Web site of some kind, fill your store or Web site with inventory and do a lot of advertising. Not having to invest in a store front or Web site is how you can best use eBay to your advantage. eBay sellers run the gamut from the person with just one item to sell to the eBay PowerSeller (those who sell at least $1,000 per month) who makes his or her full-time living selling on eBay. In between these two ends of the spectrum, you find the following types of sellers:

- Someone who would rather use eBay twice a year instead of having a garage sale.

- Someone who uses eBay to supplement his or her hobby with both buying and selling.

- Someone who has a part-time business on eBay and uses the profits to supplement a fixed income.

- Someone who uses eBay to raise money for special causes.

- A family that decides to liquidate an estate of their dearly departed on eBay instead of taking it to a consignment store or selling the house-full to a dealer.

- A brick-and-mortar store owner who is supplementing his or her store sales with sales on eBay.

Fragmented industry—within the eBay model

eBay is considered a *fragmented industry:* an industry with low barriers to entry. This means that eBay is different from traditional business opportunities for the following reasons: few economies of scale (that is, large businesses don't necessarily benefit from being large, as they do in the brick-and-mortar world), high transportation costs (but they're paid by the buyer, not the seller), a highly diverse product line (lots of different types of items being sold), and diverse market needs (people needing lots of different types of items). These characteristics definitely define almost all the small businesses and individual mom-and-pop sellers who are selling on eBay.

In the following sections, I take a look at these differences in more detail and explain why a fragmented industry within eBay means that there is the potential for you to make a lot of money without a huge outlay of upfront capital and without a whole lot of knowledge. In fact, all you will need to know to sell on eBay can be found in this book!

Low barriers to entry

Low barriers to entry means that there are not a lot of financial reasons keeping people from starting an eBay business. It also means that it is relatively easy to get into this business, and people come and go quite easily, both starting and stopping eBay businesses.

> **Moneysaver**
>
> If you can't afford a new digital camera and computer right now, you can still sell on eBay. Just buy one of those disposable cameras that's processed with a CD for transferring photos to a computer, or take a roll of real film and have the drug store put your pictures on a CD when developing. Another option is to borrow a digital camera from a friend or buy one on eBay. I bought a like-new HP 620 last month for only $60. And if you don't have a computer, most libraries offer free computer time and Internet access. eBay selling can be a very cheap business to break into.

Most importantly, you don't need a huge outlay of capital to get started. All you need is access to a digital picture, a computer, and the Internet.

You also need items to sell, but I believe most people are pack rats, and there are things sitting right now in your own home, garage, attic, or storage unit that could be bringing in big bucks. If you don't have anything to sell, pick up some items at local garage sales or thrift stores. This is a very inexpensive way to get your business started.

eBay allows us all to live the "American Dream" and own our own businesses. Anyone can be an eBay entrepreneur without spending a lot of money, and you can get started today. You don't have to go to your local bank, filter through a lot of government regulation, fill out long forms, go to school, or develop highly specialized skills. All of this adds up to overall low barriers to entry.

Few economies of scale (that is, the big players don't have it any easier)

Economies of scale are defined as being able to have the cost of doing something decline the more you do of it. This is not true about your labor to list and sell on eBay. eBay, for the most part, is very labor intensive—the average time to list an item on eBay is about 20 minutes. If you sell multiples of the same item, this time will go down and there will be some economies of scale for you. But everyone, from newbies to PowerSellers, has to spend time listing and selling items on eBay.

It can be true in your shipping that the larger you get, the more your costs and time go down for shipping and supplies. Sometimes, it takes me an hour to ship five items, but only two hours to ship twenty items. But because buyers pay for shipping, as long as you keep your shipping costs as low as possible, you likely won't be affected by the somewhat higher costs for smaller sellers. As you purchase shipping supplies in quantity, your costs can also decrease. And the more you have to ship, the more you can get into a routine that will actually save time.

What this means for you is that if you have the time, eBay can make you money. Because it is so labor intensive, many people stay out of the market, and this opens up opportunity for you. Time is money, and this has never been more true than on eBay. Often, I wish I could clone myself so that I could list more than 100 new items each week. I have tried to hire a lister (a person to take my place), but no one cares about making money for myself as much as I do! Funny how that works.

High transportation costs

High transportation costs are the costs associated with shipping one item from one seller to one buyer. This is typically the way things are sold on eBay. At The Queen of Auctions (my store on eBay), about 70 percent of the time, I sell one item to one buyer. Sometimes, though, the buyer will be enticed to purchase multiple items from me because I offer a break on shipping.

Because the items sold on eBay are typically one-of-a-kind and unique, there are not huge economies of scale in shipping charges. This is in opposition to a Web site like the Disney Store (which I happen to love!). I buy a lot of items on that site for my kids, and I never just buy one thing at a time. A large company like Disney gets economies of scale in shipping because they're shipping multiple items to one location. They save money by putting all ten of my items in one box, not using so many packing supplies, and not using so many man hours to print shipping labels, and so on. eBay, on the other hand, requires a lot of manpower and shipping supplies to ship one item. We spend a lot of money on packing peanuts, boxes, bubble wrap, and packing tape. In addition, the U.S. Postal Service (USPS), UPS, DHL, and FedEx aren't cheap. With the rise in gasoline prices, most shipping charges have done nothing but increase lately.

Traditionally, the buyer is responsible for paying the shipping charges. Some sellers add on $1 to $2 to cover the costs of supplies and manpower. At The Queen of Auctions, when I quote a shipping charge, I always add $1 to $2 to the base rate. And I call this charge "shipping, handling, and insurance." I ship 400 to 500 packages a month, and that extra $2 helps pay my assistant, Maureen, and purchase supplies. You want to always say "handling" in your quote to protect yourself. Sometimes, a buyer will receive a package from the USPS with the costs marked right on the front. Suppose the USPS charged you $5.85, but you quoted $7.50. If you didn't say "handling," the buyer can come back and ask for the difference. Believe me, this happens! When they do ask, I politely explain what a handling fee covers.

☼ Bright Idea

In all your listings make sure that you say "Save on shipping with multiple purchases." Your buyers will be enticed to check out items for sale in your eBay store that they can buy at a fixed price and add to their existing eBay auction purchase. This way, they pay only an extra $1 to $2 in shipping for each additional item.

Highly diverse product line

This strange yet wonderful marketplace called eBay definitely requires a highly diverse product line. The 147 million registered users at eBay are all looking for something different and unique. Of course, sometimes, a handful of buyers do want one certain item, and this cause an auction frenzy. As a seller, this is exactly what you want to happen!

Even though you can specialize and niche yourself as a certain type of seller on eBay, you will still be carrying very diverse products unless you are a manufacturer. As an example, suppose you decide to specialize in baseball cards. This is a well-defined niche, as opposed to a general category of all sporting collectibles. Nevertheless, baseball cards as your target market segment will still yield an extremely diverse product line. You will have diversity in baseball cards based on:

- **Manufacturer:** Who made the baseball card? Is it a Topps, Bowman, or Leaf?

- **Player:** Most people collect by player. Are the buyers looking for Lou Gehrig, ARod, or Babe Ruth this week?

- **Condition:** Are the baseball cards mint in package? Are they still sealed in the original case? Or have they been handled and torn?

- **Grading:** Has the baseball card been graded by one of the top grading companies? Is it now sealed in a plastic case with a grading from PSA like PSA5 or PSA10?

- **Autographed:** Many buyers want an autographed card. Is your card signed by the player?

- **Age:** Is this card from the beginning of the player's career or toward the end? Rookie cards tend to sell for the most.

No baseball card is exactly like any other. I just did a check on eBay for completed auctions with baseball cards, and over 400,000 were sold or listed in the past two weeks (see Figure 2.1). Now that is a highly diverse product line!

Figure 2.1. Completed auction search screen showing 408,824 baseball cards sold or listed during the last two weeks.

Diverse market needs

Buyers on eBay drive eBay's success because of their diverse needs. These diverse needs make for lots of different buyers, each desiring special varieties of a certain product. Because buyers don't want to accept a standardized version and want something unique and special, they're willing and able to pay a premium for it. This is why the auction format works so well.

To be successful on eBay (with a very diverse product line) you will spend a lot of time with certain buyers making sure that you can meet their needs. It is possible that you will work with a customer on a small amount of merchandise. In fact, most of the time, when you work with a buyer, it will be for just one item. I don't know how many times I've spent hours e-mailing back and forth with a buyer to answer his or her specific questions for a tiny $9.99 sale. Then, other times, you won't even speak to someone who spends over $2,000 for an item! Having a highly diverse product line with diverse buyers can favor the small firm over the larger one. This is why eBay works so well for so many small mom-and-pop businesses, just like yours and mine. Finally, we have the advantage over corporate America!

Diverse market needs can also stem from regional and local differences. This is another way that eBay has changed the way the world does business. It is uniting the buyer in Greece that wants a special kind of olive oil not found in his country with the seller of that type of olive oil in Spain. Another example is a child who grew up in Japan and wants an Ichiro Suzuki baseball card not typically found in his country. His diverse need is being met by the baseball-card seller in Seattle, Washington, who stocks all kinds of Ichiro cards, because Ichiro plays for the Seattle Mariners.

Another factor contributing to diverse market needs is not necessarily about the product. It is about the seller's terms. This is another way for you as a seller to position yourself as the seller of choice.

You can differentiate yourself by offering a lot of choices (I discuss these in more detail in chapters 7 and 8.)

- **Shipping companies:** Do you just ship one way? Or do you offer your buyers options like USPS for international shipments and UPS, FedEx, and DHL for the continental United States?

- **Shipping charges:** Do you automatically include insurance, tracking, and e-mail notification? Do you add a handling fee?

- **Payment options:** Do you only accept money orders and cashier's checks? Or do you take all credit cards, PayPal, and even cash?

- **Your feedback:** Do you have a high feedback rating that you work very hard to protect? This is so very important.

- **Ship time:** Most buyers want their items ASAP. If you ship quickly, you will build up a strong repeat business.

- **Customer service:** What are your terms? Do you offer a money-back guarantee?

These are all things to be thinking about as you begin to position yourself to take advantage of this fragmented market with diverse needs.

eBay creates a global marketplace that benefits both buyers and sellers. Sellers typically get more money for their items from an auction format, because they have bidders in countries from all over the world. A global marketplace also benefits the buyers, because they have more choices of items to buy and these items come from many diverse sellers offering many different items and selling terms.

Selling one item at a time

Another advantage to eBay is that you don't have to be a full-time business owner to utilize it. You can decide to sell only one item in your entire lifetime. Maybe that one item is very expensive. It could be a car, boat, or piece of property. Selling this one item on eBay could bring in top dollar and let you experience the auction format from the privacy of your own home.

As opposed to using a traditional auction house for your one item, eBay lets you react quickly and sell even faster. For example, my grandmother had a very expensive Galle cameo vase.

She had bought this vase from Lillian Nassau on 5th Avenue in New York City in the 1960s. It had been appraised in the 1980s at around $10,000.

I considered selling it, and wanted to get top dollar, and thought that taking it to Sotheby's or Butterfield's for a live auction was the way to go. I sent them photos, and then waited four weeks to hear back from them. When I did hear back, the auction estimate was only $1,000, far below what I thought the vase was worth. In this case, I decided to keep the vase. However, if I had wanted to sell it on my own on eBay, I could have named my own price by either starting the auction high or setting a reserve.

Something else I learned from the traditional auction houses was that I would have to have waited until they were having an auction that would compliment my piece, and that was three months away. Selling this vase that way wouldn't have been very convenient.

Suppose you have a car to sell. If you take it to a dealer, he may give you 50 percent of what it's worth for a trade-in. If you sell it on your own by placing an ad in your local newspaper, you may get a few phone calls, but no huge demand. But if you put your car on eBay, the world looks at your auction, and you can typically get more money. You have, in effect, cut out the middleman (the used car dealer), and that extra money goes right into your pocket. eBay is the world's largest used car dealer, and you can sell your car on eBay for a relatively small selling fee.

As an example, I sold my ex-husband's Pontiac LeMans on eBay for him, and I gave him all the money. (Really, I did.) It was in terrible condition, with a lot of rust and mold, and it didn't run. It was a classic—a 1966 muscle car. A local dealer had offered him $200, and my ex-husband wasn't interested in letting it go for that. We had tried an advertisement in our local paper for $995, but got only one interested person, who offered $500. It was time to try eBay. We sold it in October, 2002 and started the bidding at $999. If you can believe it, 2,587 people looked at this auction, and we had many inquiries. It sold for $1,875, and it was paid for immediately with PayPal. We got more than double what we would have in our local market.

The benefits of eBay for selling one item are many. You get to set your own price (you don't have to listen to anyone), and you can sell it tomorrow, if you want. You don't have to wait months and months to get the money rolling in to your pocket! You also get the advantage of a worldwide marketplace looking at your auctions. It's a win-win situation.

Finding an alternative to a garage sale

Just about everyone has taken the garage sale route. You know the drill: You do some spring cleaning, and then you're left with a huge pile of unwanted items. Do you donate to charity or try and make a few extra bucks? Most people do both at some point or another.

A garage sale takes a lot of planning and time. First, you must place advertisements in your local newspaper's classifieds or online. You try and pick a day when you think it's not going to rain. (I'll tell you, in Bellingham, Washington, where I lived for many years, it is almost easier to pick a day that you know it *will* rain.) Next, you spend days getting everything ready, and then you have to get up really early on Saturday and hang signs all over town. And then, even though you say, "no early birds," there is someone banging on your front door at 6 a.m. Not my idea of fun.

Also, after all that work, people have the gall to offer you 10¢ for a 25¢ item or to walk away muttering under their breath, "What do they think this is . . . Neiman Marcus? These prices are higher than retail." Finally, after battling the crowds and actually having things stolen, you count your money and find you have grossed $122.35. After you subtract the money spent for the advertisements, you realize that you just made about $2 an hour for your time. Who needs it? Not you and not me.

The garage sale has certainly lost its luster for me. I think I've held hundreds in my day. We used to have these huge garage sales at the antiques store—we called them the "world's greatest garage sale."

I would send out a postcard to our 1,000-person mailing list about two weeks prior to the event. My grandmother and I would spend two weeks preparing. We would price and price, and then price some more. Using grease pencils and sticky masking tape, we got boxes and boxes of items ready, and then staged them in the basement. Anything that wasn't good enough for the shop found its way into the basement. We would literally empty out the lower level of the store onto the front yard the Saturday morning of the sale. I would have to bring in extra help for that day. Usually, I hired my mom to cashier, and three other strong helpers to move boxes and furniture. We worked from dawn until dusk, hauling out items into the yard. At about 4 p.m., we started hauling everything back inside. It was exhausting. We would finally finish at about 6 p.m. My grandmother loved these days, and she could be found inside counting the loot. More often than not, though, we would end up selling about $1,000 worth from the outside junk. After she paid her five employees $100 each and deducted the cost of the postcard mailing (about $300), she was left with only a $200 profit. Yikes!

Today, with eBay, people no longer have to go through that misery. eBay has often been called "the world's biggest garage sale." (I think they stole that from me!) And it's true. It is like having a garage sale and inviting the world to come, but you have to pay only a tiny listing and selling fee. Amazing! And I've found that I can expect to get ten times more for an item on eBay than I can at a garage sale. This is definitely another eBay advantage.

In addition, you don't have to watch the public paw through your personal items—and listen to their comments. You don't have to invite them into your personal space, so that they know where you live. By contrast, eBay is a quiet and private way to do business. In fact, I hardly ever speak with a customer on the telephone; it's all done by e-mail. What an improvement!

Supplementing your hobby

Let's say you collect lions or tigers or bears (oh my!). There's no better place on earth for you to supplement your hobby than on eBay. The beauty of eBay is that it can be used to buy items that you collect, but it can also be used to sell off items that you no longer want or need in your collection. Many collectors today are using eBay to round out their collections without spending any additional money. They are, in effect, just trading or bartering items to get what they really desire.

As an example, I collect Texas Ware bowls. I have over 100 of these speckled confetti Melmac mixing bowls from the 1950s and 1960s. The common colors are browns, tans, and greens. The hard to find colors are purple and blue. I collect only purple and blue for myself now. When I find a brown, tan, or green bowl at a flea market or garage sale, I buy it cheaply, and then sell it on eBay for about $10 to $20. I then use the profit to hunt for a blue or purple one on eBay.

Along these same lines, I often hunt for misspellings on eBay and can pick up some bargains for my collection. When I just typed in "Texasware" as one word, only 70 auctions came up for sale. When I typed in "Texas Ware" as two words (which is correct), 217 auctions came up. I know that more people look for "Texas Ware" as two words and I can often pick up a bargain when hunting by "Texasware."

☼ **Bright Idea**

If there is more than one way to spell your item, like Texas Ware and Texasware, put both in the title to get more views. Also, if your item is hard to spell, like cloisonné, put all the misspellings in the title. Misspellings like cloissone, cloisoné, and cloissonné will bring more bidders!

Selling your own creations

Craftspeople and artists can use eBay to sell their own wares. Some ideas include watercolor greeting cards, acrylic and oil paintings, handmade pillows, needlepoint, and fishing flies. Crafts are hot on eBay right now. Of course, how much money you make depends on the art form, how much it costs you to make, and how unique it is. A very important factor is whether there's a demand for your craft.

The beauty of selling your own crafts, handiwork, or artwork is that you control the supply and can set the price. No one else will be doing exactly what you are doing, so you can build up a following. Remember that eBay is a fragmented marketplace where sellers can benefit from carrying diverse product lines, such as their own arts and crafts. Remember, buyers are all shopping for unique items with unique selling terms that fit their desires.

Funding for special causes

Another advantage to eBay is that you can use it for special fundraising causes. Suppose you need extra money during August to buy school clothes for your kids, or you need to raise $2,000 in April for your family's upcoming summer vacation. eBay is perfect for this. It is also wonderful for church fundraisers and people in need (like survivors of the hurricanes). In this section, I look at each of these in more detail.

Annual new clothes budget

Say you want to pay cash for your children's school clothes in August. Start in June and gather items from around your home that you don't want or need anymore. Also, hit some garage and estate sales, looking for bargains and spend about $100 on items that cost 50¢ to $1 each. (See chapters 3 and 4 for more information.) The last two weeks of July, list the 100 to 200 items that you've found. Usually, about 70 to 80 percent will sell the first time out if you price them correctly. Your average sales price will probably be $9 to $13. If you list 200 items, and 80 percent sell at an average sales price of $11, you'll have $1,501.60 ($1,760 sales price, less 9 percent in listing and selling fees, less $100 spent at garage sales) to spend on school clothes for your kids. Now that's an eBay advantage!

Family vacation

Along these same lines, get the entire family involved in raising money for your summer vacation. Your vacation may be to the coast for some beach time or even to that family reunion in Kansas. Whatever it is, assume that you need about $2,000. What a great way to teach your kids the value of money and the advantages of being an entrepreneur! Starting in April, have your partner and kids go through their rooms and get all the things that are in great condition that they don't want anymore. I'm talking about video games, DVDs, clothing, electronics, and books. Next, have them help you scour thrift stores, garage and estate sales, and spring charity sales for great bargains. (See chapters 3 and 4.)

Once you have 200 to 300 items, spend the month of May listing these on eBay. I can list 100 items each week in about 15 to 20 hours, but I do this as my full-time occupation, so I assume you can list 50 items each week.

So, at the end of May, you find that you've listed 200 items, and 70 percent have sold. Because you found such great items and many were high-ticket items, your average selling price was $22. You brought in $3,080, less the approximate 9% that went to eBay and the $200 you spent at thrift stores, so you net $2,633.60 toward your vacation. What an awesome feeling for

> ☼ **Bright Idea**
>
> Get the whole family involved in selling on eBay to earn vacation money. Have your daughter do the initial research and measure and note the condition of each item. Let your son take the photographs. Mom and dad can do the actual listings. The whole family can help ship. Get everyone involved to save time and make it a family vacation to remember.

your family, and what a great vacation you will have knowing that you all worked together to pull this off. Congratulations!

Charity fundraisers

Finally, eBay is a wonderful way for a church or other charity to raise money for a specific cause or a person-in-need. Many church congregations and other nonprofit groups rally around donating items for a good cause. Send out a flyer by regular post office mail, e-mail a request, announce it in church, or place a note in your church bulletin that you're collecting donations to benefit the specific cause. The specific cause could be to build a playground for the church nursery, supplement the church building fund, or help a member of the congregation that has fallen on hard times. It could also be to help raise medical expenses for someone who was just in an accident.

Once the request has gone out for donations, prepare yourself for a two-pronged attack. First of all, not everything will sell on eBay. There are going to be items that are just too bulky to ship and other items that will bring more money at a charity sale than on the Internet. Spend some time doing your research and dividing the items into these two different groups. Tag and prepare the charity sale items for a garage sale. Take the eBay items and have a team ready to research, photograph, list, and ship for your online auction sale. Make sure that in every listing you specify what you're doing and where this money is going to be used. Buyers will love to know that their purchase price is going to a great cause.

Running a part-time business

eBay is wonderful if you want to use it as a part-time business to supplement your income. Examples of part-timers are a school teacher who sells only in the summer, a retiree who has a fixed income but works ten hours a week on eBay, or a 40-hour-per-week person who works on eBay nights and weekends to bring in extra money.

School teachers and other seasonal eBayers

School teachers often work nine months and get paid for twelve. They also get great benefits like health insurance, and many still get the summers off (although year-round school is changing this benefit). What a wonderful way for a school teacher or other seasonal employee to get ahead—by selling on eBay.

Summers are typically the best time of year for garage and estate sales, so teachers have a built-in supply chain. Each summer, a school teacher could go to garage sales, sell on eBay for three months, and bring in an extra $1,000 to $24,000 a year. The income just depends on the teacher's motivation level and how many items he or she puts up for sale each week on eBay. I put up 100 new items each week on eBay, and this yields me $4,000 to $10,000 gross each month. It is up to you how much money you want to make.

Retirees

Suppose you're on a fixed retirement (such as a pension or Social Security), and just need a little extra money each month. Then eBay is for you. You can create your own hours and income level.

As an example, my mom's best friend, Kay, has a great retirement. However, it isn't as much as she was used to making before she retired last year. She was down about $1,000 a month. It was a piece of cake for her to make this amount each month on eBay, because she had items from her late husband that she could sell. Kay needed to sell only 100 items each month at an average sales price of $10 to bring in this extra income. Kay added $1 to $2 for each auction in handling fees, and this covered her eBay costs. So, Kay was selling 25 items each week at the $10 average and bringing in the $1,000 a month she required. Before beginning to sell on eBay, she had been bored after her retirement, but once she got started, she often e-mailed me to say, "I'm having so much fun!"

> **☼ Bright Idea**
>
> Use your eBay profits to invest in real estate, the stock market, or just put away for your retirement. You can even use the eBay profits to pay down your debt or pay off your mortgage early. It is an amazing way to help make your standard of living higher.

eBaying nights and weekends

Another example would be if you're already working full time at another job but just can't seem to make ends meet. You can use eBay nights and weekends to help become better set financially. The beauty of eBay is that you can work from home, during the night or during the weekend, and you can set your own hours. It works wonderfully as a supplement to your paycheck. Also, you decide how many items you need to list to reach your objectives (see Chapter 5).

Liquidating an estate

I can't think of a better way to liquidate an estate, which includes valuable items, than by selling it on eBay. I speak from experience. When someone close to you passes away, the last thing you want to do is dispose of his or her estate. However, sometimes, it's a fact of life.

My grandmother, Cheryl Leaf, had an amazing antiques and gift store for over 50 years, in Bellingham, Washington. I ran the store for her for the ten years before we closed it. When she passed away, I just couldn't deal with the overwhelming amount of merchandise. I brought in the best liquidator in town, Theresa Meurs. However, before I gave anything to Theresa to sell, I made sure that I couldn't get more for it on eBay.

Not everything is meant to be sold on eBay. Unique, one-of-a-kind items, and items signed with the maker's mark sell the best on eBay. Unsigned items like cranberry glass, ivory, and primitives may actually do better in a high-end estate sale.

> **Moneysaver**
>
> Most estate liquidating companies take 20 to 30 percent of the sales price. There are also companies that come in and buy the entire houseful of contents, and they will usually pay 10¢ to 20¢ on the dollar for what they expect to get. The companies that hold a sale for you price items at approximately half of the going price in reference books and on eBay. You can do a lot better for yourself and save a lot of money if you have the time to sell those items on eBay.

However, instead of paying an estate liquidator and having that person sell your items cheaply, try your hand at eBay first. Remember that most estate-liquidating companies will come in and work very hard for a week or two getting the items ready for a sale. They then hold the sale in one weekend and are pressured to move items quickly. Usually the first day, Friday, items will be sold at the marked price. Whatever hasn't moved on Saturday will go for half of the price marked, and by Sunday, many items are free or will be donated to charity.

Often, you can do much better trying your items on eBay. When we did this for my grandmother's estate, for those items we decided to sell for ourselves on eBay, we got far more than we would have at an estate sale.

Supplementing your store front

If you're already in the retail business and find your business slowing down due to the changing economic climate, eBay can really help to supplement your sales. Many small brick-and-mortar type stores have been hard hit by eBay. What this retail climate has done is to encourage customers to shop on the Internet, and on eBay specifically, to save money. So, whether you run a store with commodity items or a collectibles/antiques store carrying unique, one-of-a-kind items, eBay has affected you, but in different ways.

A store with commodity items

Let's take a look at a store carrying commodity items. What I mean by *commodity items* are stores that carry new merchandise like sporting goods, electronics, clothing, and toys. What has happened to these retailers is that a lot of their business has moved online, whether to eBay or to other online Web sites. The prices on these Web sites are typically cheaper than in a brick-and-mortar store, because the online retailer is not paying as much as the store in overhead. There's no retail building, not as many employees, not as much loss in theft and breakage, and many other benefits to this online retailer.

Looking to eBay, you find that your competition is now coming not only from these other online Web sites, but also from anyone in the world that wants to sell something. What the experts predict is that prices for new commodity items will inch closer and closer to manufacturer's wholesale.

Here's why: Suppose Sue in Smyrna, Georgia, receives a brand new set of Wilson golf clubs for her birthday. Sue really doesn't like them, but she doesn't want to offend her Aunt Lois who gave them to her by asking for the receipt to return them to Sportsmart. So, she puts them up for sale on eBay. She doesn't care what she gets for them, because it's all money in her pocket. Aunt Lois paid $300 for the clubs, and Sue would be happy with $99, so that's where she starts the auction. Robin in Houston, Texas, finds Sue's clubs on eBay, sees that they are brand new, and is thrilled to proxy bid up to $175 for them, but she ends up winning the auction for $155.

The manufacturer's wholesale price to Sportsmart was $150 plus shipping. Robin got these clubs at very close to the manufacturer's wholesale price. The eBay marketplace is making it very hard for the commodity seller to make a profit, as they are losing money left, right, and center to the online retailers and eBay businesses.

This example hurt Sportsmart and other tradtitional retailers because Robin did not go into her local sporting goods store to purchase golf clubs. She bought them on the secondary market, eBay. This huge secondary market is taking business away from retailers as more and more people are recycling and not purchasing new. And if they purchase new or like new, they still look to eBay for these items where this dynamic marketplace is bringing prices down for commodity items.

As another example, my friend Kathy owns a scuba diving store out here in the desert. She's what's known as a mom-and-pop brick-and-mortar store. She stocks a lot of expensive scuba diving gear, like dry suits and dive computers. What she has found in the past two years is that she spends hours and hours teaching students how to scuba dive. She lets them try a lot of the products for free. She is hoping, of course, that they will eventually purchase from her. However, they often come in and try items on, and then go and buy the exact item on eBay for a discount. It has been very frustrating for her.

She came to me for help, and here's what we did. We started supplementing her store sales by selling her overstocks and older merchandise on eBay. She found that with some of the hard-to-find items, she was able to get more money than the price she was asking in her store! It has been wonderful for her. Kathy also found that when she hears a customer shopping in her store mention eBay, she offers to be more competitive in price. It has been a win-win situation for her.

Antiques and collectibles store

Now let's take a look at what has happened with the antiques and collectibles brick-and-mortar stores, and how you can supplement this type of business also. When eBay really became huge, it was a boon for antiques and collectibles dealers. From 1998 to about 2001, when eBay was not as easy to use, business was great for these dealers. They had to host their own photos on their own Web sites or through a web hosting service, because eBay was not set up to store photos at that time, and there was no PayPal (see Chapter 7 for more information) to make collecting money easy.

Most dealers were getting top dollar for hard-to-find and semi-hard-to-find items. Our antique store, Cheryl Leaf Antiques & Gifts, started selling on eBay in late 1998 and used it to supplement our regular store business. Soon, we were selling about $20,000 a month on eBay, and it was responsible for 50 percent of our sales. It was a tremendous boost to our business.

If you have an open antiques or collectibles store or even a booth in an antiques mall, use eBay to increase your overall volume. Take merchandise that has been sitting in your store or booth for some time (slow-turning inventory) and try it on eBay. As you get the hang of this, you may find that certain items do better in an open store, like furniture, and others, like kitschy 1950s items, may do better on eBay. To learn more about selling antiques and collectibles on eBay, I recommend *How to Sell Antiques and Collectibles on eBay . . . and Make a Fortune,* written by yours truly and Dennis Prince (McGraw Hill).

Turning into a full-time seller

After my grandmother passed away in 2000, I spent the next two years liquidating her store/estate using eBay and an estates liquidator. At the end of that two-year period, there was still a lot of really great merchandise remaining. Instead of giving it away at 10¢ on the dollar, we decided to divide it up among the heirs: myself; my sister, Kristin; my brother, Lee; and my mom, Sharon. I wanted to remain in the antiques and collectibles business and realized that with eBay, I didn't have to have an open shop anymore. It was a very hard decision for me, but on August 2, 2002, we closed the doors of Cheryl Leaf Antiques & Gifts, established 1950.

However, this opened up a huge opportunity for me. I was able to move anywhere in the country to live and support myself as a full-time seller on eBay. I decided to move back to Southern California and do eBay full-time. It was a little scary at first, but soon I got into the swing of things. I relied heavily on the items left over from the store to begin with, but eventually I started going to garage, yard, and estate sales every Saturday. I even began to hit the local thrift stores as often as possible. (I talk more about where you can find merchandise to support yourself as a full-time seller in Chapter 4.) You don't have to rely on the secondhand market to find goods. There are plenty of new resources to tap into, like manufacturers, drop shippers, wholesalers, and even selling goods for your friends and other people.

I still put 100 new items up for auction each week on eBay, and I know that I can make a good living with that amount of merchandise. I also know that if I want to make more money that week, all it takes is more items. eBay is really a numbers game. The more items you put up for sale translates into more items sold. Price-wise, it's such a funny business. I've been in the antiques and collectibles business my entire life, and I still can't predict what will sell for $10 and what will sell for $200. Somehow, it all averages out, so that I can make about the same amount of money each week. If something is going to sell on eBay, it really depends on a lot of different market factors.

There are things you can't really control, like how many other similar items are up for sale that week, and who is looking for that item that week. Then there are the things that you can control, like how good your title, description, and photos are. And did you set your opening bid correctly? And are your terms favorable to your potential buyers? Chapters 11 through 13 get into the listing features and help you take advantage of all that eBay has to offer for a full-time seller.

Just the facts

- eBay is a very easy business to start because it is a fragmented industry.
- eBay has low barriers to entry, which means that it is relatively inexpensive to get started.
- eBay has very diverse market needs and a highly diverse product line—all good for you as a seller.

- eBay is great for just one item and much better than a garage sale.

- eBay can be used to supplement your hobby or for special reasons like a family vacation.

- Selling on eBay can run the gamut from a part-time business to being a full-time seller.

GET THE SCOOP ON...
Reviewing the top ten categories for selling
the highest volume on eBay ▪ Selling new
or used items (or both) ▪ Looking at item
specifics and key tricks

Determining What to Sell

eBay predicts that certain categories will consistently sell over $1 billion dollars per year. Now that's a lot of merchandise and opportunity! In this chapter, I look at ten of these categories and discuss tricks and tips for each of them.

Some categories are broad; others are more specific. Looking at categories is a good way for you to start thinking about where you want to take your eBay business and what items you'll specialize in. It's also a good idea to choose some type of niche and educate yourself as much as possible about the items you sell within that niche. Buy books about your subject, subscribe to publications, and join online newsletters. Remember that the only thing that you can count on in the eBay marketplace is change!

I suggest that you read each section in this chapter, even if the category doesn't pique your interest. You never know what items you may come across in the future. If you've taken the time to educate yourself about which categories are popular, you might get lucky and come across something you could sell that is out-side your niche. Items that people have passed up can sell for big bucks on eBay!

Cars and eBay Motors

If you decide to sell cars on eBay, you'll be selling on a slightly different, but still connected, site called eBay Motors (at www.motors.ebay.com). If you search on the regular eBay home page for a certain type of car, eBay automatically takes you to this connected site.

eBay is the world's largest seller of motor vehicles and was projected to sell $12.9 billion in automobiles in 2005. That means a car or truck sells on eBay every 60 seconds. This works out to over 500,000 cars sold every year. That's a lot of cars!

Fees for selling cars on eBay

The fees to sell a car on eBay are really quite reasonable. In fact, I can't understand why eBay doesn't raise these fees instead of raising fees on smaller, less expensive items. To sell on eBay Motors, you pay an insertion fee of $40 for a passenger vehicle. After a bid is placed or the reserve price is met, you pay a trans-action fee. These are all listed in Table 3.1 by type of vehicle. For example, if you sell a $15,000 passenger vehicle on eBay, you pay $40 for the insertion fee and $40 for the transaction fee, for a total of $80. As a percentage using the $15,000 example, these

---

Moneysaver

Many people today buy used automobiles that don't run, and they sell the parts. They pick up an older Honda or Mustang that still has the seats, doors, door handles, hardware, and so on in good shape, and they sell these items piece by piece. Classic car enthusiasts often will pay a lot of money to get original parts for the cars that they're working on. If you're into cars and love to work on them, check out your local auto junkyard. Remember that you will need a place (like a garage or other storage area) to dismantle these cars. Your neighbors may not like it if you do this in your driveway.

fees cost you only 0.53 percent, which is a little more than half of a percentage point!

Table 3.1. Insertion and Transaction Service Fees

Category	Insertion Fee	Transaction Service Fee
Passenger vehicles	$40.00	$40.00
Motorcycles	$30.00	$30.00
Powersports	$30.00	$30.00
*Pocket bikes	$3.00	$3.00
Other vehicles	$40.00	$40.00

*A pocket bike is a miniature motorcycle (also called a mini moto); this type of racing vehicle is very popular in Europe and Japan.

There are additional features you can use in your listings on eBay Motors. To find out more about these extras, check out pages.ebay.com/help/sell/motorfees.html. As a side note, the listing and selling fees for vehicle parts and accessories are exactly the same as those on the regular eBay site. Refer to Chapter 1, where these fees are discussed.

Selling new cars on eBay

If you deal with cars on eBay, you will most likely be selling used vehicles. However, you could enter the new-car market if you own a dealership or have access to cars at a great price from a local dealer. Also, if there's a new hot car that everyone wants and no one can get, you may be able to purchase it at retail and still make money on it. An example would be the Toyota Highlander hybrid SUVs, which were selling like crazy in late 2005. The waiting list was very long at some dealerships, and the people lucky (or forward-thinking) enough to be the first on the list made money by selling those cars on eBay.

> **☼ Bright Idea**
>
> Remember that when dealing in automobiles, you will typically be taking on more risk because the prices are higher. However, this higher risk can also lead to higher rewards. I have to sell 400 items a month to make a good living on eBay. If, however, I sold six cars a month, that's a good living, too!

The eBay Motors home page is a great resource to find out what's hot. In mid-summer 2005, the top best-selling auto types listed, in order, were:

1. Ford Mustang

2. BMW 3 Series

3. Toyota Sienna

4. Chevy Corvette

5. Harley-Davidson

6. Jeep Cherokee

7. Chevy Silverado

8. Mini-Cooper

9. Honda CR Series

10. Dodge Ram

Another great resource, if you decide to specialize in automobiles, is Joseph Sinclair's *eBay Motors the Smart Way*. It teaches you more tips and tricks for selling autos on eBay.

> **🐷 Moneysaver**
>
> All eligible motor vehicles sold on eBay are automatically protected with free purchase insurance in the rare case of fraud and material vehicle misrepresentation. This coverage goes up to a purchase price of $20,000. To find out more about it, check pages.motors.ebay.com/services/purchase-protection.html. This is a great way for eBay to make the online environment safer for everyone to trade on its site. (If you are selling a vehicle for more than $20,000, you may want to recommend to your buyers that they pay using an escrow service. I discuss escrow in Chapter 1.)

Selling cars on eBay: FAQs and answers

A common question that people ask when considering selling a vehicle is, "how do I ship it?" Generally, the buyer is responsible for paying for shipping and will want to have a say in what shipping company he or she uses, since terms from different companies will vary. Many buyers and sellers use an auto shipper, such as DAS (Dependable Auto Shippers), which is eBay's recommended shipper (call 866-DAS-eBay). Some car buyers will also fly out to pick up the vehicle and drive it to their home.

Another question is how can you get the most money for your item? Here are my tips and tricks for eBay Motors.

■ Always have your vehicle inspected by an independent third party. This gives validation to your bidders and encourages them to buy. eBay recommends two different inspection services on its site. One is SGS Automotive, which offers a 150-point condition report. This company is nationwide and charges $99.50 per vehicle, which includes interior and exterior photographs. Contact them at sgs-ebay.sgsauto.com/order_inspection.htm. eBay also recommends an inspection by Pep Boys at pages.motors.ebay.com/services/inspection/PepBoysinspection.html. The inspection is not as thorough as the SGS one, but the Pep Boys' inspection costs only $24.99.

■ Include this report in the listing or link to it and be very detailed in your description.

■ Show as many photos as possible. Show the interior and exterior from every angle. Show the trunk and the engine. When I sold a Pontiac for my ex-husband, a buyer even wanted to see photos of the floor mats! Be overly detailed.

As you decide how to set reserves or initial bids, here are some quick pointers to use when you first start selling cars on eBay. If you're selling a late model, higher priced automobile, protect yourself and use a reserve auction set at the price you hope to receive. As an example, you may want $10,000 for your

> ☼ **Bright Idea**
>
> When you start selling cars on eBay, it's a good idea to use an escrow com-
> pany to protect yourself and your buyer. I talk about escrow companies in
> Chapter 1. eBay recommends www.escrow.com, and using a company like this
> one is an important safeguard.

car. This price should be what you feel comfortable letting it go
for. It could be the trade-in price that you can get at a dealership
or what you see other similar cars selling for on eBay. (I talk about
how to do this eBay pricing research in chapters 9 and 13.) You
set a hidden reserve at $10,000 but start the bidding at $1,000.
Usually, hidden reserves are at about 10 percent of the reserve
price. This reserve protects you so that you don't have to sell
your vehicle if it doesn't meet the reserve. You can also just start
the bidding at $10,000, with no reserve. A reserve price auction
or a starting price at your asking price is what most sellers with
no experience use to sell a car.

If you have an older and lower-priced vehicle to sell, start
your auction at a lower price with no reserve. This helps get the
bidding momentum going as early as possible. This strategy can
be very effective if you're in a hurry to sell the vehicle, and the
price is not as critical. As an example, suppose you have a Ford
Mustang that's worth about $2,000 according to Kelley Blue
Book (www.kbb.com). To generate interest, you start the auction at $500. Just remember though, that if the car gets only one
bid at $500, you're obligated to sell it for that price. This strat-
egy is often used by the experienced sellers on eBay. I would
wait a while and sell several cars before trying this one!

Consumer electronics

Consumer electronics were projected to sell $3.4 billion in 2005.
This is another huge eBay category with a lot of potential. The
big-ticket items in this category are plasma televisions, which

can sell for up to $10,000. Consumer electronics encompass 19 subheadings that I list here, some of which may be new to you:

- Car electronics
- DVD players and recorders
- Digital video recorders and PVRs (Personal Video Recorders)
- Gadgets and other electronics
- GPS devices
- Home audio
- Home theater in a box
- Home theater projectors
- MP3 players and accessories
- PDAs and handheld PCs
- Portable audio
- Radios (CB, ham, and shortwave)
- Satellite, cable TV
- Satellite radio
- Telephones and pagers
- Televisions
- VCRs
- Vintage electronics
- Wholesale lots

Buying wholesale

Most of the consumer electronics being sold on eBay are new or refurbished. Many eBay sellers have worked out deals with large manufacturers to buy their returns and restocks. Another place to buy these new or refurbished items is through one of the subcategories just listed, wholesale lots. These lots are sold on eBay by many manufacturers and jobbers—middlemen who buy large

> ☀ **Bright Idea**
>
> By buying on eBay in wholesale lots, you can get great merchandise to sell at a decent price. You save time by buying in quantity. As an example, the lot of Apple iPods that sold for $164 each were probably then sold individually. There were ten blue and ten silver brand new 4GBs in that lot. The selling price on eBay for those colors ranges from $144 to $308.67. If you average it out, you can guess that the seller sold those 25 for about $224.00 each. The seller made about $60 per unit without ever leaving his house!

lots from manufacturers and wholesalers and then resell these items in smaller lots to individuals and smaller businesses. When, for example, a store like Circuit City gets several palettes of returns, it may sell them to a jobber, who in turn puts one palette at a time up for sale on eBay. I just checked completed auctions on eBay for wholesale lots in the consumer electronics category. You could have bought 25 Apple iPods for $4,100. And six pallets of high-end electronics went BIN (which means "Buy It Now"—see Chapter 1) for $3,995. The bidders then sell these items individually on eBay.

Profit margins are typically low in this category and the risk of returns is high. As an example, in the lot of 25 iPods, the seller may have had to take back two units as damaged. The seller would have been able to sell the damaged units on eBay as defective, noting the condition as "as is" and get about $40 per unit. This would lower his profit per unit (see Bright Idea, above) quite substantially, though, from $60 to $45. As a general rule, you must have some experience in electronics to sell wholesale items in this category.

Selling hot retail items

You can do well in consumer electronics by buying new right from the retail chains when a new electronic item comes out. Because the item is so hot, everyone wants it and will pay a premium. The apple-green iPod was so hot when it first came out in 2005 that people were paying double the original retail price.

Watch the news, read consumer electronics magazines, and be ready to hit your Circuit City, Best Buy, and Target to purchase some of the newest trends before everyone knows about them. Education is money.

Carrying vintage electronics

Don't pass up used electronics at garage and estate sales. Just make sure you know what you're doing and have researched the marketplace. Old 8-track players, vintage amps, and calculators from the 1950s to 1970s (see Figure 3.1) are bringing in the big bucks. This is what is known as the millennium effect. Because technology progresses so rapidly, items invented or popularized in the 1950s to even 1990 now seem ancient.

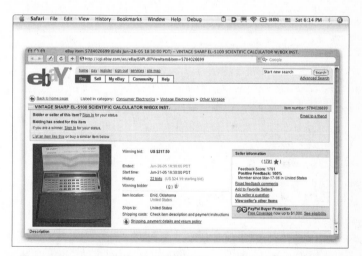

Figure 3.1. A vintage Sharp EL-5100 scientific calculator with the original box sold for $217.50. The original box helped to sell it for so much but was not the only reason. Don't you have one in a desk drawer somewhere?

Stay current on what's hot in the vintage consumer electronics marketplace by doing a completed auction search for vintage in the consumer electronics category and sorting by highest price first. First, click the **Advanced Search** link at the top right of any eBay page. On the next page, click the **completed auctions**

only box, type in "vintage" for your keyword, and choose the **Consumer Electronics** category from the drop down category box. Choose **Sort by Highest Price First** from the drop-down box at the bottom of the page, then click **Search** (see Figure 3.2).

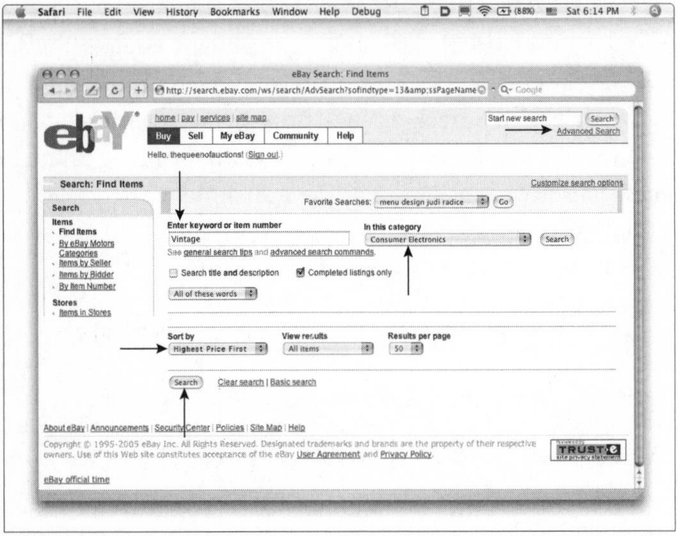

Figure 3.2. A computer screen shot showing the boxes you click to do your completed auction vintage research for Consumer Electronics

Tips for selling electronics

A tip for this category is that when you buy in wholesale lots on eBay and then resell on eBay, buy with your user ID hidden. Many of the wholesale lot sellers hold what's called a private auction. They do this so that your user ID is not shown as the winning bidder. It will say for the winning buyer: "User ID kept private." This keeps you anonymous, so that no one can find out how much you make when you break these items out into separate auctions. The Apple iPod auction was a private auction, so I couldn't search by the user's ID to see how much he sold each of those items for and how much he made.

Another way to protect yourself is to have two separate user IDs, one for buying and one for selling. I do this so that no one can see what I'm buying for resale. I also do this so that around Christmas and birthday times, my nosy friends and relatives can't see what I'm purchasing.

The electronics category tends to get a lot of new eBay buyers, who just signed up and may bid your items up very high. Without having purchased before, though, you don't know how reliable they are. You may want to say that you will accept bids only from eBay bidders with a 10 or more in feedback to protect yourself from non-paying bidders. I discuss feedback more in chapters 7 and 16.

Computers and networking

Computers and networking is another huge area of opportunity. It comes in a close third place on eBay's list, with only $200 million separating it from consumer electronics. The most expensive items in this category are networking components that sell in the $10,000 range. Most of the sellers in the upper end of this category use BIN (Buy It Now) for their items.

You have to have a general, if not technical, knowledge of how all these computer pieces fit together, so that you can convince your buyers that you're the right person to purchase from. To get you thinking about what is in this category, here's a look at the subcategories:

- Apple Macintosh computers
- Desktop PC components
- Desktop PCs
- Drives, controllers, and storage
- Input devices
- Laptop parts and accessories
- Laptops, notebooks
- Monitors and projectors

- Networking
- Printers
- Printer supplies and accessories
- Scanners
- Software
- Technology books
- Vintage computing products
- Other hardware and services

I did a completed auction search to determine whether the items selling in this category were mostly new or used. When I searched by "new" in this category, there were 250,620 items sold or listed in the past two weeks. When I searched by "like new," there were only 6,680 items. Searching by "refurbished" brought up only 1,354 items. Even more interesting was when I searched by MIB (which means mint in box), there were only 176 items sold or listed in the past two weeks. If you're going to sell new computers and networking equipment on eBay, remember to use "new" in your title, not "MIB."

To get an inventory of new computer items, work with a wholesaler, jobber, or the manufacturer directly. Or you can buy on eBay in the wholesale lot category. There were 23,862 wholesale lots sold or listed in this category in the past two weeks, so that's a great place to look for merchandise. Also, if you're interested in computers and technology and decide that this is going to be your niche, you may want to work with some of your local computer repair stores and buy their refurbished units.

A quick search told me that there were 1,815 vintage items sold or listed in this category in the past two weeks. If you can believe it, old computers, laptops, and keyboards from the 1970s to the 1980s are becoming very collectible. You can find a lot of used computers and accessories at garage and yard sales for practically nothing (see Figure 3.3). Educate yourself by using eBay to do research. Do the completed auction search by typing the word **vintage** in the computers and networking category.

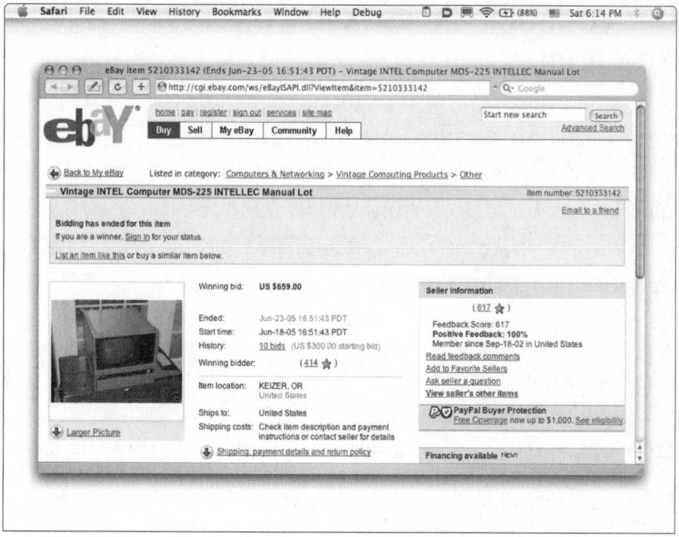

Figure 3.3. A vintage Intel computer MDS-225 from the 1970s sold for $659.00 from eBay seller Smiths4343. I bet you can find something like this at a yard sale. *Auction courtesy of seller Smiths4343.*

Shipping in this category can be tricky, because a lot of the items are huge. "Local pick-up only" can be an option, or you can arrange for shipping from a local carrier. The buyer typically pays the shipping costs.

Clothing, shoes, and accessories

I love the clothing, shoes, and accessories category, because it's a large-volume area with tons of potential for the average eBay seller—you don't have to be an electronics or computer expert to make money in this area. This category has gone over the $3 billion mark. Another reason I like clothing is because it's so easy to ship. Most clothing can be put right into a Priority Mail box or envelope that comes free from the U.S. post office (if you pay for Priority Mail shipping), and this makes your shipping a breeze. I get into a lot more detail about shipping in Chapter 8.

How clothing, shoes, and accessories sell on eBay

Taking a look at the subcategories in this area is very interesting. I took the number of listings from a two-week period and looked at them as a percent to the total (see Table 3.2). You see that there's a huge opportunity in women's clothing, as it makes up the lion's share of this category with 38 percent. The next largest category is men's clothing at 16 percent.

Table 3.2. Market Data for Clothing, Shoes, and Accessories		
Category	Number of Listings	Percent of Total
Infants and toddlers	342,383	7.19%
Boys	118,451	2.49%
Girls	252,425	5.30%
Men's accessories	244,292	5.13%
Men's clothing	791,295	16.61%
Men's shoes	158,994	3.34%
Uniforms	18,929	0.40%
Wedding apparel	63,683	1.34%
Women's accessories	459,228	9.64%
Women's clothing	1,817,671	38.16%
Women's shoes	339,064	7.12%
Vintage	131,513	2.76%
Wholesale lots	25,501	0.54%
Total	4,763,429	100.00%

> ☼ **Bright Idea**
>
> When you sell clothing, shoes, and accessories on eBay, you find two abbre-
> viations that are used a lot. They are MWT (mint with tag/s) and NWT (new
> with tag/s). I always thought that they were equal and similarly used, and,
> in fact, they do mean the same thing. But many more people use NWT than
> MWT, and you want to do the same. After doing a completed auction search
> in this category with both, I found that only 189 listings used MWT, while
> 621,360 used NWT. Always use NWT (new with tag/s).

When I searched to see whether these were new or used items, here's what I found. People who sell gently used clothing typically do not put "used" in the title, and I found only 12,588 listings with that term. "Like new" is a better term than "used," and there were only 60,104 listings (roughly 1 percent) with that in the title.

There were 1,268,521 sold or listed items in that same two-week period that had "new" in the title. Taking out the 60,104 listing for "like new" leaves us with 1,208,417 with just "new" in the title. This works out to about 26 percent being sold with just "new" in the title.

Tips for selling clothing, shoes, and accessories

When you list clothing, shoes, and accessories on eBay, make sure you describe each item very completely. Always list the size and dimensions (length from waist, length from shoulder, bust size, and so on), because sizes by manufacturer can vary. Also list the color, type of fabric, and condition (stains, rips, and so on). Many buyers also look for items from a smoke-free environment. Make sure that you say this in your listing (assuming it's true).

Clothing is a great category in which to find your niche, because it is readily available. New clothing can be picked up at department store sales, especially when items are marked down 50 percent plus an additional percentage off. Also, when the season is over, you can pick up clothes at really great prices and hold them for the next season. As an example, out here in the desert, in June and July, many of the clothing stores close up for the hot summer months. Just prior to closing for those months, you can get designer duds at 10¢ to 20¢ on the dollar. Many can be sold now, but even winter fashions can be saved for four months until fall.

Also, buy wholesale lots on eBay and sell them individually. One of my students from my Learning Annex classes in Los Angeles was buying boxes full of QVC returns on eBay, breaking them out by the piece, and making about 30 percent profit.

Keep track of the hottest trends for young girls and women, and buy these new from your local stores. These items, especially purses, can go for big bucks in bidding wars. Balenciaga motorcycle handbags were very much in demand in 2005. Furry Ugg boots were all the rage in 2004. Junior brands that (at least for the moment) are always hot include Abercrombie & Fitch, Roxy, and Tommy H. Check out styles like hoodies, ponchos, and who's making the hottest jeans this season. Watch what Hollywood is wearing and look for those styles before middle America catches on. You can make a lot of money by being ahead of the curve with fashion.

Used clothing can be found all over. Thrift stores and garage sales, yard sales, and estate sales are perfect for this. Make sure you look for clothing that still has the price tags or is in excellent condition. I bought a gently used St. John knit outfit at a consignment store (that was going out of business) for $35. If you can believe it, it sold on eBay for $480. That's the kind of return on investment that I like! Educate yourself with completed auction research to see which brands are hot. Keep a list of popular brands with you at all times when you're out shopping.

Another great idea for clothing is to sell your kids' used clothes by the lot as they grow out of them. Some of my friends do this every season and make enough money to buy their kids new school clothes. It is a great way to recycle and save yourself some money. Popular children's (toddlers and infants) brands include Gap, Old Navy, Gymboree, and Ralph Lauren.

Don't overlook the vintage category for clothing (see Figure 3.4). Clothes from the 1950s, '60s, and '70s are very hip and fashionable now. Think Hawaiiana, Western American, and Pucci.

Figure 3.4. A vintage Hawaiian shirt from the 1940s sold for $850 on eBay. Vintage clothing can be very profitable.

Books, movies, and music

The books, movies, and music category is huge, at $2.7 billion projected for 2005. eBay has grouped three large top categories together to create this monster. As you can see in Table 3.3, books, movies, and music each account for close to 33 percent of the grand total. They are really pretty equally divided.

Table 3.3. Market Data for Books, Movies, and Music

Category	Number of Listings	Percent of Total	Percent of Total
Books			
Accessories	6,220	0.49%	
Antiquarian and collectible	132,654	10.43%	
Audio books	55,625	4.37%	
Catalogs	7,414	0.58%	
Children's books	104,302	8.20%	
Fiction books	258,406	20.32%	
Magazine back issues	124,114	9.76%	
Magazine subscriptions	13,805	1.09%	
Nonfiction books	428,820	33.72%	
Textbooks, education	111,449	8.76%	
Wholesale	7,446	0.59%	
Other	21,431	1.69%	
Total	**1,271,686**	**100.00%**	**35.93%**
DVDs and movies			
DVDs	835,848	73.90%	
Film	7,545	0.67%	
Laserdisc	11,647	1.03%	
VHS	262,618	23.22%	
VHS non-US (PAL)	2,302	0.20%	

Category	Number of Listings	Percent of Total	Percent of Total
DVDs and movies (continued)			
Other formats	4,626	0.41%	
Wholesale lots	6,431	0.57%	
DVDs Total	**1,131,017**	**100.00%**	**31.96%**
Music			
Accessories	11,822	1.05%	
Cassettes	20,903	1.85%	
CDs	740,903	65.51%	
Digital music downloads	12	0.00%	
DVD audio	3,708	0.33%	
Records	341,455	30.19%	
Super audio CDs	636	0.06%	
Other formats	12,775	1.13%	
Wholesale lots	4,253	0.38%	
Music Total	**1,136,467**	**100.00%**	**32.11%**
TOTAL ALL THREE	**3,539,170**		**100.00%**

The beauty of selling books, movies, and music is that it's a category that's easily acquired and easily shipped. You don't have to know as much as you might to sell computers, and yet you still need to know more than you would to sell clothing. This is a great area to choose to acquire knowledge, because that's what makes you the big bucks. My grandmother always said, "You make your money in the buying," and she was right. She meant that if you buy correctly by knowing what is in demand and do not overpay, you will always be able to turn a profit. If you are just cleaning out your bookshelves at home, I would assume that you have already gotten your money's worth from these items and anything you make on eBay is just icing on the cake.

Storing these items is usually pretty easy, because of each item's small size. And shipping these items is a piece of cake, because you pack them in padded envelopes and ship via Media Mail, First Class, or Priority Mail. For additional safety, pack items in a strong Priority Mail box (which is free if you ship Priority Mail) from the post office. I go into more detail about shipping in Chapter 8.

Books and magazines

Fiction, non-fiction, and antiquarian and collectible books make up over 64 percent of the book category. And you can pick up these items everywhere! Library sales, estate and garage sales, thrift stores, and even eBay are great sources. Consider looking for first editions, books in great condition, and anything that looks rare or unusual. Don't overlook textbooks, because many college students buy their textbooks on eBay, and—at the end of the year—resell their books on eBay instead of selling to the on-campus bookstores. They are making more money by selling the books themselves, of course.

Don't overlook magazines. Do you know that the first edition *Playboy* from 1953, with Marilyn Monroe on the cover, sells for nearly $4,000 on eBay?

Movies and DVDs

Movies and DVDs are also another great area of opportunity. Movies includes VHS, Laserdisc, Film, Wholesale Lots, Other formats and VHS (Non US) PAL. DVDs make up 74 percent and VHS another 23 percent, for 97 percent of the movies and DVD category. The remaining 3% is made up of the other items listed above. I always see DVDs and VHS movies when I'm out at yard sales on Saturday mornings. Also check on eBay for wholesale

---

☼ **Bright Idea**

Make sure that DVDs and VHS tapes are in good condition and the right format. I learned the hard way that there is another format to a VHS tape by buying a Barbie video from eBay UK for my daughter. It came in the mail, and she was heartbroken when it was the European format (PAL) and didn't work on our system. Also, test every DVD for scratches and VHS tapes for problems before listing them. I listed some tapes that I should have tested first. One didn't work, and I had to take the entire order back for a full refund.

---

lots. Finally, talk to your local movie-rental companies. Sometimes you can work out a deal with them to buy movies after their newness has worn off. The rental companies don't need to stock as many copies several months after release as they do when movies first come out.

Music

Music is another great area in which you can make a lot of money and have fun. CDs and records are where the market is, with 85 percent of the music category. Work out deals with your local music and record companies to buy their overstocks, or buy wholesale lots on eBay. You can also pick up boxes of records at estate and garage sales for next to nothing. I recommend William Meyer and Dennis Prince's book, *How to Sell Music, Collectibles, and Instruments on eBay . . . and Make a Fortune!*

For vintage music, success comes down to how rare your particular record album is and its condition. For CDs, the same is important: condition and scarcity. Old sheet music and piano books are also something to consider. I bought a pile of vintage sheet music at an estate sale for $10 and sold just one piece of sheet music for almost $30! It was from the Supertramp *Breakfast in America* album. Easy to ship and fun to sell!

Home and garden

Another huge category projected at $2.2 billion for 2005 is home and garden. This category is really a mishmash of different items.

When eBay started growing so rapidly back in 1997 and 1998, it had to add a lot of subcategories quickly, with some of them not making much sense. You will find this in the home and garden category. Under this main category, you find such items as bedding, building supplies, food, furniture, major appliances, tools, gardening, and even pet supplies. This category has almost become a catch-all. If eBay doesn't know where to categorize something, it goes into home and garden.

It is hard to generalize this category with tips, tricks, and insider information, because this category covers everything from building a house (including the tools you would use), to decorating it, and then to stocking your pantry and bar. And don't forget the pet supplies you may need, like that huge aquarium tank, and all the plants you need for your garden. In Table 3.4, I look at all the top subcategories under the home and garden heading.

Table 3.4. Market Data for Home and Garden

Category	Number of Listings	Percent of Total
Bath	48,747	2.94%
Bedding	119,707	7.23%
Building and hardware	39,644	2.39%
Dining and bar	57,451	3.47%
Electric and solar	6,216	0.38%
Food and wine	46,163	2.79%
Furniture	70,976	4.29%
Gardening and plants	182,011	10.99%
Heating, cooling, and air	14,465	0.87%
Home décor	364,643	22.02%

Category	Number of Listings	Percent of Total
Home security	11,433	0.69%
Housekeeping—vacuums	38,569	2.33%
Kitchen	152,525	9.21%
Lamps, lighting, and fans	53,322	3.22%
Major appliances	9,786	0.59%
Outdoor power equipment	33,614	2.03%
Patio and grilling	26,542	1.60%
Pet supplies	129,416	7.81%
Plumbing and fixtures	22,293	1.35%
Pools, spas	18,984	1.15%
Rugs and carpets	32,093	1.94%
Tools	141,419	8.54%
Window treatments	22,933	1.38%
Wholesale lots	13,287	0.80%
Total	**1,656,239**	**100.00%**

What you can't sell on eBay

Whenever I do a radio interview, I am invariably asked, "Is there anything you can't sell on eBay"? The answer is yes and generally applies to alcohol, food, and plants.

eBay doesn't permit the sale of alcoholic beverages on its U.S. Web site, except for certain pre-approved sales of wine (see additional information at pages.ebay.com/help/policies/alcohol. html) and certain sales of collectible containers. You can sell food

---

☀ **Bright Idea**

Live animals and live pets are not allowed to be sold on eBay. However, don't overlook the huge opportunity to market to pet lovers. The pet supplies sub-category accounts for 7.8 percent of the home and garden category. Pet lovers go nuts for their animals. In fact, if you can believe it, ferrets have their own category, and I recently saw 1,182 items listed—items like cages and toys.

---

on eBay, but the sale of food is regulated by the federal government. If you plan to list food and food-related products, familiarize yourself with these laws before listing items on eBay. This information can be found at pages.ebay.com/help/policies/food.html. Finally, some federal, state, and local laws prohibit the sale of a select few types of plants or seeds that are considered "exotic" or "noxious" weeds. More on this can be found at pages.ebay.com/help/policies/plantsandseeds.html.

Growing or making your own auction items

Even with all the regulations listed in the preceding section, there is still a lot of opportunity in the food and gardening categories. Keep in mind that you don't always have to purchase items to sell on eBay. You can, instead, make them or grow them. Many creative eBayers are selling their recipes and home-baked goods on eBay. I just saw an auction for 2 pounds of homemade Italian cookies that sold for $14.

The gardening subhead is another huge area at almost 11 percent of home and garden. The plants, seeds, and bulbs category has the most listings within this subhead. Who knew that you could grow plants and sell them? An area to take a close look at is bonsai growing. These live plants can sell in the $500 range. Please see Figure 3.5 for a lovely live Bonsai. I have also found that anything with a bonsai shape is highly collectible. I have sold ceramic, glass, and plastic bonsais on eBay for $15 to $100.

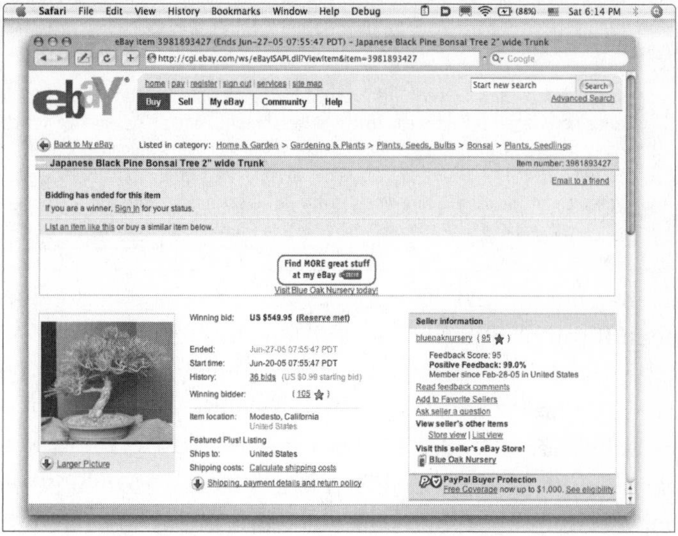

Figure 3.5. A Japanese black pine bonsai tree with two-inch trunk sold on eBay for $549.95.

Descriptions of other home and garden categories

Home décor is the largest subhead, at 22 percent. This includes anything and everything you can think of to decorate your home. Picture frames, wall hangings, clocks, candles, and throws are just a few of these items. You can pick up a lot of these items at garage, yard, and estate sales and also in thrift stores. If you want to sell new items, check the wholesale lot category on eBay, as well as stores like T.J. Maxx, Marshalls, Kohl's, and Ross for bargains.

In home and garden, you also find silverplated flatware. Flatware is a great item to pick up at thrift stores and at garage sales. If you can identify the pattern, this is a huge area of opportunity. And don't overlook stainless steel flatware. Some patterns are very hard to find, and once you have identified them correctly, can sell for a good profit.

> **Moneysaver**
>
> The challenge to selling furniture is the shipping. If you decide to specialize in furniture, start working with some major shipping companies to get rate discounts. If you can ship furniture for a reasonable price, your sales potential is huge in this subcategory. You can always state in your listing, "Must be picked up at location." This works quite well in a major metropolitan location like Los Angeles or Houston, where people aren't afraid to drive.

Furniture is another large subheading, at 4 percent. In new furniture, people are selling anything and everything. Kitchen tables, children's bedroom sets, you name it. Among vintage items, mid-century modern items are very hot. Anything from the 1950s to 1960s that looks space-age sleek is going for big bucks.

Finally, there is the builder/contractor aspect to this category. Tools accounts for over 8 percent and kitchen for 9 percent of the main category. If this is your niche, look into setting up some accounts with manufacturers to resell their goods. Also, check out your local builder's co-op or re-store looking for bargains. If you can believe it, I found a seller who sold an entire kitchen on eBay for $11,211.11—lock, stock, and barrel. He buys homes and redoes them, and he sold the kitchen "as is" for a lot of money. He said "Must be picked up at my location," and he told me that the buyer came and took it all down at his expense. They are now friends. eBay is such an interesting place!

Collectibles (and antiques)

This is my favorite category of all. eBay just calls it "collectibles" and estimates it to be a $2.2 billion business for 2005. A lot of what is in this category could be considered antique, which is defined by the dictionary as "an object of ancient times" or "a work of art, piece of furniture, or decorative object made at an earlier period and according to various customs laws at least 100 years ago."

> ### 🚗 Watch Out!
>
> Most of the items in the collectibles category are used (not new) and are very fragile. This makes shipping critically important in this category. Often, these items are irreplaceable, and that makes it even more important to ship and pack them safely. You don't want to disappoint your customer in Duluth who spent three years searching for that special cup and saucer, another week waiting to see whether she won the bid, and the last 5 seconds bidding up the price sky high. I talk more about shipping in Chapter 8.

Most dealers consider items 100 years old to be true antiques. Some countries have changed their customs laws to be just 50 years, which takes you to right around 1950, a time known as Mid-Century Modern and Eames era, so named for the famous architect Charles Eames, who designed his famous chair during that time period. Eames-era items, which are sleek, modular and space age, are very collectible. I believe that people are trying to rebuy their childhoods. The baby boomers (who now have disposable income) grew up in the 1940s and '50s, and these items are hot!

I typically call anything from the 1940s and earlier "antique," and I call items from 1940 to 1980 "vintage or collectible." To antiques dealers, "vintage" is a term used for something that is not antique but still has some age to it. Vintage is a great term to use in an auction title.

Here's a look at the subheads that eBay uses for its collectibles category:

- Advertising
- Animals
- Animation art, characters
- Arcade, jukeboxes, pinball
- Autographs
- Banks, registers, vending
- Barware
- Bottles and insulators
- Breweriana, beer
- Casino
- Clocks
- Comics
- Cultures, ethnicities

- Decorative collectibles
- Disneyana
- Fantasy, mythical, and magic
- Furniture, appliances
- Historical memorabilia
- Holiday, seasonal
- Housewares and kitchenware
- Knives, swords, blades
- Lamps, lighting
- Linens, fabrics, textiles
- Metalware
- Militaria
- Pens and writing instruments
- Pez, keychains, promo glasses
- Photographic images
- Pinbacks, nodders, lunchboxes
- Postcards and paper
- Radio, phonograph, TV, phone
- Religions, spirituality
- Rocks, fossils, minerals
- Science fiction
- Science, medical
- Tobacciana
- Tools, hardware, locks
- Trading cards
- Transportation
- Vanity, perfume, and shaving
- Vintage sewing
- Wholesale lots

These subhead categories are varied, so you have a lot of options for selling in this category.

Think about what you collect. Then think about what others collect. Almost anything in the world could be considered collectible. I have friends and family who collect trains, Blenko glass, hot sauce, Steiff teddy bears, figural dogs, princess items, restaurant menus, and even matchbooks. The potential in this area is staggering.

Animals and ephemera

I want to point out a few areas in collectibles that are always good. The animals subhead is a great place to focus. There is another layer of subcategories under animals, and if you can believe it, eBay lists about 100 breeds of dogs. Each dog has its

☼ **Bright Idea**

Don't sell any antique or collectible on eBay without knowing what you have. Do your research. If you can't find it on eBay with completed auction research, there is a great new service called www.priceminer.com. For a small monthly fee, Priceminer takes data going way back in time on eBay, and adds it to data from Tias and Go Antiques. It then gives you prices and information. It is a great service, and I use it all the time!

own final category number. People who collect by their breed of dog spend money on vintage and unusual items. I sold a bulldog brass letter holder for over $150. Don't pass up any dog items, but make sure you can identify the breed.

Another important area within collectibles is ephemera. Ephemera is paper goods used in everyday life, such as ticket stubs, maps, magazines, menus, postcards, and even trading cards. This is a growing area. Don't throw away any of that old paper in the attic without trying it on eBay first. Some examples of ephemera that I have sold are an amusement park map from 1970s Disney World for $21.55, and an Imperial Glass catalog from 1950 for $77.50. Also, some people sell advertisements from old magazines. I should know, I am the buyer for any that have my last name, "Dralle," which is a famous German perfume company. I love buying those old advertisements for $10 to $20 (most come from Germany), and I frame them and display them in my guest bathroom. One of the biggest benefits to ephemera is that it's easy to store and easy to ship.

Pottery and glass

I also want to discuss pottery and glass. It is its own top-level category on eBay, but fits in well with antiques and collectibles, too. This is a great area to specialize in and have fun with.

Within pottery and glass is dinnerware. I use www.replacements.com to identify the pieces I pick up while at yard sales. One of the best sets of dishes I ever purchased at an estate sale was a set with a stylized "f" on the back side. The woman I

> **Watch Out!**
>
> There are some fakes and reproductions in the pottery and glass area, so educate yourself. A great book to learn more about this area is *How to Sell Antiques and Collectibles on eBay . . . and Make a Fortune* by Dennis Prince and myself (McGraw Hill).

bought the set from told me that they were Fabrik, made by a Seattle company. I got on the Replacements Web site and identified the pattern as Ptarmigan (a type of bird). I had paid $20 for the box and broke the auctions out into two dinner plates, two mugs, two salad bowls, and so on. (I never sell my dinnerware or flatware as a set, but instead break it out into pieces). All told, that box sold for over $1,000 on eBay!

Also in pottery, think California pottery, Rookwood, Weller, and Roseville. In glass, consider art glass, carnival, Depression, and EAPG (Early American Pattern Glass). You can even sell glass insulators, used in power lines to prevent the flow of electricity. I sold a Westinghouse insulator on eBay for $72.99! It sat in our antiques store for 20 years, with no takers at $8.50.

Sports

Sports items are another huge area of opportunity, with $1.9 billion projected in 2005. Just about everyone is a sports fans on some level. I know that I buy anything related to my alma mater, the University of Southern California. In fact, my father makes fun of me and says my blood runs cardinal, not red (USC's colors are cardinal and gold). Anyway, this is a great category and can be a lot of fun to specialize in. eBay has combined the two sports categories (sporting goods is one, and sports memorabilia, cards, and fan shop is the other) and has just called it "sports," with expected sales in 2005 to top $1.9 billion.

I won't analyze the sporting goods category by subhead, because it includes too many different sports—covering everything from A to Z, or at least from archery to wakeboarding and waterskiing. Sports include baseball, billiards, camping, fishing, golf, paintball, scuba diving, snowmobiling, and triathalon. Fishing and golf are two of the biggest subhead categories, and you can find items related to these areas practically anywhere, even in your own home.

Sporting memorabilia has subhead categories (see Table 3.5).

Table 3.5. Market Data for Sporting Memorabilia

Category	Number of Listings	Percent of Total
Authenticator pre-certified	1,006	0.07%
Autographs–original	120,672	8.85%
Autographs–reprints	4,616	0.34%
Cards	752,040	55.15%
Fan apparel and souvenirs	482,933	35.42%
Wholesale lots	2,328	0.17%
Total	**1,363,595**	**100.00%**

The areas to focus on in sporting memorabilia include cards and fan apparel and souvenirs. This is a huge chunk of the business; both of these areas, combined, account for over 90 percent. It takes some expertise to become proficient in card trading. I know this from first-hand experience. I bought eight apple boxes full of baseball cards at a yard sale for $50. I was so excited. Most had never been touched. I had my dad (the baseball nut) choose all the ones that he thought were worth a lot of money. The best card he found was a rookie Ken Griffey, Jr. card that looked to be in mint condition: if these have a PSA (Professional Sports Authenticator; www.psacard.com) rating of 9 to 10 they can sell in the $2,000 range.

What a coup! Or so I thought. I was so naïve that when I sent the card off to PSA for grading, I spent $50 for 48-hour turnaround. (Hey, I needed the $2,000—my mortgage was due!) The PSA graders first determine whether the card is authentic (not counterfeit) and whether it has been altered. Once they establish that it's real, the graders then focus on the characteristics of the card, such as the strength and quality of the corners, color, edges, centering, surface, print clarity, and overall eye-appeal. My card came back with a PSA rating of 4.5. It was hardly worth the paper it had been printed on and would sell for about $2. Who knew? However, if you have a really rare card, a low PSA rating can still bring in big bucks. Please see Figure 3.6 for a Lou Gehrig card (rated PSA 5.0) that sold for over $6,000. Wouldn't you like to find one of those in an old trunk in your attic? Notice that the PSA rating was only 5. In this case, it didn't matter that the rating was low, because the card was so scarce. If you're going to specialize in sports cards, educate yourself, and then educate yourself some more.

In the sporting card business, most sellers don't take bids from new eBay users who have zero feedback (see Chapter 1 for the basics on feedback). Sometimes, on expensive items, sellers pre-approve their bidders. This is a good way to protect yourself from someone that just wants to mess around with your auctions.

According to eBay, based on its research, more than 50% of unpaid items come from new users with a feedback score of less than 5. For this reason, you may want to say in your listing, "Only bidders with a feedback score of 5 or higher."

☀ **Bright Idea**

To save yourself from phony bids on an expensive item, only accept pre-approved bidders. You may do this for each of your listings individually by creating a list of pre-approved bidders who may bid on that item or purchase it with BIN (Buy It Now). If a bidder is not on your pre-approved list, he or she can contact you by e-mail and ask to be pre-approved and added to your list.

Figure 3.6. A rare 1925 exhibit Lou Gehrig rookie card sold for $6,360!

Fan apparel and souvenirs is another fun area. It includes anything you can imagine from your favorite sports and sporting teams. When a team is hot, you can usually purchase new items and make good money on eBay. This is especially true if you live in the area where the team is from. If you were in Boston in 2004 for the World Series, for example, you could have cleaned up by buying memorabilia and new clothing locally, and then selling it on eBay. Thrift stores and garage sales are another place to check for these items. Often, old jerseys and vintage sporting memorabilia, like pennants, do really well at auction.

Toys and hobbies

Toys and hobbies is another big category, with $1.7 billion projected in sales for 2005. This category encompasses both new and used/vintage items. When I searched with "new" in the title, 219,776 items came up for the past two weeks, and when I typed in "vintage," 85,166 items came up. This is a high percentage of vintage being sold in this category. Remember that people are trying to buy their childhoods, and this is especially true in the toy category (see Table 3.6).

Table 3.6. Market Data for Toys and Hobbies

Category	Number of Listings	Percent of Total
Action figures	311,682	16.31%
Beanbag plush–Beanie Babies	62,210	3.25%
Building toys	38,300	2.00%
Classic toys	18,696	0.98%
Diecast, toy vehicles	374,192	19.58%
Educational	19,314	1.01%
Electronic, battery, wind-up	16,418	0.86%
Fast food and cereal premiums	27,706	1.45%
Games	152,916	8.00%
Model RR, trains	124,463	6.51%
Models, kits	94,467	4.94%
Outdoor toys and structures	14,525	0.76%
Pretend play, preschool	53,753	2.81%
Puzzles	25,109	1.31%
Radio controlled	118,444	6.20%
Robots, monsters, space toys	8,740	0.46%
Slot cars	24,413	1.28%

Category	Number of Listings	Percent of Total
Stuffed animals	29,047	1.52%
Toy soldiers	19,283	1.01%
Trading card games	161,420	8.45%
TV, movie, character toys	174,714	9.14%
Vintage, antique toys	35,110	1.84%
Wholesale lots	6,454	0.34%
Total	**1,911,376**	**100.00%**

This year, I met a woman at eBay Live (an eBay gathering) who makes a living doing the toy-store route looking for hot new items. She is always at Toys 'R' Us and other chains when the doors open. I asked her how she knows what to buy, and she said she researches. She reads magazines and the front pages of eBay to see what's hot. If you're interested in this category, get to know your local toy shops and see if they will sell you their overstocks and slow-turning inventory at a bargain price.

Vintage toys

Vintage toys are everywhere, especially considering that vintage can be as recent as the 1980s and 1990s. I see toys, games, and trading cards at every garage sale. This isn't my area of expertise, so I don't check the items over that well. However, if you decide to specialize in this area, I believe you can do very well.

Bright Idea

There are two abbreviations used for new toys on eBay: MIB (mint in box) and MIP (mint in package—vinyl, plastic, and box). Looking at completed auction research, there were 36,633 listings with MIB in the title and only 10,051 with MIP in the title. If mint in box applies, then use MIB instead of MIP because more people will be looking for it.

Buy as many books as you can and subscribe to trade publications. I subscribe to the *Antique Trader* for general information about antiques and collectibles, and it is super. I also know of a toy magazine called *Toy Shop*. From vintage tin toys to the latest action figures, Hot Wheels, and board games, *Toy Shop* features the latest news, up-to-date market trends, auctions, comprehensive coverage of pre-1980s toys, price guides, and reports from toy dealers and toy shows nationwide. You can get more information on these publications at www.krause.com.

Action figures and die cast toys

Looking at Table 3.6, you see that action figures, die cast toys, toy vehicles, trading-card games, and characters from TV shows and movies are the largest subhead categories.

- An action figure is a posable plastic figurine of an action hero, superhero, or a character from film or television. *Star Wars* action figures are always in demand. See Figure 3.7 for a Star Wars action figure that sold for a lot of money.

- Die cast toys are formed from molten metal in a die (mold). Die cast toys run the gamut, from antique to current. This is the largest subhead category and although the proper spelling for die cast is "die cast," on eBay, twice as many auctions are listed with it as "diecast" in the title. New die cast items to watch for are NASCAR, *Star Wars*, and in vintage, Dinky toys and Ertyl.

- Trading card games to watch for are Pokemon, Yu-gi-oh, and Magic. However, the demand for these different games is constantly changing, and you need to know what you are doing in this subhead before you dive in.

- TV, movie, and character toys are always in demand. Disney, Popeye, and the Flintstones sell well. More recently, Disney (again), Thomas the Tank Engine, *Harry Potter,* My Little Pony, and *The Simpsons* are selling well.

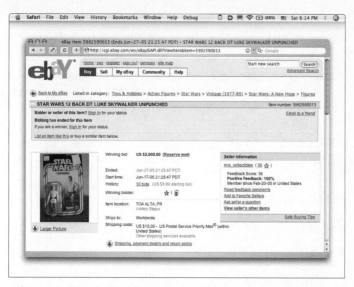

Figure 3.7. This Luke Skywalker *Star Wars* action figure in the original package sold for $2,000. The seller used the term "unpunched" in his title. He told me that unpunched means that this item never found its way onto a rack in a toy store. The hole was never punched out to hang it up. That makes it even more rare.

Jewelry and watches

Jewelry and watches are projected at quite a lot of volume: $1.6 billion for 2005. This is another of my favorite categories, because everyone has jewelry and/or watches in their homes. It is also an easy category to find when out thrift shopping or at garage sales. Another great feature of this category is that it's easy to ship.

However, I have had challenges selling in this category over the years. My brother is GIA (Gemological Institute of America) certified, and that has helped us immensely when selling gemstones and expensive items, because I've found that people want some sort of guarantee. For a while, we weren't selling much jewelry on eBay, and then it really picked up. The only explanation we can give is that, back in 1998, people were afraid to buy something so personal without being able to feel it and try it on.

Now, as more and more people join the eBay bandwagon, it has become more comfortable for bidders to buy jewelry pieces. In Table 3.7, you can take a look at where this market is.

Table 3.7. The Current Market for Jewelry and Watches

Category	Number of Listings	Percent of Total
Bracelets	116,800	4.69%
Charms and charm bracelets	343,146	13.77%
Children's jewelry	4,574	0.18%
Designer, artisan jewelry	37,193	1.49%
Earrings	63,708	2.56%
Ethnic, tribal jewelry	243,318	9.76%
Fashion jewelry	243,318	9.76%
Jewelry boxes and supplies	69,397	2.78%
Loose beads	201,523	8.09%
Loose gemstones	130,617	5.24%
Men's jewelry	78,843	3.16%
Necklaces and pendants	225,354	9.04%
Pins, brooches	33,495	1.34%
Rings	246,016	9.87%
Sets	11,340	0.46%
Vintage, antique	157,978	6.34%
Watches	231,463	9.29%
Other items	9,502	0.38%
Wholesale lots	44,452	1.78%
Total	**2,492,037**	**100.00%**

The number-one subhead category is charms and charm bracelets. This is due to the overwhelming popularity of those Italian charm bracelets that everyone seems to be wearing. Next is the ring category, at almost 10%. What you see lately is a lot of diamond engagement rings being traded on this site. Typically, when people would get divorced, they would take their rings into the local jeweler and get pennies on the dollar. Now these same people can get a lot more money by selling rings themselves on eBay. Another great thing about this is that if you're in the market for an engagement ring, you can get amazing deals. Diamond rings with from 2 to 4 carats, set in platinum (depending on color and clarity of course), are selling in the $10,000 to $12,000 range. What a bargain!

The next largest subhead categories are ethnic/tribal jewelry and fashion jewelry. There is a lot of ethnic jewelry and tribal jewelry that has been imported from Afghanistan, Egypt, and Africa. African trade beads are also very popular on eBay. Fashion jewelry is very popular, and designers like L.C. Tiffany, Louis Vuitton, and Cartier are bringing in high-dollar bids.

The watches being sold on eBay are typically new and expensive. However, vintage watches, including pocket watches, can do quite well. I sell a lot of beads in the loose bead subhead category. Italian millefiori (1,000 flowers) and other beads made for trade with Africa in the early 1800s do very well. If you're an artist, another option is to sell your own handmade beads.

Moneysaver

If you do decide to sell an expensive ring or piece of jewelry on eBay, pay for a professional appraisal. Find a local jeweler in your area who is GIA (Gemological Institute of America) certified or certified by another reputable company, and pay for a thorough inspection and valuation. The appraiser will grade and weigh the stones and give you a value. This way, you can put all that information in your listing and include the appraisal with the sale. You get more money for your item this way, and your bidders will feel much more comfortable knowing that the ring has been inspected by an expert.

eBay has a lot of policies concerning jewelry to keep people from selling something that has been misrepresented. Check out eBay's policies at pages.ebay.com/help/policies/jewelry.html and learn about what you can and can't say in your titles and listings.

The jewelry area requires a certain expertise and knowledge level. If you decide to specialize in jewelry, take time to educate yourself. Buy books, subscribe to publications like the *Lapidary Journal* at www.lapidaryjournal.com, and join a local bead club.

Just the facts

- Make sure that you read and learn about the top ten eBay categories.

- Do your research within each category so that you know what to search for when out hunting.

- Pick one or two of these areas of opportunity to focus on.

- Spend time learning about your niche so that you can become an expert.

- Since eBay is constantly changing, go on the site on a regular basis to gather data.

- Don't overlook any item that looks interesting when you are out buying—especially if it jogs your memory and is a a bargain.

GET THE SCOOP ON...
- Finding items to sell right in your own home -
Buying secondhand - Buying new and in bulk

Chapter 4

Acquiring Your Merchandise

I hope you realize the incredible opportunities waiting for you when you start amassing inventory. As my grandmother said, "You make your money in the buying." This is so true! If you buy correctly, there will be a market for you to turn a profit. Be conservative when starting out. Your money will be made in finding unidentified treasures, buying in bulk, arranging relationships with suppliers, making your own goods, or by bargaining for the best price.

I believe that most of us have a lot of clutter in our lives, so don't overlook all the wonderful items that may just be sitting around your own home. Use eBay to make some money and clean up the mess in your life!

Your house

As you know, I've been very fortunate because my grandmother, Cheryl Leaf, owned and operated an antiques store for over 50 years. Can you imagine how much stuff I still have? I am probably the exception, not the rule. But I believe most Americans are pack rats, and the first place to look for merchandise is in your own house, your parents' house, and your friends' houses.

Get a big box and start a pile. As for what sells and what doesn't, you just never know. I was listing some incredible antique Majolica jardinières the other evening, and as I did my research, I found that they sell only in the $20 range. On the other hand, I had a new creamer/sugar in the shape of a trailer and Nash automobile that was going for $44. Kitschy, unusual, and strange often sells for more than authentic and antique. In general, look for the following:

- Items you don't use or need anymore
- Items in good condition
- Items that are still in the original box (MIB: mint in box)
- Anything with a brand name or signature
- New or like-new clothing, new with tags (NWT)
- Unique or unusual items
- Items that were very expensive originally
- Shabby chic, vintage, and antique items
- Items made in the United States, Europe, and sometimes Japan (stay away from items made in Hong Kong, Korea, and Taiwan)

Go through your home and look in the following places for possible items:

- **Garage:** Toys, sports equipment, hunting and fishing items, golf items (really hot right now), car parts (I know someone who got $8,000 for a rare car part!), and so on
- **Attic:** Antique clothing, ephemera (paper goods like Victorian scrap, letters, and postcards), old magazines (my ex-husband's skateboard magazines from the 1970s sold for $20 to $50 each!), old toys, collections, and anything that has been put away for a while

- **Kitchen:** China, dinnerware, silverware, appliances, and refrigerator dishes are desirable now. Watch for anything that has a brand name or is signed, old tins, and so on.

- **Bedrooms:** Clothing with brand names that are in good to excellent condition, brand-name purses and scarves, signed costume jewelry, and Bakelite. Look in your kids' closets for clothing that is gently worn with brand names like Baby Gap, Old Navy, Gymboree (see Figure 4.1), Tommy Hilfiger, or anything new with tags (NWT).

Check in your child's toy cabinet, too, looking for brand names and anything you can put back in an original box. Little Tykes, Barbie, and Thomas the Tank Engine are all good. Think trains, cars, dolls, books, airplanes, and so on.

- **Bathrooms:** Old perfume bottles, medicine bottles and vintage (1970s) cosmetics (I sold a Faberge dusting powder set from the 1970s in the original box for $25!)

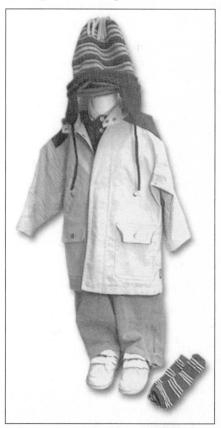

Figure 4.1. Three lots of my son's used Gymboree clothing sold on eBay for $99.14. Notice how well the one outfit is displayed.

☼ **Bright Idea**

When selling clothing, new or used, never model it yourself or on your children. Buyers do not want to see that. Purchase a cheap mannequin form on eBay and display it professionally or stack neatly and take photos that way. See the picture in Figure 4.1 that shows my son's clothing on a hanging half mannequin that I bought on eBay for $10. Pretty cute!

- **Bookshelves:** Old books, especially those with unusual titles, that are author signed, and that are first editions; also look for magazines.

- **China cabinets:** Antiques, glassware/china/porcelain, and pottery that is signed; stemware like Waterford; also Lladro, Precious Moments, and Boyds

- **CD/cassette/record cabinet:** Old LPs and CDs (I just sold a James Bond Casino Royale Album for $31!)

- **DVD/video case:** Videos and DVDs (a girl in one of my classes was making $1,000 a month selling her old videos and CDs on eBay)

Here is a list from eBay (and they should know what sells!) that recommends some items to look for. eBay's list is by top-level category, whereas my preceding list was by room.

- **Antiques:** Dolls, clocks, pocket watches, lamps, furniture

- **Art:** Original comic art

- **Business and industrial:** Laboratory equipment (microscopes, oscilloscopes, signal generators)

- **Cameras and photo:** Camcorders, darkroom equipment, digital and film cameras, lenses

- **Clothing:** Wedding dresses and formal attire, designer garments, purses, shoes, scarves and belts, designer maternity wear

- **Computers and networking:** Computers (PCs, laptops, Macs), PDAs, flat-panel monitors, inkjet printers, routers,

UPS backup batteries, popular software (Microsoft Office, Adobe Photoshop, and so on)

- **Consumer electronics:** Audio components (receivers, tuners, amps, speakers, CD players, turntables), video components (TVs, DVD players, TiVo), portable players (DVD and MP3 players)

- **Home and garden:** Bathroom fixtures and faucets, electronic toothbrushes, high-end cookware and utensils, china, crystal, dinnerware, glassware, barware, small appliances (blenders, bread machines, espresso makers, microwave ovens), chainsaws, table saws, high-end vacuum cleaners

- **Jewelry and watches:** Diamond jewelry, pearl jewelry, pocket watches, rings, designer wrist watches

- **Musical instruments:** Accordions, guitars, violins, clarinets, saxophones, synthesizers, studio equipment (mics, mixers, power amps, speakers)

- **Pottery and glass:** eBay does not itemize this category, but you know what to look for from Chapter 3.

- **Sporting goods:** Camping and outdoor gear (backpacks, tents, sleeping bags in excellent condition), binoculars and telescopes, high-end bicycles, golf clubs and bags by name brands, scuba gear, skis and snowboards in new condition

- **Sports memorabilia:** eBay does not itemize this category, but I hope you can remember key items from Chapter 3.

- **Toys and hobbies:** Teddy bears, model trains

- **Travel:** High-end luggage, steamer trunks

- **Vehicles parts and accessories:** Audio components, GPS units, radar detectors, parts for vintage and luxury cars, performance tires

- **Video games:** Game consoles (Playstation 2, Xbox, etc.)

Of course, this isn't an exhaustive list, but it does give you some idea of what eBay sees selling for over $50 and gets you thinking in that direction.

Buying items to sell on eBay

I have some rules for buying items to sell on eBay. When shopping for inexpensive items that are second-hand—thrift stores, garages sales, and estate sales—I usually expect to get at least ten times what I pay. If I pick up a vase and it's marked $1, I ask myself, "Can you get $10 for this on eBay?" This works out to a 900 percent profit margin ($10 minus $1 cost equals $9 profit, divided by the $1 cost equals 900 percent). When I buy higher-end antiques that cost $30 to $450, I try and get three times what I pay. When I purchase any item for over $50, I try to double my money.

When buying wholesale lots or direct from a retailer or manufacturer, the rules change dramatically. When I buy a wholesale lot of gift items or clothing, I try to double my money (100 percent margins). I just bought a wholesale lot of 50 pieces of new women's clothing on eBay. I paid $72 plus $40 shipping. That works out to $2.24 per item. I will try to average $5 per item, or about double what I paid. Keep in mind that key word, *average*. eBay is a numbers game, and one of my clothing items may sell for $100 and the rest for only $2.99. Overall, it will average out to what I expect (based on years and years of experience), which is $250 total.

This rule changes drastically if you're buying electronics or computer items. The margins on these lots can be very small—10 to 50 percent. As an example, if you pay $100 for a computer part, you expect to sell it for $110 to $150.

When I buy directly from a retailer or manufacturer, my margins vary a lot. As an example, I sell Christmas plates that I buy directly from the manufacturer. I pay $40 for these wholesale, with shipping. They typically sell for an average of $50. The margin on this is 25 percent ($10 profit divided by the $40 cost). You will need to spend some time and figure out what margins you need to achieve to ensure that your eBay business is profitable for you. I discuss this in more detail in Chapter 5.

Garage, estate, and yard sales

These days, garage-sale season in the United States is almost a year-round event. I spotted about ten after taking my kids to school this past Friday, and boy did I want to stop!

In my video series, *Trash to Cash,* I show how $74 spent at garage sales on a Saturday morning can turn into over $500 in cyberspace. You can be successful at this, too, especially if you follow my proven techniques.

Get a newspaper and map your route the night before

The most important way to ensure your success at garage sales is to be organized. Pick up your city's newspaper the night or day before you intend to hit the sales (most garage sales are in the paper at least one day before). Or print your city's newspaper's online listings of sales. Sit down with this information and look first for the sales that promise to have the most merchandise (and the most potential treasures). Key words like the following indicate large sales:

- Estate
- Moving
- Neighborhood
- Kiwanis or other organization
- Church sale or rummage

Also, look for sales that mention items that pique your interest or that you specialize in, for example, toys, sports memorabilia, clothing, glassware, and so on. Organize sales by starting time. Choose which 7 a.m., 8 a.m., 9 a.m., and 10 a.m. sales you think best. Plan and map a route around your starting times. By doing this the night before, you save critical time and get to the best sales ahead of the other garage salers!

Believe it or not, sometimes I don't take my own advice. If I have had a busy week, the last thing I want to do on a Friday night is map out my route. Those Saturdays when I don't have the route mapped are a big time waster, and my mom gets so mad at me for making her drive all over the city. With gas at an all-time high, planning a route and getting proper directions ahead of time is the smartest thing you can do!

Get there right on time

After you've mapped your route, getting to the most important sales on time will be a breeze. Garage sale etiquette requires that you do not start banging on doors early. As someone who has held a lot of garage sales in her day, I can tell you that jumping the gun is very rude. The majority of sales will not let you in early anyway, so trying is generally a waste of time. However, if the sale sounds amazing, try driving by it early to see if it has started—you don't want to miss out on the big one. Charity sales at churches and schools typically always start right on time, but you want to get to these early to get a good place in line.

This strategy really paid off for me in 1998 when I got to a Kiwanis Club sale right when it opened. No one else had even been there yet. I was able to get many great deals, including a large metal tray for $1 and a covered Mexican pottery hen for $2. The metal tray turned out to be from World War II, and I sold it on eBay for $51! The covered hen sold for $27.99. These were just a few of my finds that day! See my book *The 100 Best Things I've Sold on eBay* (All Aboard, Inc. 2003) for more information on these items.

As you're looking through each sale, carry a mesh shopping bag or box with you to scoop up bargains ahead of the next guy.

What to look for

In general, look for the following (since most of these are the same as what you looked for in your own home, I am only including new ones; refer back to pages 92–95 for the rest of the list):

- Good designer-brand clothing in gently used condition
- Items that are not priced too high (I never buy any item for more than $5 unless I know something about it)

■ Anything that reminds you of your childhood (if you look at something and say, "Wow, remember these from when we were little," buy it!)

How to bargain for the best deals

After you have your pile of treasures chosen, always try to get a slightly better deal. You don't want to offend anyone, but it certainly can't hurt to ask very politely. I usually add up my items with the owner of the sale. Suppose I've picked out ten items, and they added up to $17.55. I might ask, "Would you consider $15 for everything?" Usually, they say "yes"!

When my video series was finally finished and I was watching the garage sale portion with my father, he said to me, "You are just like your grandmother." That was the highest compliment he could have paid me! She was such a savvy businesswoman and a shrewd negotiator.

Take some risks

I often tell people in my classes to take some risks at sales. If items are only 50¢—or even $5—what do you have to lose? Not a whole lot.

The more you can buy and try on eBay, the more money you will make and the more you will learn. I have learned my best lessons by making mistakes. Just last week, I made a painful mistake that hit me right in my pocketbook. I paid $67 each for three Department 56 Dickens villages. I thought I was being so smart! They were over ten years old and mint in box. Now, I

☼ **Bright Idea**

Survey the sale quickly when you first arrive. If everything is marked "Made in Taiwan" or "Made in Hong Kong" the sale may be a waste of your time. Get to the next one quickly. If you get to a sale and everything is marked "Made in France" and/or "Made in the USA," and the items look like they were expensive originally, grab a box and start putting in anything that looks good. You can edit later. Time is of the essence, but don't be rude.

have seen some of these go for over $1,000. Because they were over $20 each, they exceeded my $5 rule, so I should have called a friend with computer access and had her do some research. Or I should finally buy that cell phone with Internet access. I thought I was so smart and spent $200 on these villages. They sold last week for $40 total. I just lost $160 and believe me, I will not buy anything over $5 again without doing my research (at least for the next six months until my memory fades . . . again).

Check back at the end of sales

The beginning and the ending of sales are the best times to buy. Go back to the best sales close to their closing times. Many sellers are really willing to deal at about 3 p.m. on a Saturday or Sunday. I have gotten many items for next to nothing and even a few things for free. This is the time to do your best negotiating. At one estate sale, I got a darling round table and chair set for $25. She had been asking $125 during the previous two days, but at the end of the sale, she probably would have paid me to haul it away. It was a horrible 1970s wood color, so I just painted it white and recovered the upholstered chair seats with darling Waverly fabric. I ended up selling it for $250 in my antiques store. It probably would have sold for close to that on eBay with a heading like, "Country Chic Round Table—3 Chairs—Waverly—DARLING!!"

I was at a huge estate sale this past weekend run by a professional. The man who runs it typically prices items too high for me to make a profit. However, it was a famous estate out in Palm Springs, and my mom and I decided to go just to see the home that supposedly Bette Davis used to stay in when in the valley.

☼ Bright Idea

It is a good idea to carry generic business cards to give to a professional estate liquidator. I typically don't give them my eBay card but use a card that just says "Buy and Sell," and then I list what my interests are. If you identify yourself as a dealer, those running garage sales will usually work with you and know that you're serious, with cash to spend.

The estate was incredible, and there were some very lovely dishes that I was interested in purchasing.

Well, I got to that sale at the right time last weekend, and everything was 50 percent off. It had been going on since Thursday, and we were there on a Saturday. There was a set of Royal Albert china priced at $900 and a lovely set of antique Spode Hunting dishes at $800. The person running the sale told me he would take $475 for the Royal Albert and $350 for the Spode. I started to walk away and he said, "Talk to me." I said "I could go $400 on the Royal Albert and $300 on the Spode, because I need to make a profit." There were 90 pieces of Royal Albert and 50 pieces of Spode. This worked out to $4.50 a piece for the Royal Albert and $6 a piece on the Spode. I know that was over my $5 limit, but I just had a feeling. The people who owned this estate had money, and they only bought the most expensive items. Anyway, he said "Fine. Let's talk about the rest of the china." He offered me two other sets (priced at $300 and $100) for only $100! Then he offered me three full tables of silver for only $200. I spent $1,000 that day and got some amazing treasures. I was there at the right time and was very pleasant. There's another rule here: Always be nice!

Garage sale buying is a quick way to get merchandise

My mom and I still go out every Saturday morning to garage sales, and I take about $200 in cash. I can fill her van full in about two or three hours with about 100 items. Garage sale shopping is fast. We start at 6:30 a.m. or 7:00 a.m., and often by 10:00 a.m., we're done. Time goes by slowly when you're dashing from one sale to another. We often look at one another and say, "Can you believe it's only 8:00 a.m.?" That vanful usually turns into anywhere between $1,000 to $2,000 during the next week on eBay. As a side note, not every week is as good as every other week. Some are awesome, and sometimes, there's nothing. The weeks of nothing are when you need to supplement what you have found with items from other venues, such as thrift stores.

Thrift stores

There are about ten thrift stores in my area. Eight of them consistently overprice, but there are two where I find great bargains. Take some time in your city to figure out which thrift stores are the best. Make a list and schedule to hit your best thrift stores on a consistent basis. I try and hit the eight overpriced stores in my area once every two weeks. The stores where I find the best merchandise, I try to be in every other day, if not every day. You just never know what is going to get put on the shelf that second before you walk in. Please see Figure 4.2 for a wonderful vase that was on my lucky shelf in my favorite thrift store. This is the same shelf where I found the $2 bird that turned into over $2,000 on eBay (see Figure 1-4).

Keep in mind that thrift-store shopping is just like garage-sale shopping. Look for the same items and follow the same rules. Most thrift stores don't negotiate on price, but they do have special tag sales every so often. The one in my neighborhood sometimes decides to put up a "50 percent off housewares" sign, and that's when I can really do well. They don't advertise it, and it's up

Figure 4.2. A Tappio Wirkkala vase from Venezia Italy got put out on a shelf in my favorite thrift store just as I was walking in. I paid $4, and it sold on eBay for $365!

to the manager's whims, so this is another reason to constantly visit your favorite stores. Chains like the Goodwill and Salvation Army have more rigid rules regarding sales. Typically, each

> ☼ **Bright Idea**
>
> Get to know the workers and managers at your favorite local thrift stores. Let them know what types of items you're looking for. More often than not, they will wait to put something out if they know that you're a good buyer and are in the store often.

month, they take 50 percent off a certain colored tag. Watch for these markdowns.

Auctions

Live auctions are a fun place to pick up merchandise. There are auctions for everything imaginable, including furniture, cars, antiques, and livestock. Well, I won't talk about livestock auctions in this section because (remember from Chapter 3), you cannot sell any live animals on eBay.

You can learn a lot from a live auction, but they can take a lot of your time. You can end up spending several days at an auction and never get anything great. However, if you're patient, you can score big, but it can be a waiting game.

The best way to buy at a live auction is by the box lot. I love when I can pick up boxes of china and antiques for $5 to $50. I can break these items out individually and make good money.

Always attend the auction preview and mark on your program which auction lot numbers you're interested in. Go home or to a place with a computer and do your research. Never buy without checking to see what similar items are currently selling for on eBay. Once you know your maximum bid, write this down

> 🐷 **Moneysaver**
>
> Keep in mind that most auction houses charge an auction premium. It usually runs 10 percent, so figure this into the total amount you're willing to pay. If you forget about the 10 percent premium, that could be your profit margin!

on the program. Don't get caught up in the auction frenzy and go over this amount. I know it is very tempting in the heat of the moment, but remember that you're trying to make a profit.

Some of the best live auctions are held in rural areas. Check the Internet, local newspapers, trade magazines, and your favorite auctioneers to see when and where auctions will be held.

Jobbers and wholesalers

There are many companies dealing with the disposition of overstocks. Overstocks occur when a manufacturer gets a cancelled order or just made too many of a certain item, or a retailer buys too many items, or a distributor gets stuck with slow-moving merchandise. These overstocks can be a huge opportunity for you. These jobbers and wholesalers are always looking for new buyers that won't infringe upon their existing sales channels.

Just remember that you're going to have to buy in bulk to get a good price. You'll also likely be buying multiples of a single item. eBay really favors the unique one-of-a-kind item, so I encourage you to proceed cautiously or try and buy pallets full of unique items. Another option is to put a lot of this merchandise at a fixed price in your eBay store. I do very well by doing this, because the listing fees are a lot lower in an eBay store, and this merchandise can sit there relatively cheaply until it sells. See Chapter 17 for more about running an eBay store.

Overstocks.com is a site that has a special wholesale area. If you go to www.overstockunlimitedcloseouts.com, you can see what's being offered. The way this division of Overstocks.com works is that you can buy by the case at a fixed price, bid to buy by the pallet, or bid to take all of the items. I've shown a screen shot of one of their offerings in Figure 4.3. If you want to buy just 24 of these trucks, you can get them at $20 each. This works out to $480 total. If you want to bid on the 312 units available on one pallet, you would start your bidding at $6.90 per unit. This works out to $2,152.80 total. Or you could buy them all (and make the seller very happy), spending $6.00 per unit and purchasing 1,944 items for a total price of $11,664. You will also pay shipping on these items. I did a search on eBay, however, to find what similar trucks are selling for and couldn't find anything close enough in price to make the purchase worthwhile.

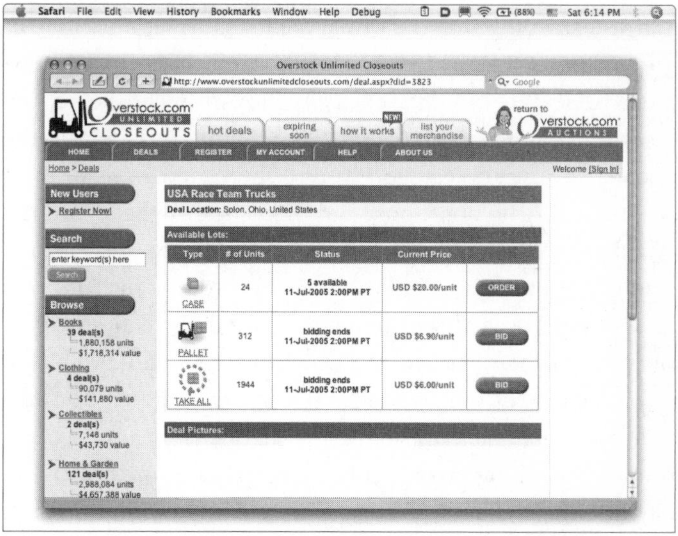

Figure 4.3. Screen shot from www.overstockunlimitedcloseouts.com. This listing is for a USA Race Team truck. Note that you can buy by the case at a fixed price, bid on just a pallet, or bid on all of the items.

When buying on sites like this one, keep in mind that these are typically huge quantities, so you need to find items that you think you can sell, with reasonable quantities.

Another option in the jobber/wholesaler category is to check with your local wholesalers. You may be able to get some great deals right in your own back yard. I know that in my hometown of Bellingham, Washington, there is a jobber named Pace. If I were still in that area, I would try to forge a relationship with the owners and let them know the kinds of items I am looking for: gifts, antiques, collectibles, and so on. This is a great way to find items that aren't going to cost you an arm and a leg in shipping.

On eBay

You can buy wholesale on eBay, and this is a great way to purchase smaller lots with more unique items. I just typed in **wholesale lot** in a current auction search by title, and over 18,000 items came up.

If you sit and watch the wholesale lot subcategory in the category in which you're specializing, you can pick up some bargains. To search this way, click on the Advanced Search link near the **Search** button. When the Search: Find Items screen appears, choose the category you're interested in from the In this category drop-down box, and then click the **Search** button. Click on the Wholesale Lots link in the Categories section at the far left, and then use the Sort by: feature to sort by Time: ending soonest. You will see the auctions ending in the next few hours, if not the next few minutes. You may be able to pick up some bargains, especially during the slower summer months.

You can also pick up some great bargains with misspellings on eBay. A spelling error can be a big bargain for you. Use the eBay Favorite Searches to store searches for some of the more popular misspellings for your area of expertise. eBay will automatically e-mail you when an item comes up for sale with that misspelling. I just made a huge mistake and listed an item with a misspelling in the title. I could just kick myself. I found this incredible pair of Foo Dogs at my local thrift store for only $4. I thought that they would have sold in the $100 range. Well, the auction ended, and the winning bid was only $9.99 (see

---

☼ **Bright Idea**

Store the searches you use most frequently using eBay's Favorite Searches feature. To use it, just enter your search keywords as usual. When the search results are returned, click on the Add to Favorites link on the right-hand side of the page. On the Add To My Favorite Searches page that displays, you are asked to name the search. You're also given the option of having auctions that meet your search criteria e-mailed to you daily. After the search is saved, you will be able to access it through My eBay.

Figure 4.4). I couldn't figure it out until my mother pointed out that I had typed in "Food Dog" by mistake. Darn!

Figure 4.4. Foo Dogs that I sold recently for $9.99 on eBay. If only I had checked my spelling in the title and hadn't listed them as Food Dogs, they should have sold in the $100 range.

Manufacturers' goods

There are manufacturers of goods in every city in the United States and abroad. Nearly every manufacturer would love to find a non-traditional selling channel to move some pile of slow-turning inventory or returns. What I mean by *non-traditional* is that it won't compete with its existing channels of distribution and make existing customers angry.

Check the Yellow Pages in your city for any manufacturing company that interests you. Then see whether you can find a contact in common. In my hometown of Bellingham, Washington, there is a large manufacturer of CD and DVD accessories called Allsop. The mother of my best friend, Melanie, used to be the secretary to the president. Now, if I were interested in this type of product, I would see whether she could get me an appointment. Perhaps I could strike a deal with Allsop that I would sell their items for a certain percentage or just buy their returns on a regular basis. Be creative when forging these relationships. Think outside of the box.

Regular retail and going-out-of-business sales

You can buy from regular retail stores and do well on eBay. One of the most important ways to ensure your success is to watch for deep discounts and clearance tables. There is a Macy's here in Palm Desert, and I watch the 50-percent-off clearance racks and tables, because they eventually go another 40 percent off. Not bad! This is like buying at 70 percent off of regular retail. You can usually turn around and get 50 to 60 percent of original retail. For example, suppose you buy a Ralph Lauren sweater that retails for $100. It was marked down to $49.99, and by waiting for the right time, say you get another 40 percent off. You pay $29.99 for it. You might expect to get between $49.99 and $59.99 for it in the right season on eBay.

Be sure to buy good brand names. Brand names sell well, and customers search for items to buy using their favorite designer's name. Here are just a few examples in clothing:

- **Kids:** Baby Gap, Old Navy, Gymboree, Jacadi, Ralph Lauren, Tommy Hilfiger
- **Teens:** American Eagle, Gap, J Crew, Levi, Polo, Abercrombie & Fitch
- **Men:** Polo, Structure, Gap, Kenneth Cole, Gucci, Prada, Hugo Boss, Versace, Banana Republic, Tommy Bahama
- **Women:** Express, Ralph Lauren, Liz Claiborne, Donna Karan, Missoni, Kenneth Cole, Giorgio Armani, Ann Klein, Lord & Taylor, Ann Taylor

Keep in mind that size does matter! You never know which sizes people will be looking for, so try all different sizes. The beauty of eBay is that many people shop for hard-to-find sizes. From size 0 to 5X may all be great possibilities.

Try to buy outfits or collections. Often, on eBay, you'll see clothing sellers selling in lots. By doing this, they get much more than by piecing it out. Just make sure that the lot or collection is all the same size range, so that one person can wear it all.

Don't forget to shop clearance stores in addition to regular department stores. Stores like T.J. Maxx, Ross, and Marshalls can be great places to find bargains. Last year, I bought my son a Scooby Doo backpack on eBay for $19.99 BIN (which means Buy It Now). I went shopping at T.J. Maxx a few days later and found the exact same backpack for $7. That seller was doing quite well buying at clearance stores and selling on eBay.

Finally, don't forget to buy off-season. Purchase Halloween costumes on November 1st, for instance, when stores want to get rid of these items at whatever price it takes. Watch for Toys 'R' Us and other large chains to take deep discounts on items the day or week after Halloween. Last year, I bought 40 costumes at Toys 'R' Us after Halloween. Many of the costumes were 75 percent off; some were even being sold at 99¢. Put them away and sell them next year about two to six weeks before Halloween. You can sometimes make ten times your investment, especially if it is a popular costume. Think the same for Christmas, Independence Day, and Thanksgiving.

Want-to-buy and for-sale classified advertisements

Placing a want-to-buy ad in your local paper or one of the national publications can be a lot of fun! The main thing is to try to catch trends before they happen. If you think that the next biggest thing is going to be 1980s hearts and rainbows, place an ad in a publication like *The Antique Trader* and let sellers from all over the world contact you. Everything is cyclical, and I can see the 1970s and 1980s coming back into favor.

An ad in your local paper can bring you numerous sellers. As an example, a want-to-buy-dinnerware ad would work very well for me. I love to sell china and dinnerware, and I know that there is a lot of it out here in the Valley. Keep in mind, though, that if you place the ad, sellers may want you to name the price. This can get tricky. I tend to overpay when I have to name the price. My grandmother always said, "Whoever names the first price loses," and she was right. Any good negotiator lets the other side speak first. Therefore, always ask the seller what he or she wants for the item. If the seller doesn't know, tell the seller to do some research and get back to you. It is better to have your seller see the reality of the situation by doing his or her own research.

Suppose the person with the dinnerware goes onto Replacements.com (a great Web site for researching china and silverware) and finds that the set would sell for $1,000 on that site. So the seller calls me back and wants $500. Now we have a starting point. I can then explain to him or her that when I resell china, I typically get 30 percent of what Replacements asks. So, I would expect to sell the set for $300 on eBay. To handle an entire set of dishes, I expect to double my money. I would then be able to tell the seller that if all the pieces are in perfect condition, I'll pay $125 to $150. If the seller is interested, I would then go and see the set.

Consistently check the classified ad section of your local paper. You can find anything imaginable. Phone sellers ahead of time and get more information before you actually drive out to

 Watch Out!

Whenever you buy from individuals, do your due diligence to make sure that the items are not stolen. This is a very real concern when dealing with secondhand goods. If you ask all the questions recommended in this section, and the seller is skirting the issue and not answering directly, the goods may be stolen. Trust your instinct. You don't want to be involved in a crime.

see items. I have been on enough time-wasting appointments to know that I had better ask specific questions, like:

- What exactly do you have?
- Where did you acquire these items?
- What is the condition?
- How many pieces do you have?
- What is the price?

If a seller won't name a price on the phone, he may be looking for a free appraisal. If he asks you to name a price, don't do it; ask politely to get a call back when he has a price in mind. The seller may just use your bid to get $5 more from the next buyer. You can usually feel out the seller to find out how motivated he is to move the goods, and whether the transaction will be worth your while. If you do decide to go and inspect the merchandise, always take someone with you for safety reasons.

Selling homemade goods

If you manufacture your own items, whether you are a cook, a seamstress, a bead maker or an artist, eBay can be very advantageous to you. You get to control everything about your business: how many items you make, how much you're going to charge, and when you're going to sell them. You also get to be your own R&D (research and development) department. You can constantly be on the lookout for new ideas and new designs and be doing completed auction research to see what is actually selling in your field. And then, because you're your own manufacturer, you can react quickly to what the market wants. It really is a win-win situation.

Remember to always put out a quality product and stand behind your items. Your reputation is your most important asset on eBay. Don't get discouraged if it takes a while to build up a following for your items. Just keep doing your best, making the highest quality products, positioning them correctly, and offering fantastic customer service—you will, in time, do great!

Selling for others

eBay started a *Trading Assistant program* three or four years ago. It lets sellers (like myself) be official Trading Assistants. When a seller goes to list an item on eBay, there is a little button labeled **Let a Trading Assistant Sell for You.** You are then directed to a page like the one in Figure 4.5. Trading Assistants charge a percentage to sell items for others. These percentages are set by each individual Trading Assistant and vary widely. To be listed in eBay's directory as a Trading Assistant, you must meet the following requirements:

- You've sold at least four items in the past 30 days.
- You have a feedback score of 50 or higher.
- Ninety-seven percent or more of your feedback is positive.
- Your eBay account is in good standing.

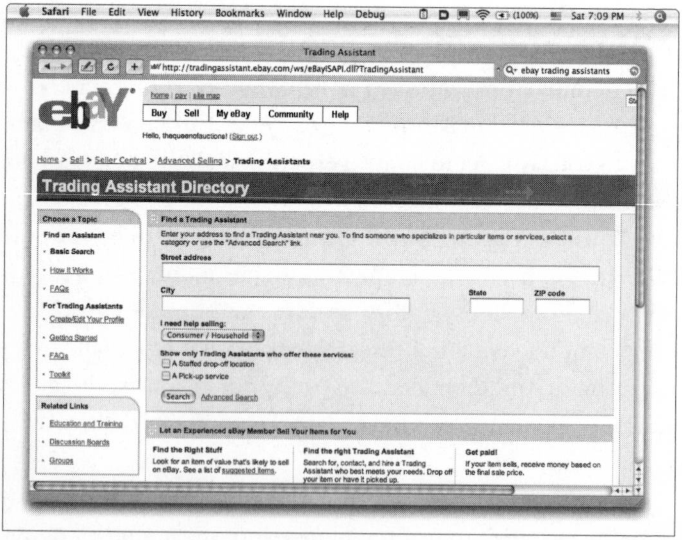

Figure 4.5. The eBay screen showing what you have to type to find a Trading Assistant. Sellers can find an expert in a certain category and ask for a staffed location or pick-up service.

I signed up and tried it for about six months, but it really didn't go anywhere for me. I found that the time wasted talking to sellers about their one item (which they think is worth $20,000 because of *Antiques Roadshow*) could be better spent finding my own items and making up to 900 percent returns on them. However, if you absolutely can't find anything to sell, sign up to be an eBay Trading Assistant after you have met the requirements.

Another way to sell for others is starting your own consignment business. You don't even need a store front. You can do it from your home and take items from your friends and neighbors. Start spreading the news with a flyer or business card and offer to sell items for a 20 to 30 percent commission, plus the eBay selling fees. This is in line with what the drop-off stores are charging, and if you are approaching friends and relatives, your reputation should be stellar (at least I hope it is!).

Just the facts

- Go through your own home with a fine-tooth comb before you go out and buy any merchandise to sell on eBay.

- Buying at garage, estate, yard sales and thrift stores is a lot of fun and can bring in big returns.

- Forge relationships with wholesalers and manufacturers to buy overstocks and slow-turning merchandise at good prices.

- Don't overlook regular retail as a place to pick up the hottest new items and great bargains.

- Want-to-buy advertisements and selling for others can also keep you rolling in goods.

How to Get Started
Selling on eBay

PART II

GET THE SCOOP ON...
Writing a business plan ▪ Knowing what it
costs to get started ▪ Estimating taxes,
licenses, and insurance

First Steps to Building a Business

M any eBay PowerSellers got to where they are today without a roadmap. It just kind of happened to them and one day, they woke up with a full-blown business. Now that eBay is much better developed, it is very important for you to have a compass to get you where you want to be—you should have a plan and follow it. However, also know that there are times when you must re-evaluate where you're going and make new decisions. Keep in mind that your business plan is a work in progress and not written in stone. The beauty of running a business on eBay is that feedback from buyers comes in so quickly that you can change direction with that good data in a New York minute (and that's fast!).

Thinking about your business goals

The most important thing you can do when you start a business is write a working plan and a mission statement. (This is my inner MBA coming out.) Think about some key questions:

- Are you going to be a part timer?
- Will you do it as a hobby?
- Is this going to be your full-time business?

eBay is a numbers game. The more items you list, the more money you'll be making. It's that simple. The best way to figure out how many items you need to list each week is to ask yourself how much money you need to bring in each month. Would you be happy with an extra $50 in gross sales each week? That works out to $2,600 per year. Not bad. Or do you want to do $1,000 in gross sales each week ($52,000 per year) and make it your full-time business? Every seller will have a different strategy. On average, the items that I sell on eBay gross between $10 and $20 each. Obviously, some sell for a lot higher, others for a lot lower, and some don't sell at all. This is just my average, and I'm closer to the $20 end of the range.

As you start out, you'll probably be closer to the $10 average price. As you learn more and get into your area of expertise, you can hope to increase this number. Also, if you choose automobiles or another high-ticket area, your average ticket price will be much higher. However, for the purposes of this book, I assume that $10 is your average sale. Keep in mind that this doesn't mean every item you list on eBay will sell. It does mean that during one week, if you list 100 items, maybe 70 percent will sell the first time listed. So, of those 70 items that sell, 67 of them will likely sell for your starting price of $10 ($670), one will sell for $125, one will sell for $150, and the last one will sell for $50. That adds up to $995 divided by the 100 items listed works out to $9.95 average for each *listed* (but not necessarily sold) item. Very close to the $10 estimate.

When you have an average selling price, you can figure out how many items you need to list each week. If you're a part-timer who wants to bring in $50 a week in gross sales, you need to list five new items every week. If you're a full-timer who wants to do $1,000 per week, you need to list 100 new items every week. Please remember that this is just an estimate and your numbers will of course vary, but it's a good starting point.

Starting with a working plan

A *working plan* is a commitment to a particular work ethic. Write down how many hours you will spend on eBay each week, how many new items you will list each week, and how much you hope to produce in gross sales. Also list your specialty and where you plan to find your merchandise. This is a goal-affirming process that can keep you on track when the going gets tough. As an example, I show my working plan.

It takes me and my assistant, Maureen, about 20 minutes to deal with each item on eBay. This includes the time required to find it, photograph it, list it, answer questions about it, accept payment, and ship it. When you're starting out, assume you'll spend about 20 to 30 minutes per item. My 45 hours a week (total for Maureen and me) works out to 135 items at 20 minutes each. This is about right, because we are not only listing the 100 new items but also selling about 30 items a week from my eBay store. If you're going to be listing 100 items each week, count on about 33 to 50 hours per week. This is, of course, just a rough estimate, and your time will vary, but it's a good staring place.

> 66 I am committed to spending 45 hours per week total (20 hours for me and 25 for my assistant) doing eBay. I will list 100 new items each week. It will produce approximately $2,000 per week in gross sales. I will specialize in glass, pottery, and tabletop items. My inventory will come from garage sales and thrift shops. Selling on eBay will be one of my streams of income. 99
>
> Lynn Dralle's working plan

Developing a mission statement

The next thing you need to formulate is your mission statement. A *mission statement* takes your vision (where you see your business heading) and core values (attitudes and beliefs that will help your business to succeed) and boils them down into a two- or three-sentence plan. It should include the following:

- What will your concentration or niche be on eBay?
- What are your goals?
- What benefits will this business yield in your life?

❝ I will sell high-quality, unique items on eBay to customers from all over the world as a supplement to my income. This business is exciting to me, because I enjoy treasure hunting and finding bargains. Family is very important to me, and eBay enables me to keep my grandmother's memory and business alive while spending all day at home with my young children. ❞

Lynn Dralle's mission statement

A great mission statement puts into words what it is that makes you want to jump out of bed in the morning and start working ASAP! I show an example of my mission statement so that you can get a feel for what one looks like.

When times get rough, a clear mission statement is a wonderful thing to read. It helps you focus and reinforces your sense of purpose.

Writing a business plan

A *business plan* is a written blueprint and communication tool for your business. It helps you plan how you intend to operate your business. It is almost like a road map to show yourself and others how you intend to get to your goals. Research has shown that a business with a written plan consistently does better than a business without—sometimes ten times better. The plan can be quite simple.

The whole purpose of writing a business plan is to get you thinking and put your thoughts down on paper, but a written business plan can eventually be used to acquire investors and get financing, too. The plan should include the following sections:

- An overview
- A description of your niche
- An analysis of where eBay is heading with your niche
- Your staffing and operational plan
- Your marketing plan
- Your finances

Overview

First, you need to write an overview. Take your mission statement and working plan and expand them into more detail in this portion of your business plan. As an example, my overview is as follows:

I intend to sell $8,000 worth of merchandise every month on eBay by doing garage and charity sales every Saturday morning (and spending $200 on 100 items) and by hitting my thrift stores on a weekly basis. I plan to gross $100,000 this year from my eBay business alone.

Description of niche

Next, describe your niche. Here's mine:

I will specialize in antiques and collectibles, because this is where my expertise lies. I will focus on dinnerware, flatware, and unique collectibles.

You may also want to explain why you have chosen this niche and what credentials make you highly suited for this area.

Analysis of eBay and your niche

In speaking about your niche in relation to eBay's plans for this area, think about and quote some of the statistics in Chapter 3. For me, *eBay sees antiques and collectibles as a growth area and expects to sell over $2.2 billion in collectibles alone for 2005.*

I would also note that everyone collects something, so there will always be a market for unique, hard-to-find items. Be sure to expand on eBay's statistics with information from other sources.

Staffing and operational plan

This is where you describe how an employee or employees will help you, or whether you're going to go it alone. A section of my staffing and operational plan looks like this:

I plan to have one part-time assistant do all my paperwork and run the office. She/he will keep track of what auctions are ending, check on the payments, keep control of the inventory, and ship the items. She/he will be responsible for ordering shipping supplies and our new gift items. She/he will answer all questions relating to our merchandise and keep our customers advised of their shipping dates and tracking numbers. My assistant will be in charge of re-listing all items that don't sell at auction. I will be responsible for finding merchandise, photographing, and listing items on eBay.

You would also explain the operational flow of merchandise in this section.

Marketing plan

In your marketing plan, discuss how to find and keep your best customers. Here's an example:

I will do special marketing campaigns for my repeat customers. I also have a growing e-mail list to which I will send special promotions on a regular basis. I will also put a nice note with a newspaper article about my grandmother into every box shipped and thank customers for their business!

Your marketing plan should detail what sets you apart. Explain why you will be successful in your efforts.

Finances

Now it is time to talk about finances and making some real money!

Planning for start-up costs

Another great benefit to selling on eBay, besides not having to own a brick-and-mortar store, is that your initial investment can be next to nothing. Because you're most likely working from your home and you probably already own most of the expensive equipment (like a computer and digital camera), running an eBay business doesn't have to cost much.

As you start out, keep your overhead low by deferring as many expenditures as possible until you absolutely need them. My grandmother always taught me to keep my overhead low. She would wait months and months before buying anything expensive. It took me six months of constant convincing to get her to buy the first computer for her antique store in 1993 (computers then cost about $5,000, with all the bells and whistles). Boy, it was sure worth my effort! But she was a very savvy businesswoman and always took her time when making big monetary decisions. Table 5.1 shows a sample start-up costs worksheet.

Table 5.1. Sample Start-Up Costs Worksheet

Research books	$55
Periodical subscriptions	$72
Business cards	$45
Remodel work areas	$120
Digital camera	$75
Computer	$0
Licenses	$100
Legal/tax advice	$150
Miscellaneous	$0
Grand total	**$617**

I always recommend investing in your education, which is why I've put in an amount of $55 for guidebooks and another $72 to subscribe to periodicals in your field.

Business cards are a must (see Figure 5.1). I actually have two different business cards: One is my eBay business card that I give to everyone *except* the people I buy from. Why? People having garage, estate, and yard sales don't want to know that you're going to make money off of their items on eBay. They don't mind if you're an antiques dealer, but for some reason, taking their items and selling them on eBay tomorrow for ten times what you paid them rubs them the wrong way. Maybe it makes them feel bad that they didn't sell the items on eBay themselves. I bought a set of china from a woman at a garage sale several weeks ago and she asked me, "What are you going to do with that, resell it?" I told her that I was, and she asked, "Are you going to make money off of me?" and I answered honestly, "I hope so." She wasn't happy. Whatever the reason these sellers feel uncomfortable, to combat it, print up two different business cards, one to advertise your eBay business and one with the types of items you're looking to purchase.

I also have a section in Table 5.1 for you to budget for remodeling your work area (see Chapter 7). I estimated $120 to purchase shelving and a table. However, your area may be fine just the way it is, and you won't need to spend anything. I also assume that you need a digital camera and can buy a great one on eBay for $75. I did just that several months ago: I had received an HP 620 digital camera as a Christmas gift several years before from my friend Peter and had loved it. When it broke, I was heartbroken until I realized that I could find the exact same camera on eBay for a bargain—only $62!

Finally, I list $100 for licenses and $150 for legal and tax advice. This is money well spent. Protect yourself and talk to an expert (most likely your accountant) in the small business field. The SBA will also give you plenty of information and advice for free. Check them out at www.sba.gov.

Figure 5.1. My two different business cards. One card is for The Queen of Auctions and one for my antiques business, Cheryl Leaf Antiques (named after my grandmother).

Looking at cash flow

For the final portion of the finance section of your business plan, project out your monthly cash flow for the next year. This should be based on your past experiences (or predictions) and your estimated monthly sales. In Table 5.2, I give you a sample cash flow for my business. I did not include my assistant's salary in this because you probably won't be hiring help—at least at first. I have help because half of my time is spent selling on eBay and half of it is spent writing books and lecturing. It is very feasible, however, that you could do this volume on your own in a 35- to 50-hour week.

Table 5.2. Cash Flow Example—Ongoing Monthly Expenses

Cash in	
Gross sales	8,000.00
Shipping/handling fees collected	4,750.00
Total cash in	**12,750.00**
Cash out	
Research books	20.00
Inventory	800.00
Auto expense	45.00
Packing supplies	
Bubble wrap	50.00
Packing tape	25.00
Packing peanuts	105.00
Tissue	20.00
Boxes	135.00
Flyers/business cards	40.00
eBay fees at 9%	720.00
PayPal fees at 3.5%	224.00
Batteries	10.00
Shipping fees	
UPS	2,125.00
DHL	0.00

Cash out		
	FedEx	0.00
	USPS	450.00
	Other	0.00
Overhead		
	Electricity	30.00
	Internet access	52.00
	Gas	16.25
	Telephone	62.00
	Water	9.50
	Garbage	13.75
	Insurance	35.85
Repairs		12.00
Supplies		37.00
Miscellaneous		0.00
Total cash out		**5,037.35**
Cash in (+) or out (−)		**7,712.65**

At the top portion of the cash flow, I show cash coming in: $8,000 in gross eBay sales and another $4,750 collected in shipping and handling fees. I talk more about shipping in Chapter 8, but I do want to point out that I charge $2 to $7 above the actual shipping cost per package on shipping, and I use this money to pay my assistant and to pay for shipping supplies.

Then I deduct the cash spent. Of course, I have to continue doing my research, and there is a line item for purchasing books. I buy inventory each month, and mine is about one-tenth of my final sales price, or $800. Because I travel around to garage sales and shops, I list an automobile expense here. I also include packing supplies, which can really add up. I spend about $335 per month on these (see Chapter 8). You will need flyers or an advertisement to put in each box, and I pay about $40 per month for this. eBay fees have increased recently, so I estimate 9 percent of the total gross sales price, or $720. PayPal accounts for about 80 percent of my sales, so I take 80 percent of $8,000 and then 3.5 percent of that ($224) to PayPal. I go through batteries like crazy for my digital camera, so I estimate $10 for that big box I buy at Costco every month. (You know, I think some of these batteries may be going to my kids' toys. Oh well!) As you can see, I pay about $2,575 to UPS and USPS, so I'm making a nice amount on the shipping charges to offset my packaging costs, labor costs, and other eBay fees.

Next are the expenses associated with running a business from my home. My accountant does not want me to take the home-office deduction. I get the interest write-off anyway (because I itemize), and he has other reasons for not wanting me to do this. In your case, however, the situation may be different. (I can't stress enough how important it is to work with a professional accountant in setting up your business.) I do write off 25 percent of my utilities, because I am using 25 percent of my home for my business. I also write off the entire cost of my business phone line and Internet access. (I have a separate business phone and fax line. It makes the business appear much more professional.) The insurance cost is 25 percent of my homeowner's policy, and I discuss this in the "Insurance" section later in the chapter. Finally, I include a small amount for repairs and supplies.

Inventory: Purchases and sales

Keeping track of your purchases and sales—that is, the movement of your inventory—is a critical part of your business. You must keep excellent records of every item you buy and sell. A simple ledger system, a computer spreadsheet, or my record-keeping notebook called "I Sell on eBay" (available at www.the queenofauctions.com or in the eBay store at http://www.thee bayshop.com/Catalog228/Default.asp) all work well.

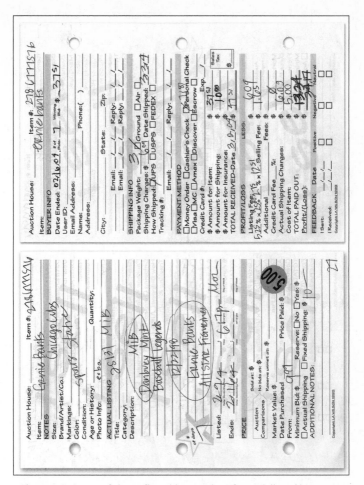

Figure 5.2. A copy of the profit and loss section of my I Sell tracking sheets. I go through at least 100 of these sheets each week. It's a great way to keep all of your item's information in one easy-to-find location. I just hand them to my accountant at the end of the year, and he can do my income taxes!

To keep your records in a simple ledger, mark the date and the item purchased, along with the price paid. It is best to do this the moment you return from making your purchases, while it is still something you can remember! Otherwise, all items start to look alike. Make columns to record the price the seller pays

> ### ☼ Bright Idea
>
> When I started buying and selling on eBay in 1998, I realized that I needed a way to get organized and to keep track of all those unique one-of-a-kind items I was purchasing and selling. I invented the "I Sell on eBay" three-ring binder loose-leaf tracking system to keep track of what I was selling and "I Buy on eBay" to keep track of what I was buying. Each I Sell sheet contains a place to fill in the date the item was purchased, from whom it was purchased, and the price paid. Once the item sells, there is a profit/loss statement on the back side. It has been a lifesaver, and eBay loved both binders so much it carried them in its online eBay store for three years. My binders, I Sell for selling and I Buy for buying, are currently back in the eBay store. What a fantastic honor. Check them out at http://www.theebayshop.com/Catalog228/Default.asp.

and any direct expenses, such as eBay and PayPal fees. You can also set up a simple computer spreadsheet and fill it out just as you would a handwritten ledger.

Business licenses and sales tax

As far as all the legalities involved in starting a business, the first thing you need to do is apply for a master business license. A great place to start looking for license requirements is on the SBA (Small Business Administration) Web site at www.sba.gov/hotlist/license.html. It has a list by state, and when you click on your state, you're directed to additional Web sites that show what's required for your area. Typically, you file forms for a master business license application through your state's department of licensing or through your county or city business tax office.

You need to apply for a sales tax (reseller's) permit if you live in a state that charges sales tax, and this permit is typically through your state's department of revenue. You're required to collect sales tax on items delivered within your state. What this means is that if your business is located in California, and you ship a vase to a man in Florida, no sales tax is collected. But if you sell a plate to a lady in California and she picks it up or you ship it to her, you must collect sales tax, because the item is being used in your state. This amount will usually be such a low

> ### Watch Out!
>
> If you decide to hire employees, make sure you file all the appropriate forms. You need to have a Federal Tax ID number and withhold Social Security and Medicare from your employee's paychecks (the employee pays half, while you, as the employer, pay the other half). You will also be responsible for withholding a portion of each employee's wages for federal income tax liability and you're required to pay unemployment and liability insurance to your state government (and once-yearly unemployment taxes to the federal government).

figure (because most goods will be shipped out of state) that you may be required to file forms for this tax only once a year.

A reseller's permit also enables you to buy inventory without paying sales tax, because you're purchasing for resale. What this means is that if you go to a retail location to purchase inventory and they want to charge you sales tax (you are in a state that charges sales tax) you can tell them that you have a resale permit. You will be asked to fill out some forms and will not be charged sales tax, because you are buying for resale and the final buyer (that you sell to) will be responsible for the sales tax.

If any federal forms are required, you can find out by calling the Internal Revenue Service at 800-829-3676 or going to the Web site at www.irs.gov and ordering Publication 583: "Starting a Business and Keeping Records." Typically, you need federal forms only if you're planning to hire employees or if you need to be paying estimated quarterly income tax on your earnings (see the following section).

Legal fees and income taxes

Speak with an accountant or attorney to determine how to set up your business. Will it be a sole proprietorship, corporation, or LLC (limited liability corporation)? The majority of people starting out selling on eBay run it as a sole proprietorship. However, you should speak to an expert about your personal situation.

Do you pay income tax on your eBay sales? And the answer is, of course! I run my eBay business just like I ran our antiques business when we had a store. I keep very good records and report all sales to the state and federal government. Just remember though, that the beauty of running your own business is that you can take a lot of legal deductions for your car and mileage and using your home as a business. Because you're probably running your business out of your home, you can deduct a percentage of your utilities, a percentage of your phone, a percentage of your mortgage, and many other expenses.

My accountant has advised me to set up a completely separate checking account for the business. He wants me to pay for all of my eBay expenses through this account and keep very good, separate records. Again, I recommend that you speak to your accountant about how he or she will recommend setting this up for you. You might want to consult *The Unofficial Guide to Starting a Small Business,* 2nd ed. (Wiley Publishing, 2004).

Insurance

With all your merchandise stored in your home, you want to have some sort of insurance for your inventory. It doesn't have to be overly expensive and may already be included with your homeowner's insurance. I turn my inventory so quickly that I probably only have $2,000 to $20,000 worth of goods at any one time. You will probably do the same with your inventory. My homeowner's insurance covers $400,000 worth of goods in my home, so I feel that this is sufficient coverage. However, I am learning that you must check with your agent to make sure your particular circumstances are covered.

A rider to your policy, called a home-based business rider, may be just what you need. I have found that if you're running a home-based business, some activities and property won't necessarily be covered under your current homeowner's coverage. Often, the policies exclude business use. You can probably upgrade to cover the increased risks caused by the business. You'll pay a little more for a business rider, but the peace of mind will be worth it. Talk to your insurance agent as soon as you can.

Other types of insurance include general liability, business interruption, key man, and automotive.

- General liability protects you against a lawsuit if someone is injured at your place of business.

- Business interruption insurance provides funds to compensate your company if there is some event that causes business to be lost.

- Key man insurance enables your company to continue to operate if an owner or manager becomes ill or dies.

- Automotive insurance protects your business if one of your employees has a car accident while on the job.

From my experience, these last four types of insurance are priced rather expensively and the cost is not worth the risk.

Just the facts

- Make sure you take the time to write a mission statement and business plan.

- Do a preliminary start up cost and cash flow estimate as this will help you make the best plans for your business.

- Keep good track of your inventory purchases and sales for tax purposes.

- Make sure you get the proper business licenses and legal forms filed and filled out prior to becoming a full blown business.

- Take the time to make sure your business is covered with the proper insurance.

GET THE SCOOP ON...
Assessing the state of your equipment ▪ Making
your work station comfortable ▪ Setting up a
flow for your merchandise

Chapter 6

Get Your Work Space Organized

The first step to getting your work space organized includes taking a look at what computer equipment you own. As you read this chapter, you'll be able to evaluate what you own and decide whether you need to purchase new items. You also want to take a look at how you're connecting to the Internet: How fast is your connection speed? When selling on eBay, Internet speed is super important. Another important consideration is your computer work station: Is it set up to keep you as comfortable as possible? You will be spending a lot of time at your desk, so your workstation setup is very critical to your health and happiness.

You also need to figure out how your merchandise will flow through your home, office, and/or garage. You may be bringing in merchandise from outside your home or office, and you need a place to stage it and do your write-ups for your listings. You also need to photograph and store your merchandise. Finally, you need an area from which to ship. I go over all of this in more detail throughout this chapter.

Evaluating your hardware needs

The hardware that you should evaluate includes your computer, monitor, keyboard, printer, and digital camera. These items are imperative to your success on eBay, but you don't necessarily need to rush out today and purchase them. My grandmother was always cautious with her capital expenditures; and you want to be careful, too.

Your best bet is to take stock before you start selling, take stock again as you get some experience selling, and *then* make a decision about what equipment you need. However, your equipment may be so antiquated and frustrating that you'd be better off replacing it right away. My mother's computer, for instance, is eight years old, and it "hangs" for ten minutes at a time. She got so frustrated last week that she came over and said, "I quit. I can't do eBay." I said, "Yes, you can. It's just your equipment. You can purchase a new computer tower from HP for about $500." Keep in mind that my mom has about $30,000 worth of stuff to sell on eBay, and it makes sense for her to purchase a new computer before getting up and going with her business. With the right equipment, she can get started without all the frustration of an antiquated system.

In the following sections, I walk you through the hardware and Internet questions to ask yourself before and during your eBay selling experience.

Computer requirements

Take a look at your computer equipment first. You need to have a relatively quick computer, one that won't get hung up when you're listing items online. I can do a typical listing (after all my research is done and the photos taken) in about two to four minutes on my fast computer. If you have a slow computer it can take ten minutes for the same thing. Three months ago, I had a five-year-old computer that finally got to that ten-minute point, and at that time, I invested in a new computer. It was the best decision I ever made for my eBay business. At 100 items a week, that extra wasted eight minutes would be 800 minutes or 13.333 hours. My brother, the computer expert, claims that in time saved, I paid for that new computer in about two weeks! He's right!

Each computer is unique because of its configuration. There are so many different factors that go into making each computer—parts, manufacturer, software, what is stored on the hard drive, and so on—that your computer will need to be evaluated on an individual basis.

If you have a relatively new computer (purchased in the last two years) that's running slowly, I recommend that you have a friend or family member who is a computer whiz (don't we all have one of them?) check it out for you. Or hire someone to take a quick look at your system.

66 If your computer is running slowly, one of the best upgrades you can do is to add more memory. I recommend 512 MB RAM at a minimum. It will help everything run more smoothly and should be enough for the limited image editing needed for eBay. Of course, hire a specialist to help you with this. 99

Lee Dralle, computer expert

If your computer is over two years old and is running slowly, it's probably time to upgrade your current system or buy a new computer. Often, it's cheaper to buy new if your computer is very sluggish. The best advice I can give you is to try using your current computer to list items on eBay and time yourself. If you're going through the listing screens and it takes longer than 10 to 30 seconds to load the next page, you probably want to start investigating upgrading your current system or purchasing a new computer. Before buying new, get estimates from a specialist and evaluate the costs versus benefits of upgrading versus replacing.

New computers are coming out almost monthly, and there are always great deals. I recommend Kim Komando's Web site at www.komando.com for great tips on computers, hardware, and software. Another great Web site comes from *PC Magazine* at pcmag.com. I also recommend Dan Gookin's *Buying a Computer For Dummies* (Wiley).

It doesn't matter whether you use a Mac (Macintosh) or PC (personal computer) for selling on eBay. Both work fine. The choice between Mac and PC depends only on what you prefer and are the most comfortable with.

Monitor resolution and brightness

The size of your monitor is important, because you can show more text or images on a larger display, thus speeding up your listing and searching processes. Also consider getting a high-resolution monitor, which enables you to display finer and more detailed images and text. Remember that selling on eBay requires a lot of computer time, and you want to make it as comfortable for yourself as possible.

If your display is 14 inches or less (measured diagonally across the screen), has a resolution of less than 640 by 480, or is more than four years old, it may be time for a replacement. CRT (tube) displays lose their brightness over time. If yours has become dingy or dark, consider buying a new one. You can find a nice LCD (flat panel) display for under $200 and a CRT (tube) display for about $100. I recommend 15 inches as a minimum size for your display; if you can afford 17 or 19 inches, that's even better.

Keyboard comfort

Is your keyboard comfortable? An eBay business requires a lot of typing, and you don't want to injure yourself. Recently, I

☼ Bright Idea

OSHA (the Occupational Safety and Health Administration) shows how your monitor should be placed to reduce excessive fatigue, eye strain, and neck and back pain at www.osha.gov/SLTC/etools/computerworkstations/components_monitors.html. This Web site is a great resource.

found that my wrists were getting weak and achy, and it felt like I was developing carpal tunnel syndrome. A friend recommended that I purchase a gel-like wrist pad, and this has helped immensely.

If you're doing a large amount of typing, it may be worth upgrading to a higher quality keyboard. Some people like the ergonomic angled keyboards, and some people can't stand them, so try out some keyboards at a local store, and then buy what is comfortable for you. Keyboards are very reasonably priced and can save a lot of strain on your hands and wrists.

Printer needs

Any standard printer should work fine as long as you can print UPS and USPS (post office) labels. If you do large quantities of prints, consider investing in a black-and-white laser printer, because the price per sheet printed on a laser printer is far less than on an inkjet model. If you do small quantities and want to print color photos, an inkjet may be your best choice.

Camera requirements

Most digital cameras these days are suitable for taking photos of eBay products. The default picture size on an image hosted by eBay is 400×400 pixels; larger images (called supersize, which cost more money in your listing) can be up to 800×800. Higher resolution cameras are useful for *printed* photos, but the display on the Internet does not need a super-high-resolution camera.

A 35 mm camera will work for eBay. I used mine one week when my digital camera was in the shop. The main problem is that you will spend a lot of money on film and developing. You also won't have a viewfinder to see how your pictures are turning out until you have already paid to have them developed. This option is pricey if you take hundreds of photos each week like I do. That week I spent over $100 on film and processing. (I should have just bought a new digital for that kind of money.)

If you will be using a 35 mm camera, make sure that when the photos are developed you have the images put on a CD so you can access them from your computer.

If you currently own a digital camera, try using it to sell on eBay for a few weeks and see how well your pictures are turning out. And keep in mind that if the pictures don't look great, it may not be the camera's fault, but user error!

Most point-and-shoot digital cameras (that is, cameras without a lot of adjustment options) do an adequate job. Some special uses do require more specialized cameras, however, such as photographing jewelry or anything else that is small and detailed. Even a maker's mark on an antique requires macro (close-up) capabilities.

One consideration when choosing a new camera is the software that comes bundled with your camera. The main use for your camera's software is to crop and resize photos, with some adjustment to contrast and brightness. Most cameras come with a software program that's suitable for these tasks. Many cameras are now shipping with Photoshop Elements, a limited yet very capable smaller brother to Photoshop (which is frightfully expensive).

If you decide to purchase a new digital camera, remember that new cameras are coming out almost weekly. To keep up with the changing technology, check out a camera review site on the Internet. One I recommend is www.dpreview.com. Another suggestion is to buy your camera at Costco or Sam's Club. This is what I did when I was first starting out. Costco, in particular,

Moneysaver!

Before you buy a new digital camera to replace your old one, read the manual cover to cover and try some of the suggestions. I had a great little camera for over six months, and only then realized how to use it correctly. When I finally took the time to read the manual, I found that it had a zoom feature and a lighting feature that made my pictures look amazing! I still use this camera, and it's now over 3 years old.

Watch Out!

I don't recommend using a camera phone to take photos of an item you're going to sell on eBay. These won't give the same quality as a regular point-and-shoot digital camera.

has a great selection at great prices. The first one I bought was not right for my business, but Costco took it back for a full refund, no questions asked. This enabled me to get the perfect camera without a lot of hassle.

Network access

If you're planning to run a small business on eBay, a high-speed (broadband) connection is a must, because page-load times on eBay will be must faster, as will image uploads and downloads. A faster network connection also makes your research much faster, and you can view more auctions in less time.

The two main types of broadband today are DSL (which runs over phone lines) and a cable modem from your cable company. Some companies give you a break if you have more than one type of service with them (such as bundling your DSL service with your phone bill or bundling your cable modem with your cable TV service). Check with your phone company and cable provider in your area and compare prices.

I use high-speed cable access from Road Runner. It costs me about $45 per month and is worth every penny. In fact, I just couldn't go back to dial-up. Last summer, when I stayed at my mom's house on the beach in Washington, I was forced to use dial-up. It took me four times as long to do a listing, so I finally gave up. I packed up my laptop and went to Kinko's in Bellingham to plug in to its free cable service. (By the way, if you have your own laptop and there is a desk available, high-speed Internet connection is free at Kinko's! This will most likely change in the future.) I spent most of my summer days at Kinko's listing my items quickly.

Most new laptop computers come with built-in wireless capabilities. You are then able to access the Internet from many different locations without actually plugging in to a cable. As an example, Starbucks offers T-Mobile wireless in all its cafes. You will have to have an account with T-Mobile and pay to use this, but it sure is handy. I have also noticed that some airports around the country are offering free wireless Internet access. This makes it easy to work when you are traveling.

Set up your computer workstation

The best way to set up a computer workstation is to first understand the concept of neutral body positioning, which means being in a comfortable working posture so that your joints are naturally aligned. If you can work with your body in a neutral position, you will reduce stress and strain on your muscles, tendons, and skeletal system and lower your risk of developing a musculoskeletal disorder like carpal tunnel syndrome.

The OSHA (Occupational Safety and Health Administration) Web site has much more important workstation information and can be found at www.osha.gov/SLTC/etools/computer workstations/positions.html. The best thing I learned on that site is that your elbows should be bent between 90 and 120 degrees. Mine were bent at about 70 degrees, and this was causing strain on my hands. I needed to purchase a desk chair that would go higher. Please take a look at the OSHA site and really study the pictures and tips. It makes a lot of sense.

Setting up your other work areas

You also need to evaluate how merchandise will flow through your work area. Keep in mind that all of your merchandise storage does not have to take place in one room; it can happen in different areas of your home or even your garage. And if you're selling on eBay only part-time or as a hobby, you won't need as large of an area as someone who is doing this full-time. There are four key areas in my basic merchandise flow chart:

1. **The staging area:** This is where you put items when you first acquire them and where you measure items, note the condition, clean them, and do any repairs.

2. **The photography area:** This must be a place with a good backdrop for taking crisp pictures.

3. **The storage area:** This is where you store items until they're paid for and can be shipped. Remember that items could be stored for as long as one month for an auction item or much longer if you have them listed in your store. (I usually give my buyers up to a month to pay, especially if they have e-mailed me to make these arrangements.) As far as the items that I have listed in my store, my rule of thumb is to leave it in the store for one to two years.

4. **The shipping area:** This is where items are packed for shipping.

I do two of these processes (the staging and storing) in my office. My office is about 20 feet by 30 feet (approx. 600 square feet). It has been converted from my family's rec room into my workspace. I also have two computer work stations in this space, one for me and one for my assistant. The photography I do outside, and the shipping is done in a portion of my garage. You can definitely utilize your home to its best advantage.

Set up your staging area

When I bring items home from garage, yard, and estate sales, I stage them on a table in my office that I bought at Costco. It's about 3 feet by 8 feet and very sturdy. This is where I write up my I Sell sheets for each item. When I first started buying and selling on eBay back in 1998, I realized that I needed a way to keep track. I invented a system of tracking sheets, I Sell for selling and I Buy for buying. These sheets have been a lifesaver, and many people use them to stay organized. These binder systems can be purchased from eBay in their eBay shop at www. theebayshop.com/Catalog228/Default.asp. It has been a huge

> **Watch Out!**
>
> Try to keep your eBay business out of your living space. I know this is difficult—sometimes (well actually a lot of times), my business spills over into my dining room and my family says, "Oh my gosh, it's starting to look like Grandma's house!" My grandmother was an antiques dealer, and her house looked just like her shop. This is when I get really scared and quickly move everything into its proper place! It will be best for your mental well-being to keep your business and personal life separate.

honor that eBay recommends my products! You will find samples of both I Sell and I Buy in the Appendix.

On the I Sell sheets, I note condition, size, color, manufacturer, age, brand, and any history. Once my items are written up, I place them in a box with the sheets next to each item, and then take them out to my photography area.

When I buy items by the pallet, I stage the pallets in my garage. Sometimes, when I've gone a little crazy with overstock purchases, I can't even park in my two-car garage (and I have only one car). Yikes! I break down the pallets in the garage and try and get as much of the merchandise moved into the inside staging area as possible. If the items are super-huge, like the pallet of toys I just purchased, I just leave them in the garage and forget about bringing them into my office staging area.

For your staging area, consider using a laundry or utility room, a spare bedroom, a corner of your office, or even part of your garage. If you don't have a lot of merchandise or if your items are small, you may even be able to convert a small closet or cabinet. Use your imagination.

Set up your photography area

After I have my boxes of items all catalogued, they're ready to be photographed. For many years, I took photos inside and the photos were okay, but not great. About two years ago, I started taking them outside in indirect sunlight, and they are fantastic!

> ☼ **Bright Idea**
>
> I store items by classification, so that I can find them easily when they sell. This way, my assistant and I don't waste any time looking for lost items. I have shelves set aside for dinner sets, metal items, cloth items, dolls, lamp parts, collectibles, Christmas and collector plates, other Christmas items, figurines, plastic items, flatware, and unusual items.

What a difference it has made. Of course, I live in sunny southern California, where it hardly ever rains, so you probably want to take a look at some other options.

On nice days, have an area set up where you can shoot outside. A great place is on a covered porch, covered patio, or under an overhang of your roof. Remember that indirect sunlight is what you're looking for. In my outdoor area, I've put a wooden roof over a portion of my patio and hung fabric drapes behind a rustic table. (See Figure 6.1.) The drapes are off-white canvas painter's tarps that I hung with clip-on curtain rings. (I had to make it really simple, because I don't sew.)

In inclement weather, have a place in your home where you can shoot photos. There are a lot of great tools on the market to get professional-looking photos inside, and I discuss these in Chapter 11, which is all about photography. Just start thinking about where you could make a studio outside and where you have about 3 feet by 3 feet of space inside.

Set up your storage area

It is very important to have a super-safe place to store your items. It could be shelving that's secured to the wall with anchors, built-in shelving, cabinets with doors, or another form of safe storage. You can even box your items up and stack them in the garage as long as you clearly mark what's in each box. I use shelving that's secured to the walls of my office—quite a lot of them, actually, because I typically have 2,000 items for sale at auction or in my store (see Figure 6.2).

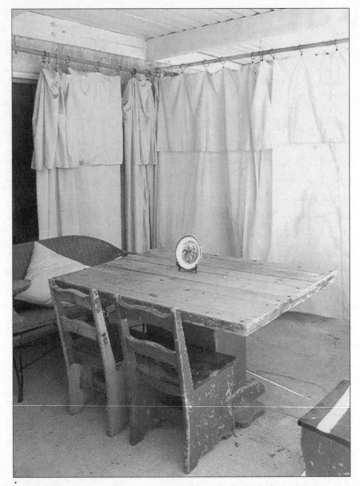

Figure 6.1. This is a picture of my outdoor photo studio. I use it even on rainy days, although we don't get many!

Because I live in earthquake country, I will be adding a small width of wood to the front ledge of each shelf. The wood pieces are about ½-inch tall and will protect items from slipping off the shelf in case of an earthquake.

Figure 6.2. This is a picture of one of the shelving units in my office. I have ten more.

Set up your shipping area

Your shipping area should be in an area of your home or garage that can get messy. Shipping is an untidy business, especially if you're shipping using packing peanuts. (And anything break-able should be shipped with packing peanuts or an air pillow system. I discuss this in Chapter 8, which is all about shipping.) You also have to store boxes, bubble wrap, and packing tape, so choose an area that can accommodate all of this. Finally, you need some type of table or counter on which to wrap your items.

When I bought my house here in the desert, I made sure that it had a large rec room for my office and a two-car garage to house my extra merchandise. I also have a third garage door that's smaller than the other two, because it was built for a golf cart. It works perfectly for my shipping needs. There, I keep all of my shipping supplies and even have a packing peanut dis-penser that hangs from the ceiling.

Just the facts

- Make sure you have a fast computer and digital camera that you can operate.
- Sign up for high speed internet access if you are going to be spending a lot of time online.
- Get your workstation set up so that you are comfortable at your desk—with eBay you will be spending a lot of time here!
- Plan your merchandise flow for staging, photographing, storing, and shipping.
- Make sure your shipping area is in a place that can get messy.

GET THE SCOOP ON...
Choosing a catchy user ID ▪ Getting a feel for
eBay as a buyer ▪ Show me the money

Chapter 7

First Steps to Starting Your eBay Business

O ne of the first steps to starting your eBay business includes spending some time on the Internet. Get used to doing that! Much of what I do
as an eBay PowerSeller is done through the Internet
and includes hours spent in front of my computer. I
spend my time answering e-mails, doing research, and
listing items. To get started, you need to choose a user
ID, get registered as an eBay buyer, learn the ropes,
build up your feedback rating, and upgrade to an
eBay seller's account. You also need to know the ins
and outs of the ways you can be paid. This is the fun
part! This chapter gives you the basics.

Start by spending time on eBay

eBay may seem a little intimidating at first, but it
isn't. It is a very user-friendly site, and it's getting
more so every day. Spend some time on the site just
surfing around to get a feel for it. Do some basic
searches using the blank search box at the right-
hand top of every page. This is the same search box

that you would type in an eBay item number if you wanted to search that way. As an example, if you have always wanted a Partridge Family lunchbox from the 1970s, type in "Partridge Family lunchbox" and see what comes up (see Figure 7.1). What a great way to revisit your youth.

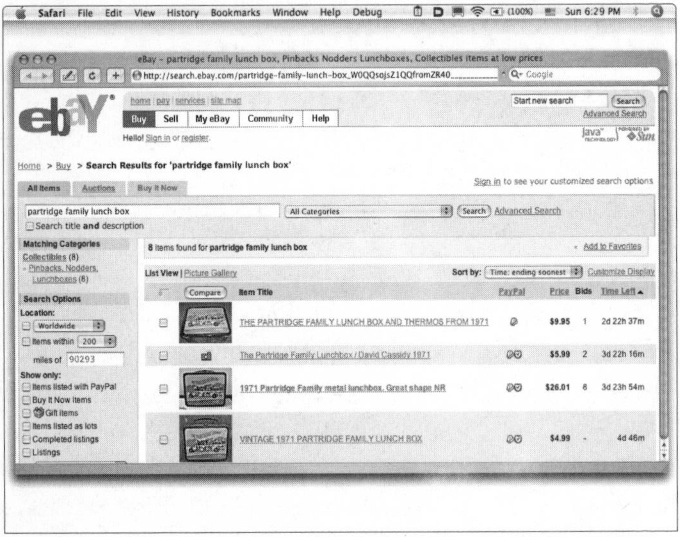

Figure 7.1. There are eight vintage Partridge Family lunchboxes from the 1970s available for sale on eBay. You could pick one up for as little as $4.99. But remember the auctions are not over yet. When I checked completed auctions, two similar boxes sold for $75.00.

eBay is a fun site, and I encourage you to get better acquainted with it. As you're checking it out, take a close look at the buyer user IDs and seller user IDs, because in the next section, you're going to start brainstorming for ideas.

Pick a user ID

Before you register on eBay, you need to think about what you will choose for your user ID. This needs to be a catchy phrase that your customers will remember easily.

As you may know from trying to get an e-mail address through Yahoo! or AOL, many of the good names are already

> ☼ **Bright Idea**
>
> Remember to write down at least five to ten different user IDs before start-
> ing the registration process on eBay. This will save you time in the long run,
> because you will have made the effort to think of names that work for you
> from all different angles ahead of time. Rank them in order of your preference.

taken. This is why you want to make a list of possible options
beforehand. If you don't do this, you can get flustered when
you're registering and end up picking something—anything—
just to complete the process.

I started out selling on eBay as LAWilson (my initials and last
name) in 1998. After my divorce, I wanted something more
descriptive of my business. My publicist called me the Queen of
Auctions, so I went on eBay to change it to QueenofAuctions.
Guess what? It was already taken. Luckily, I had written down
some other options, and TheQueenofAuctions was available.

Remember that you can change your user ID on eBay, and
your feedback points and information will follow you. Keep in
mind, though, that eBay will refer customers to your new ID for
only 30 days, and for those 30 days, you will have a changed user
ID icon next to your ID. It is not a good idea to change your ID
because you may lose business if former customers don't search
for your auctions during that 30 day window. Instead, choose
the right user ID from the get-go.

Here are some hints for choosing your user ID:

■ If you plan to specialize in one area, choose an ID with
  that category in your name. As an example, a bookseller
  may choose BooksRFun, Books4U, Books4You, BookLover,
  Book$, BookstoYou, Books2You, Books!, BookReader,
  Read4Fun, and so on.

  Normally, I wouldn't recommend adding "the" or an
  exclamation point to an existing user ID, but because eBay

has grown so huge (with almost 150 million registered users), this approach has become a necessity. Add punctuation (! or $) and/or real numbers (such as 4 or 2) to make your ID different from other people already registered on eBay.

- Don't make your user ID too long, unreadable, or with too many numbers. Some sellers like to use their birth year or favorite numbers in their ID. This can get confusing and hard to remember. User IDs like 2976Porsche, Hamilton1955, and 789546821 are not easily remembered (and these are actual user IDs from eBay).

If your current user ID doesn't make sense after reading this section, I recommend changing it. Just like getting a new ID, make a list of ideas before making the change. eBay asks that you consider the following before changing your user ID:

- If you change your user ID, eBay members may have trouble finding or recognizing you.

- Do consider changing your user ID to better represent what you do on eBay.

- You can change your user ID only once every 30 days.

- The **Changed ID** icon will appear next to your user ID for 30 days (even for current listings.)

- You can't use an e-mail address or Web site as a user ID.

Here is where you go to change your user ID: cgi4.ebay.com/ws/eBayISAPI.dll?ChangeUserId or you can follow the string home > my ebay > change user id.

Register on eBay

Once you have your list of favorite user IDs, it's time to actually register on eBay. On the home page of eBay, there is a greeting at the center top that says, **Hello! Sign in or register. Sign in** and **register** are hyperlinks; click on the **register** link. The Register: Enter Information page that comes up looks like Figure 7.2.

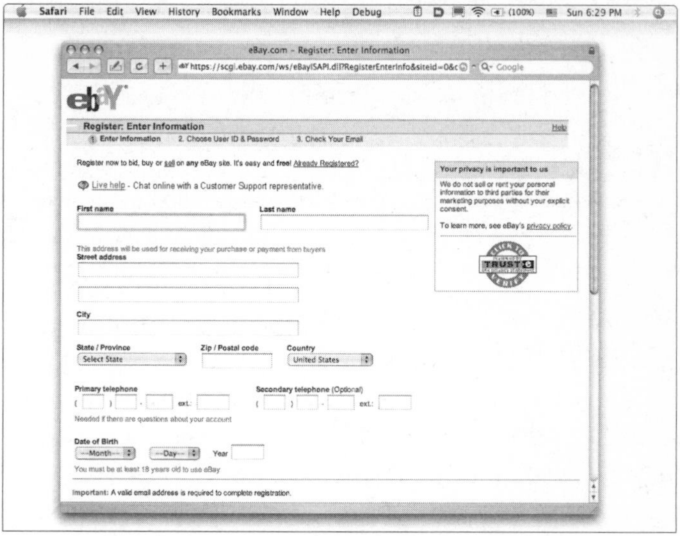

Figure 7.2. The front page to register as a new user on eBay.

eBay will ask for your name, street address, telephone number, and date of birth. A valid e-mail address is required to sign up. You're also asked to read the eBay User Agreement and Privacy Policy. This is very important, because there's information in the agreement and policy that you must be aware of when selling on eBay. Click on the printer-friendly version and print it out to read (at the time of this writing, it's ten pages long). An example of some of the important items you find in the agreement includes:

- eBay's services are not available to persons under the age of 18.

- Children under the age of 18 may use the site in conjunction with, and under the supervision of, a parent.

- If you earn a net feedback rating of –4 (minus 4), your membership may be suspended.

After agreeing with the policy, check the box at the bottom of the page. The next page that comes up asks you to choose

> ### ☼ Bright Idea
>
> On almost every eBay page, there is a yellow question mark icon next to a **Live help** hyperlink. Clicking on the **Live help** link opens up a new window that allows you to chat online with a customer support representative within minutes. Please utilize this feature if you get stuck. Don't be embarrassed to ask for help. I've been an eBay PowerSeller since 1998, and I still use this service at least once a month.

your user ID. eBay gives you three suggestions or lets you create your own. I encourage you to create your own (you should have all your choices already written down). When I signed up for a third account, I was given three terrible choices: Lynn2005, Lynn3376, and 123Lynn. (By the way, I tried to take two of the user IDs that were recommended, just for the purposes of researching this book, and by the time I got to the next page, they were already taken by someone else!)

After you choose your user ID, eBay asks you to choose a password, and it must be at least six characters long. eBay now has a really cool feature, where they show a meter with three bars: If your password is not very secure, the three bars won't light up. Test various passwords until you get a secure one.

The next page shows whether or not your user ID is available. If it isn't, eBay suggests some others or lets you keep inputting until you get one that isn't taken. Don't get frustrated here. (Let me tell you, I did. It took me seven tries to find a user ID that was available. I was about ready to give up. Now, don't you do the same!) Keep trying. Some ID will eventually be accepted, but make sure that it's one you really want. Finally, the screen comes up that says you have a unique user ID.

If you register with an anonymous e-mail address, such as a Yahoo! or Hotmail account, you need to keep a valid credit card number on file to verify your identity, but your card will not be charged. eBay says that if you register with a paid address like the one tied to your home service (@verizon.com or @dc.rr.com), you won't need to give a credit card number. However, when I registered with my e-mail address, lynn@thequeenofauctions. com, which is an e-mail address I pay to have, eBay made me give a credit card number.

eBay then asks you to go to your e-mail inbox and open a special e-mail message from eBay to finish the process. You follow a link back to eBay and confirm your account. Congratulations! However, you're not done yet. Read on.

Buy ten items and build up your feedback

Before selling on eBay, you want to build up your feedback rating. You may have already been buying on eBay for years and already have a nice high number next to your user ID. If so, good for you! But if you don't have feedback points, I suggest that you buy ten cheap items to build up your feedback rating.

These items don't have to cost more than 99¢. One idea is to buy a downloadable e-book, which means that you pay the purchase price, and then the buyer just sends you an e-mail link to an e-book, so you pay no shipping. It's also good to actually buy a few items that will be shipped, because then you get a better feel for how eBay works. You can take a look at how other sellers are doing things and take notes about what you like and what you don't like. It is a great way to become initiated in the ways of eBay.

Finally, make sure that the sellers you buy from have a good history of leaving feedback for their buyers. To do this, click on the feedback number next to the seller's user ID. This takes you to the seller's Member Profile page. Once there, click on the tab button that says **Left For Others** to see the actual number of feedback that the seller has left for buyers. For example, I have received 12,965 feedback ratings and have left 17,024 feedback ratings for others. It is a good bet I will leave you positive feedback if you buy from me. Check out my auctions at user ID TheQueenofAuctions.

Set up a seller's account

In the old days, once you registered on eBay, you were registered for everything. These days, you need to register again to become a seller by setting up a seller's account using your eBay user ID.

To be able to sell on eBay, you have to enter a credit or debit card number and checking account information. eBay requests this information to keep eBay a safe place to buy and sell, because eBay is able to verify who you are. eBay also asks for this information because when you list items to sell on eBay, eBay charges fees and needs a way to collect.

In setting up a seller's account, eBay first asks for your credit or debit card information. You will need the three- or four-digit security code to do this. It then asks for your bank name, routing number, and checking account number. Finally, it asks you how you would like to pay your selling fees. Do you want them to come from your checking account or be charged to your credit card? I like to use my credit card because I earn frequent flyer miles, but this is up to you. After that, you're done. Finally, you have a seller's account, and you're ready to start selling.

If you're unsure about giving all this financial information to such a large Web site like eBay, I can tell you that I gave this information back in 1998 and I have never had a problem with eBay misbilling me (that they didn't straighten out later) or using my personal information for the wrong reasons.

Know how money is collected on eBay

Even before you acquire merchandise to sell on eBay you must think about how you are going to collect money and get signed up for these services. It's my favorite part of the entire process—actually collecting and receiving the money! It's what makes it all worthwhile.

Buyers on eBay will pay you many different ways. When I first started selling on eBay in 1998, almost 50 percent of my sales were paid for with checks (personal, money orders, and cashier's), and 50 percent were by credit cards processed in my family's antiques store. Today, those numbers have changed dramatically. The biggest reason for this change is because of online credit card processing sites like Billpoint and PayPal. Billpoint was eBay's way of enabling a non-traditional business to collect money by credit card, but it never really took off. However, PayPal, founded in 1998, was brilliant in its marketing, offering you a $5 credit for anyone you referred to its site. Sellers were all enamored with PayPal, and it really started to take off in the 2000s. About that time (October 2002), guess what happened? eBay acquired PayPal, buying up the competition and putting Billpoint to pasture (it no longer exists).

These days, about 90 percent of my payments come through PayPal (at a fee, of course), and only about 10 percent are run through the antiques store's credit card processing or received in the mail in the form of cash or check. In the following sections, I look at all these money-collecting options in more detail.

PayPal

In 2005, PayPal had over 70 million registered users, about half as many as eBay itself. eBay owns PayPal, and all of its systems are integrated on the eBay site. It really does make selling on eBay a lot easier than in the past. However, PayPal does take a chunk out of your profits.

PayPal allows any individual or business with an e-mail address to securely and easily send and receive payments online. These payments can be charged to a credit card or taken right out of a bank account. PayPal keeps all of your personal financial information private so that both the buyer and seller can feel secure using this service.

PayPal charges a fee to process these payments. On average, it costs me about 3.5 percent per month. This is higher than what I pay for my business credit card terminal, which costs about 1.9 percent. However, PayPal saves me time. When I had my antiques store and took 50 percent of all transactions over

☼ **Bright Idea**

Not only does PayPal save you time by processing credit card payments, it saves you time because it's completely integrated with eBay. Once someone pays you with PayPal and you go to your item's auction screen, it will say, "The buyer paid with PayPal" and give the date. That's a great feature.

the phone by credit card, I had to pay employees to answer phones, record the information, and hand-process the credit cards. If the customers wanted to chat, this wasted our precious work time. Also, sometimes, we would write the information down and miss something, so we'd have to call the buyer back to verify all the info. In this way, PayPal saves time and mistakes, and I believe it is worth the cost.

PayPal accounts

In this section, I discuss how PayPal is set up and how it calculates these fees. There are three type of accounts:

- Personal
- Premier
- Business

A personal account is free: You can send money for free, and you can receive money for free if it's coming out of a person's bank account. With a personal account, you won't be able to accept credit cards from any customers, however. And as a seller, you want to be able to accept credit cards from your buyers.

To accept credit cards, you have to upgrade to a premier or business account. I've had a premier account since 1999. (The business account is something to consider when you get to a higher level of sales, because it enables you to limit areas of your PayPal account to different employees.) I'm still very comfortable with my premier account, and this is what I recommend for you to begin with. When you do sign up for the premier or the business account, you can send money for free, but to receive funds is going to cost you.

> ### ☼ Bright Idea
>
> PayPal is accepted in 38 countries. This means that it's now easier than ever to get a payment in U.S. dollars from countries like Canada, Europe, and Japan. Also, PayPal offers $1,000 protection to buyers and sellers who meet certain requirements. Please visit the site and go to www.paypal.com/us/cgi-bin/webscr?cmd=_pbp-info to find out more about this feature.

For up to $3,000 in total PayPal transactions per month, PayPal charges 2.9 percent plus a 30¢ fee per transaction. Some of my items sell for $9.99; add the $8 shipping/handling/insurance fee to this, and you get $17.99. PayPal charges me 52¢ plus 30¢, for a total of 82¢. This works out to 4.55 percent. As the prices of my items go up, this percentage comes down a little.

If you go over $3,000 in total PayPal transactions per month, you can apply for a merchant rate account. The fees go down slightly. For $3,000 to $10,000 per month, the amount changes to 2.5 percent plus 30¢ per transaction. So on that same $17.99 sale the fees would be 2.5 percent or 45¢ plus 30¢ for a total of 75¢ or 4.16 percent. Not a huge difference but every little bit helps. This 7¢ savings times my 500 transactions per month is $35.00. I just applied for the merchant rate account.

Having PayPal is a great selling point for buyers; in fact, many buyers won't buy from someone who doesn't accept PayPal. As a seller, you can't live without PayPal.

Sign up for a PayPal account

PayPal claims that it takes less than two minutes to sign up. It does take longer than that, but it isn't difficult.

On the front page of the PayPal site at www.paypal.com is a hyperlink in the top right-hand corner that says **Sign Up.** Click on this, and you're taken to a screen that asks you to choose which type of account you'd like. Select the button next to **Premier Account.** The screen asks you your country name, and then you're taken to a page that looks an awful lot like the eBay sign-up page. See Figure 7.3.

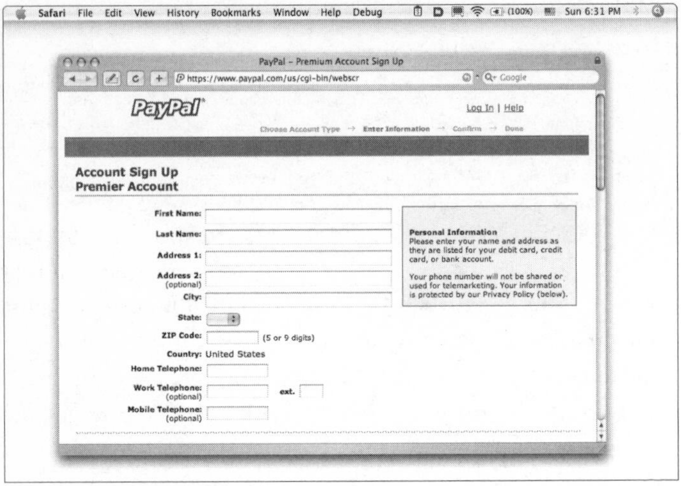

Figure 7.3. This is the PayPal sign-up page. It is very similar to the eBay sign-up page.

You input your name, address, and telephone number, plus your e-mail address and a password that's at least 8 characters long and case-sensitive. You're prompted for two security questions in case you lose your password.

Finally, you must consent to the User Agreement and Privacy Policy. I recommend that you print this document out and read it (it's about ten pages long). Do read it carefully. I found a few interesting items in the User Agreement that I didn't know about. For example, even though American Express cards are accepted by PayPal, American Express has decided to decline any credit card transactions that are funded with a corporate Amex card.

Once this page is completed, a page comes up that says, **Thanks! You're almost done!** All I had to do then was go to my e-mail account and open a message from PayPal, click on the link that takes me to the PayPal site, and input my password. That was all! It really did only take two minutes.

However, at this point, PayPal records my status as unverified. I knew two minutes were too good to be true! PayPal needs to add a bank account and confirm its existence before I can become verified. Being verified is an important security feature that makes your buyers feel much safer. Also, for you to be able to transfer your PayPal funds into a bank account for your use, you need to complete this step. Click on the **unverified** hyperlink, and then click on the **add bank account** hyperlink. Type in your bank name, bank routing number, and your account number. Now you must confirm the verified account, which can take a few days. The reason this process takes a while is because it's a several-step process:

1. PayPal makes two small deposits into your bank account (and they do mean small—usually 2¢ to10¢ each!).

2. You check your online bank statement or call your bank in two to three business days to find out these exact amounts.

3. You log in to your PayPal account, click the **confirm bank account** link, and enter these two amounts.

Now you are really signed up on PayPal. So, I was right—it does take longer than two minutes.

Visa/MC/Amex/Discover terminal

Back in the old days, a business would have had to have a credit card terminal (those machines that an employee swipes your card through) to accept credit cards. This is no longer the case, because PayPal has become such a huge factor in credit card payment acceptance. However, if you have your own business outside of selling on eBay, you may still choose to have your own terminal. I've kept my terminal, because I still get a few customers every month who want to call or fax in their credit card information and don't want to use PayPal.

I currently use Costco for my credit card terminal processing, and it costs me $20 per month plus a 1.9 percent fee per transaction. It's much cheaper than PayPal on a large volume item, but I'm selling lots of small volume items, so the extra work of processing credit cards myself can add up. The number of customers calling in their credit card information is dwindling, so I may give my terminal back to Costco in the near future and go exclusively with PayPal.

Money order/cashier's checks

One of the safest ways for your potential buyers to purchase with a check is to use a money order or cashier's check. Note that I said, "safest way *to purchase with a check*," not simply, "the safest way to purchase." The safest way for a buyer to purchase is by using a personal credit card through PayPal. This way, the buyer is protected by his or her credit card company and by PayPal. However, many buyers still prefer using some type of check, and a cashier's check or money order ensures that a buyer isn't sending her personal and bank account information to a stranger.

As a seller, you will receive quite a few money orders and cashier's checks. For a small amount (such as less than $100), it is not usually necessary to hold these checks and wait for them to clear because they are payable on demand.

Personal or business checks

I'm still seeing quite a few personal and business checks being used for eBay purchases. However, the USPS fraud division tells me that it's not wise to send a personal check—it just has too much information on it in these times of rampant identity theft.

 Watch Out!

If you receive a cashier's check or money order for a rather large amount (say, $500 or over) and you get a funny feeling about the buyer or the transaction, wait two weeks for the check to completely clear before sending the merchandise. This gets tricky because cashier's checks and money orders are payable on demand and your buyer won't understand why you are holding it. If you're going to do this, though, notify your buyer. There have been some scams recently with large (over $500) and fake cashier's checks being used to purchase cars. The bank sees them as payable on demand since they are money orders or cashier's checks, but when they turn out to be fake, guess who is responsible? You. Be careful!

Many sellers have a policy stated very clearly in each listing, "We hold personal and business checks for 10–14 days to make sure that they clear." If you decide to accept this form of payment, this is a good policy for you to state in your listings.

I've been taking personal and business checks for eBay purchases since 1998. Out of the 5,000 or so checks I have received, only one has ever bounced, and I redeposited it the next week, and it was good. Of course, if I get a personal check for a large sum of money (over $100), I always check the buyer's user ID and feedback. If it's stellar and the buyer has been on eBay for a while, I go ahead and ship the product before the check clears. If something is questionable, I e-mail the buyer and convey that, due to the large dollar amount of the check, I need to wait 14 days to make sure that it clears. Most sellers say to wait 10 days to clear, but from my experience in my antiques store (where I've had more than my share of bad checks), some checks take 14 days to come back. Wait 14 days to be safe.

Cash

Yes, believe it or not, buyers actually do send cash, and it happens quite regularly. About twice a month, my assistant, Maureen, hands me a wad of bills that have come in the mail. More often than not, they are brand new and super-crisp, coming from overseas. A U.S. money order can be very expensive in some countries, and some countries also cannot use PayPal. It is pretty easy, on the other hand, to get U.S. dollars in many foreign countries. Also, if someone can't sign up for PayPal (the buyer doesn't have a checking account, for example), cash is an option.

These buyers usually send the money by registered mail or send it in a regular envelope but wrap the cash in aluminum foil. Receiving cash is just fine with me! I've never had someone claim to have sent me cash and then not received it. Also, I've never received counterfeit bills. Most of my cash arrives in $20s, $10s, $5s, and $1s, but if you do happen to get a $100 bill in the mail, it might be worth your while to take it to your bank and make sure it's authentic before shipping the item.

Just the facts

- Sign up to be a seller on eBay and pick a catchy user ID.

- Build up your eBay feedback rating so that you don't look like a newbie.

- Sign up for a PayPal premier account and be ready to accept payments by credit card.

- Figure out your payment terms.

- Let your buyers know that you will be holding all checks for 14 days to make sure that they clear.

GET THE SCOOP ON...
Knowing how to ship your type of item ▪ Finding
the best carrier for you ▪ Obtaining packing
supplies ▪ Organizing your shipping area

Shipping

Shipping is one of the most important steps in becoming a stellar seller on eBay. Your shipping expertise and speed is what keeps your customers coming back for more, so spend the extra time to become really good at this. It can make or break you.

One touch that buyers love is when you e-mail them and let them know when and how the item shipped (or let the UPS, DHL, or FedEx software do it for you). Big-time online stores (like Amazon.com, Target.com, and so on) do this, and you can, too. If you keep buyers in the loop, they'll be happy returning customers. These are the best kind of customers to have!

I have an assistant, Maureen, who does many things for me, but the biggest task she does is that she saves me from doing any shipping! Maureen loves her job and enjoys getting packages shipped out immediately. She gets her enthusiasm from knowing how excited our customers get when they receive their items quickly. Maureen ships items out the day or day after a person pays, which is very quick! If you read our feedback comments, many are about how fast the item was shipped, how well it was packed, and what a great experience this was for them.

In this chapter, I talk about the different carriers, focusing on the big ones: the U.S. Postal Service (USPS), UPS, FedEx, and DHL. I will discuss how to pack and ship different items, and let you know what types of shipping supplies you need to purchase. I'll even tell you the best way to set up your shipping station. Finally, I show you how to decide what to charge for shipping. Keep in mind that I do try to make money on my shipping. My fee averages from $2 to $7 per package, which is considered very reasonable. The reason I do this is to pay for all the shipping supplies, and to pay part of Maureen's salary.

One more note before you get started: Always place a business card or thank-you note into each box you ship. This extra step shows your customers that you care and are, in effect, asking for their repeat business. I also put an *Antique Trader* article that was written about my grandmother and me into each box, along with an order form for items that we carry in quantity. Many of my customers take the time to e-mail me and tell me what a wonderful grandmother I had and how lucky I was to have grown up in the business. They are right!

Comparing shipping companies

The rates among UPS, FedEx, DHL, and USPS for shipping in the United States are pretty comparable. Every company seems to be getting a little bit more competitive and trying harder.

☼ **Bright Idea**

At the top of each *Antique Trader* article, it looks like I have handwritten a note that says, "Dear eBay Customer: We have packed your item with care and want you to be satisfied. If you're happy, please leave us positive feedback. Thank you so much for your business! Lynn. E-mail me at LDralle@dc.rr.com." Of course, each sheet doesn't have my real handwriting on it. I had my local print shop copy 1,000 of them so that it looks as though it was handwritten. This extra touch ensures good feedback and encourages repeat customers.

They all want a bigger piece of the huge eBay shipping pie, which has turned into a very big business. Who knew that eBay would not only make a ton of money itself, but would also yield such huge windfalls to the shipping companies? A few years ago, you would have been very smart to buy both eBay and UPS stock.

When choosing among these companies, it basically comes down to which one you prefer working with. I hear so many different comments about each company. Some people love UPS, and others hate it with a passion. Some sellers swear by the USPS, and others would rather not use the postal service. FedEx is an up-and-coming shipper for regular ground service and has a stellar reputation for overnight service. DHL (previously called Airborne Express) is giving all the other companies a run for their money in the international marketplace. The choice is really up to you. You may want to try them all before making your decision. Ship a few packages with each carrier and keep track of all the costs and benefits, and then make your decision. You may end up using a combination of two or three. In fact, I use a combination of UPS and USPS.

Each company has some size and weight restrictions—see Table 8.1. Note that length plus girth is the same as adding the length (L) plus two times the width ($2 \times W$) plus two times the height ($2 \times H$). See Figure 8.1.

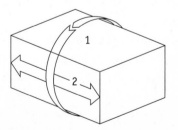

Figure 8.1. This figure shows you how to measure length plus girth for determining your package's size: 1 + 2 = length + girth.

Table 8.1. Regular Service to the Continental United States: Weight and Size Restrictions

Company	Maximum Weight	Maximum Length + Girth (or L + 2W + 2H)	Maximum Longest Side
USPS	70 lb.	130″	NA
UPS	150 lb.	165″	108″
FedEx	150 lb.	130″	108″
DHL	150 lb.	NA	72″
Greyhound	100 lb.	30″ x 47″ x 82″	82″

The pallet of overstock toys that I recently purchased had two huge toy boxes that UPS, FedEx, and USPS would not take. DHL wanted $900 to ship one of them! Yikes. I can't sell a $200 toy and charge $900 shipping. A nice eBayer recommended Greyhound—I had forgotten! Greyhound is a great shipping service to use for oversized items, as long as the package doesn't weigh more than 100 pounds. To ship an 80-pound item across the country costs me only $70. Just keep in mind that, to use Greyhound, you need to drive the package to your local station and, in turn, your customer also needs to drive to his or her station to pick it up.

Finally, if you're sending something breakable, most companies have restrictions on how it must be packaged so that the insurance will be valid. Check with each company for its specifications. However, based on my experience, every item must be either double-boxed or bubble-wrapped, and then have two inches of foam packing peanuts on all six sides. In the following sections, I take a look at the pros and cons of these companies in more detail.

UPS

UPS is my carrier of choice. Sure, I've heard the horror stories about how a package can arrive looking like a gorilla stepped on it, but you know what? I pack my items really well, and we rarely have breakage. When we do have breakage, UPS is quick to pay a claim as long as the box was packed according to its requirements: As mentioned before, two inches of foam packing peanuts on all sides of your item, and your item should be double-boxed or wrapped in bubble wrap first.

- **Pros:** Daily pickup from my home, which costs between $8 and $12 per week depending upon your shipping volume. UPS will stop by daily even if you don't have anything sitting out in your designated pick-up area. Your shipment is automatically insured for up to $100 for each package. UPS has great software that actually e-mails your customer his or her tracking information. A free tracking number provided automatically. UPS is really great to deal with for breakage; they pay claims immediately.

- **Cons:** Not as fast as USPS or FedEx, but they are working on it. Shipments take typically five working days from coast to coast. Not available for shipments to Hawaii, Alaska, Canada, and Mexico, unless you go air (very expensive). It's too expensive for most other international shipments, and UPS always requires complicated customs forms— your international customers won't go for this. UPS charges by volume weight or actual weight, whichever is *larger*. (On the UPS input screen, you're asked to enter the dimensions of your package if it's very large. Let's say that your package only weighs one pound, but the dimensions are 20" by 20" by 20." UPS will charge you a volume weight of 30 pounds, because they take into consideration how much space it will take up in their trucks. I learned this lesson the hard way.)

> ☼ **Bright Idea**
>
> UPS requirements say that each item must be wrapped individually and be at least 2 inches away from other items. Also, each item must be at least 2 inches from the walls of the outer container. Newspaper is not acceptable and they recommend packing peanuts and other foam based items. Rumpled kraft paper can be used for non-fragile items, but these must have 4 inches from each wall. Fragile items may require additional cushioning or double-boxing. (See the UPS site for more information: www.ups.com/content/us/en/resources/prepare/guidelines/prepare_package2.html.)

USPS

I ship smaller items in the USPS flat-rate cardboard Priority mailers. The postage is just $3.85 and is perfect for heavy books, paper items, and DVDs. I also use USPS for all my international packages and packages to Alaska and Hawaii. Their rates are fair, and USPS doesn't ask for a whole bunch of customs forms the way UPS, FedEx, and DHL do. USPS does ask for one simple form per international shipment, not the multiples that are generated when you do a shipment with one of the other carriers. Maureen goes to the post office about once or twice a week, and we try and coordinate our shipments so that we don't wait in line with fewer than ten packages.

The USPS will pick up for free in some areas when they are delivering your mail. You can request this service online. They will only pick up domestic Overnight and Priority shipments, and the postage must already be on the box. If you make a mistake in calculating postage, your item will come back to you and cause a major delay. The USPS will also pick up some international shipments if you choose Global Express. This is very expensive and we hardly ever use it.

- ▪ **Pros:** Free boxes if you are shipping Priority Mail, which is a huge money-saver. Quick service (two to three days across the United States); in fact, by the time I get ready to e-mail a customer that her shipment has gone out, it has already arrived! Best choice for international shipments. First Class and Media Mail can also be cheap alternatives for your customers.

- **Cons:** USPS will pick up from you only if you call or schedule the pickup online, and it is only free if the carrier shows up for your regular mail delivery. If you want them to pick up at a specific time it will cost you $12.50 per pickup. Also, if your package weighs more than 16 ounces, your return address must be the address it was picked up at—something I don't recommend at all. I only use a PO Box as a return address on all my shipments—UPS and USPS included. It's not safe to have anyone know where you live or where your expensive merchandise is stored. This is not as handy as having a daily pickup from UPS, FedEx, or DHL. A daily pickup from one of these carriers means that a driver comes to your home or place of business every day at about the same time. My UPS driver shows up at 2:00 p.m. and if he doesn't see any packages in our normal staging place, he will ring the doorbell to make sure we don't have anything that day.

  If you're shipping airmail or surface mail internationally with the USPS, you must fill out a form and wait in line at the post office with your package. This can be a big time-waster. The USPS will only pick up international shipments that are shipping Global Express (the most expensive option).

  If you want your package insured you will pay extra for insurance, and it's pretty pricey. You must also pay extra for a tracking number if you want one. Not only do these two features cost extra, but you will have to fill out a separate form for each one! Finally, if something goes missing, you may never find it, and collecting from the USPS for breakage or loss is a nightmare. I'm still waiting on a claim that was filed six months ago.

FedEx

FedEx has become a leader in the overnight shipping business. This service is too expensive for most eBay sellers to use for larger items. FedEx has recently become a ground competitor with FedEx Ground and is a company to watch and experiment with on your shipping. I have heard good and bad things. They are not up to the standard that UPS has set but are working towards it.

- **Pros:** Rates are slightly better than those of UPS. Software is comparable to UPS. Delivery is slightly faster than UPS to major metropolitan areas. One of FedEx's companies, FedEx Freight, is a good alternative if you have LTL (less than a truckload) of larger items to ship.

- **Cons:** Not as reliable for delivery to rural areas. They sometimes contract out to smaller trucking firms, and I have heard that packages can get lost for weeks at a time.

DHL

DHL's strong suit is the rapid delivery of documents and shipments by airplane. If you don't want to hassle with the USPS and are doing a lot of airmail to overseas destinations, I recommend contacting DHL (which used to be Airborne Express). If you ship a significant volume, DHL will usually work with your small business to help you get better rates.

- **Pros:** Great at rapid airmail deliveries. DHL can be very competitive with the USPS for international shipments.

- **Cons:** Ground is too expensive. The rate for a one-pound package from 92211 to 87120 with tracking, residential delivery, daily pickup, and insurance for $100.00, was $10.23 (UPS was $5.10). DHL requires a lot of customs forms and paperwork, which can turn off your international buyers who hate to pay duty.

Greyhound

Greyhound serves more than 2,000 destinations in the United States and offers freight service from terminal to terminal at reasonable prices.

- **Pros:** You can ship an oversized item for less than $100 coast-to-coast. Will a customer mind spending $100 for an item that they have to drive to Greyhound to pick up, when the only other option is $900 by FedEx freight? I don't think so. The item doesn't have to be crated or in a box. It just needs to be protected from anything it might come up against in the freight hold (under the bus).

- **Cons:** You must drive the item to the terminal, and your customer must also drive to pick it up. The item cannot weigh more than 100 pounds. Packages take 5 to 7 days to arrive, and if you are shipping Greyhound you obviously must spell out the fact that the buyer must go and pick it up ahead of time. I also charge a $40 handling fee to get the item to Greyhound. Only use Greyhound when your item is too expensive to ship any other way—such as the oversized toys I spoke about earlier. There is no e-mail giving the buyer a tracking number.

Shipping different types of merchandise

It might be that you ship only one type of merchandise. For example, maybe you're going to specialize in DVDs. If that's the case, you will only ever need to buy one type of packing container, or you can use the flat rate Priority Mail envelopes for free from USPS. You will always know the weight of your item, and your shipping routine will be a breeze.

Most people, however, sell a much bigger variety than that. When I do radio interviews and they ask me what I sell, I answer, "Anything that I can make money on." Because of this, I often

> ### Watch Out!
>
> Shipping is critical to your feedback rating. Most feedback deals with the speed of shipping, how well the item was packed, and how accurate you were in describing it. So make sure that you wrap professionally, ship quickly, and let your customers know as soon as each item is shipped. Get in the habit by setting up a good routine for this early on in your eBay business.

have to figure out how to ship unique and unusually-shaped items. It just happened to me this week with a batch of huge toy boxes. But, with the help of the eBay community, I was able to figure it out and quote reasonable shipping using Greyhound.

The following sections take a look at some of the different items you may be shipping.

Large items: Computers and electronics

For items up to 150 pounds and not oversized, like most computers and electronics, UPS and FedEx are the way to go. Many of these items are in the factory-issued boxes when you receive them, which makes shipping them out a breeze. Just make sure you take measurements and know the item fits within the size constraints. Some televisions are larger than the requirements, so you may need to utilize Greyhound for these—as long as they weigh less than 100 pounds.

If your computer or electronic item is not in a factory-sealed box, you will need to wrap it very carefully. I suggest Styrofoam on all sides—just like in the factory boxes. If you can't get ahold of Styrofoam, wrap it in bubble wrap and place it in a snug inner box. Then place that inner box in an outer box that has 2 inches around it on all sides, filled with packing peanuts.

Large items: Furniture, machinery, etc.

Furniture and items over the weight restrictions for the carriers listed in this chapter can get tricky. (Don't forget about Greyhound for items under 100 pounds.) There are a couple of

> ☼ **Bright Idea**
>
> You can say in your listing, "Must be picked up at my location." (There is a button for this when you do your listing.) Taking this approach has worked well for me on several occasions, because I live only two hours from Los Angeles. People do drive out to my location to get their items, especially if it is something that they really want.

companies specializing in the packing and shipping of furniture and other large items. One is Craters and Freighters, and it can be found at www.cratersandfreighters.com. Craters and Freighters will come to your location and wrap or crate the piece of furniture and arrange for its delivery. This service is quite expensive, but it is an option. I had the company give me a quote on a round glass china cabinet going across the country, and I was quoted a price of $700. FedEx Freight is another company doing LTL (less than a [truck] load) shipments.

Contact your local freight companies and get quotes. If you use a local freight company, you will likely have to wrap the item for shipping. Crates, material padding, and lots of cardboard are required to protect your item.

Another option, if you're going to specialize in large items, is to invest in a cheap truck and offer to deliver within a 100-mile radius for a small fee. This is great customer service, but may only work well if you live close to a large metropolitan area.

Non-breakables: Clothing, shoes and accessories

Oh, the beauty of shipping non-breakable items: no packing peanuts and no bubble wrap. What a joy! If your clothing item is small, it can fit into a flat rate Priority Mail envelope, which you can ship for only $3.85. If it is too big for the envelope, try using the flat rate Priority Mail boxes, which cost $7.70 for unlimited weight.

> **Moneysaver**
>
> Remember that Priority Mail boxes are free from the USPS, and this saves money! If you're shipping USPS, you can print labels right from your PayPal account. This can save a lot of time, because you don't have to write labels. It used to cost an extra 20¢ to do use this feature, but now it's free.

I send lots of lightweight clothing First Class. This is a very inexpensive way for your customers to receive their goods. If you're selling kids' clothing at $2.99 a piece, a buyer will not want to pay $5 for shipping, so offer them the First Class alternative. Just place the item in a manila envelope, and if it weighs one-half pound (eight ounces) or less, it is only about $2. As you get closer to one pound, the prices get closer to the priority rate of $3.85—so you will probably want to convert your packages from First Class to Priority Mail at that point.

I recommend buying tissue paper to wrap clothing items prior to shipping. It adds a nice touch, instead of just throwing the items into a box. If you're going to ship clothing, shoes, and accessories by UPS, invest in standard-size boxes that you know will accommodate the different-sized items you will be shipping.

Media items: Books, movies, music, and paper goods

This is another great category of easy-to-ship items. Although you can't call these non-breakables, they are pretty close to being non-breakable. However, jewel cases on CDs and DVDs can crack, and LPs could break. Because of this, please bubble-wrap these items prior to shipping. USPS makes great Priority Mail boxes that fit videos perfectly and, once again, these are free.

You may decide to ship all of these types of items in padded manila envelopes—a great alternative and much cheaper than boxes. You then have the option of shipping them First Class, Media Mail, or Priority Mail. Media Mail is a cost-efficient way to send books, sound recordings, recorded video tapes, printed music, and recorded computer-readable media (such as CDs, DVDs, and diskettes). Media Mail cannot contain any advertising expect for incidental announcements of books (according to USPS). You save money in shipping, but the shipments can also take a lot longer. The best compromise between Media Mail and Priority Mail is First Class. It costs a little more than Media Mail (and less than Priority Mail, up to a certain weight) but arrives faster. Also, I've had several Media Mail packages go missing, and this doesn't seem to happen with First Class.

Small breakables: Antiques and collectibles

This is a tough shipping category. Glassware, pottery, china, and porcelain are all very fragile and easily broken. You want to make sure you wrap your items very carefully. Make sure that you bubble-wrap each item and tape the bubble wrap around it securely, or put it in a small interior box (wrapped in tissue), and then put two inches of packing peanuts around all the edges. Please see Figure 8.2 to see how this should look.

Also, if someone is buying multiple items from you, such as six plates, wrap each plate individually in bubble wrap, and then use a piece of cardboard to separate every two plates. If someone is buying a large bunch of fragile items, I break the items out into two or three separate boxes to ensure safe arrival. Maureen and I tend to err on the cautious side, and I urge you to do the same.

Winning Bid Printout,
Note, or Business Card   Packing peanuts

Bubble wrap

Figure 8.2. A vase wrapped in bubble wrap with at least 2 inches of packing peanuts on all sides. The box just needs popcorn to the top edge and it will be ready to tape up and ship to your customer.

Setting up your shipping station

Your shipping area is very important and will work best for you if you lay it out ahead of time and plan where you'll keep all the items you will be using. We keep all our Priority Mail flat-rate envelopes, stamps, and international forms inside next to Maureen's desk. These are used quite a lot and are handy to have close by. She also bubble-wraps every item on a counter that we designated for shipping. She keeps tape guns filled with tape there also, so that she just has to grab one.

Once Maureen has an item bubble-wrapped and taped securely, she writes the customer's name on the bubble wrap in marker and then carries the item out to our garage shipping area, where we have stacks of cardboard boxes and our packing peanut dispenser. Maureen then tapes up the proper size cardboard box, places packing peanuts in the base of the box, and puts the item inside. Then she surrounds the rest of the box with packing peanuts, places our article and order form on the top, and seals the box shut. She writes the customer's name on the outside of the box, weighs the package, and writes down the weight on our tracking sheet.

After she's done packing all her boxes for the day (usually 20 to 30 packages), Maureen brings the tracking sheets back to the computer area and uses the UPS software to create labels. Once the labels are printed, she puts the labels on the boxes, stacks the boxes outside, and at that point, we're ready for UPS to pick up.

If packages are going USPS, Maureen prints the labels inside and fills out the forms at her desk. She goes to the post office only once or twice a week. (You can arrange for free USPS pickup on the Internet—but only if you ship Priority or Global Express International and don't mind that your return address must be your home address—not a good idea). Start thinking about how you can set up your shipping station to work for you.

If you don't have a lot of space, keep the supplies that you use the most nearby, and store the rest in your garage or back room. It's very nice to have a tape gun or dispenser to use both inside and out. If you buy your packing tape from Uline (www.Uline.com), you get a free tape gun every time you buy a case. I think we have about 30 tape dispensers around here!

Purchasing shipping supplies

Recycle as much as you can when shipping. Ask your friends, family, and neighbors to donate boxes and packing supplies that they receive. This not only saves you money but also saves our planet. Maureen worked part-time at a restaurant, and every day she would come over with a car filled with free boxes. It was fantastic! Go to your local liquor store, grocery store, and/or strip malls and talk to the store owners about picking up their freight boxes once they are empty.

You will most likely need to purchase the following:

- Tissue paper
- Packing tape
- Cardboard boxes
- Bubble wrap
- Packing peanuts

You may eventually want to purchase a packing peanut dispenser like I have in my garage. These run about $150 but are worth it when you get to a certain level of shipping. For tissue paper, packing tape, and cardboard boxes, I buy from Uline. They are located in select major metropolitan cities and have great prices. I do pay a lot in shipping costs for these items, but their prices are so reasonable that the shipping supply companies in my city can't compete. However, I do recommend that you do go through your phone book and call all your local shipping supply wholesalers to get quotes on the items you use the most.

Bubble wrap and packing peanuts are items that cost too much to ship because they are oversized. Find someone in your local market to purchase these items from. I buy 14-cubic-foot bags of peanuts and pay $17 each, wholesale. This is what you should be shooting for. I buy large bubble wrap in 12-inch-wide rolls, with perforations every 12 inches. A 750 ft. roll costs me about $38. This gives you some idea of prices.

> **Moneysaver**
>
> Consider buying your shipping supplies on eBay. I've read several success stories about eBay PowerSellers who are making a great living dealing in shipping supplies. Take some time and do your research on eBay: You may find some great packaging deals and save yourself some money. You may even be able to start a business relationship with a PowerSeller and get all your supplies from one dealer. Try searching for shipping supplies by location—this way, you won't spend a lot on shipping.

You also need some type of scale. I bought a scale that goes up to ten pounds on (you guessed it) eBay. It cost me about $15 and has been great. For anything over ten pounds, I use my bathroom scale. However, if you're consistently shipping large packages, invest in a bigger professional scale.

Charging for shipping/handling/insurance

Knowing what to charge for shipping, handling, and insurance is tricky. You can make mistakes when you estimate weight, dimensional weight, and the cost of shipping supplies—among other variables. Some sellers are adamant that they don't charge for handling. That's fine. If you want to do that and can absorb your handling expenses and still make a good profit, that's fantastic. However, I am of the mindset that since every major catalog and online retailer has been adding handling charges for years, I am going to do the same.

> **Bright Idea**
>
> Always quote a price for shipping in your listing, instead of saying "actual." This is a huge time-saver. If you say "actual," you'll have a hundred eBayers e-mailing you and asking, "How much to zip code 87120?" If you don't want to charge a handling fee, price the shipping and insurance as close to the cost as you can. It will all average out, but save yourself hours in aggravation by quoting a price up front.

In the late 1970s, well before eBay, I was shipping collector's plates that we sold mail-order from advertisements in the *Antique Trader*. I was a kid, but my grandmother used to pay my 10 percent for everything we would sell out of one of those ads. Some weeks, I would make $200 in commission! Here is how I have figured my charges for shipping items after all these years of experience.

I stick to using UPS, and I know that I can ship a small item (about one pound) for $4 to $6 anywhere in the country. I know that a medium item (one to two pounds) will run me $5 to $7, and a larger item (three to four pounds) will cost me $6 to $8. I take the average of those prices and add $2 to all of these for my handling fee. Because UPS automatically includes $100 of insurance, I quote small items at $7 s/h/i (shipping/handling/insurance), medium at $8 s/h/i, and larger at $9 s/h/i. On items over 4 pounds, I weigh them and check my UPS charts for worst-case scenario—say across the country—and this is what I quote, with my handling fee added in. I have quoted $12, $15, $20, $25, $45, and on up for s/h/i on larger items. Once in a great while, someone will complain about my shipping rates, but such customers are few and far between.

I state in my auctions that buyers can save on shipping with multiple purchases, usually $1 to $2 for each additional item, and this helps sales. Once auctions end, there is a button on the My eBay page that says **buyers with multiple purchases** and tells how many. This feature shows up only if you have buyers who have purchased more than one item from you and you pay for Selling Manager or Selling Manager Pro. Click on this button, and it will list all the buyers and how many items they have bought from you. Click on each user ID, and you're taken to a page where you can send the buyer a combined invoice. This feature is so handy! I use it all the time.

I ship USPS only if it's something that I can get in a flat-rate envelope or that I know will weigh less than one pound—like clothing, a book, a small piece of jewelry, and so on. When I do this, I quote $5 s/h/i, because I know that the Priority stamp is $3.85, and I am making an additional $1.15.

International shipments

I do not quote prices for international shipments in my listings. It would be too time-consuming, because every country has a different rate. However, when someone does e-mail to ask a quote to a certain country, I use the USPS international chart (pe.usps.gov/text/pub51/51tblb.html#_Toc498745161), rounding up to the nearest pound and adding on $2 to $3 for handling. Then I post the question with my listing so that other international buyers can see it.

There are many options to shipping overseas with the USPS, including airmail and surface for items under four pounds (there are certain size restrictions; this is called letter post) and airmail and surface for items over four pounds, or larger than the size restrictions (this is called parcel post). USPS also has global (this is what they call them) flat-rate envelopes. It is beyond the scope of this book to talk about all of them, so I suggest you spend some time on the USPS Web site (www.usps.com) and check out your options.

Don't get discouraged with international shipping costs in the beginning. It is a whole new world, and you will learn as you go. Just remember, I've been doing this for years, and I still mess up, especially with foreign shipments. It never fails, no matter how good I am in estimating foreign costs, I still make mistakes. That is why I round up the weight to the nearest pound and add on $2 to $3. We just shipped a Risk game to Sweden: I had quoted $20 s/h/i airmail, and when Maureen got to the post office, it was $27. What do you do? You ship the item, eat the difference, and keep your customer happy.

Just the facts

- Check out all the shipping companies and choose the one or two that will work best for you.

- It is a sure bet that the USPS will play a part in your shipping experience. Get familiar with them at www.usps.com

- Always add on a small handling fee for packing supplies and an employee's time.

- Always pick a flat rate to use in your listings so that you are not quoting shipping to 100 different buyers. Remember that it will all average out.

- Pack your items according to your shipper's specifications. Always pack carefully and professionally.

- Ship quickly and e-mail a tracking number.

- Add a kind note, newspaper article, or order form to ensure repeat business and add a personal touch.

Building Your Business

PART III

GET THE SCOOP ON...
Cleaning and measuring your items ▪ Noting all
the details of your merchandise ▪ Assessing
an item's condition

Preparing Your Items for Sale

In previous chapters you've learned where to find merchandise, what types of merchandise to look for, how to set up your work areas, and how to ship. Now, you're ready to get your items ready to sell on eBay. I'm assuming that you have gathered up some sellable items and are raring to go. In this chapter, I show you my routine—what works for me. I encourage you to try this process, and then modify it to work for you.

Establish a routine

First, I spread out all my items on my staging table (see Figure 9.1). All but one of these items were acquired at garage sales for a total of $118. The large brass scale in the background was on an overstock pallet from a high-end San Francisco retailer. Its original retail was $600, and I paid $138. I hope to double my money on this.

Figure 9.1. Lynn's staging table on a recent Saturday morning.

Next, I get a stack of my I Sell sheets (see Chapter 3 for more about these sheets—or the Appendix for blank sheets) and sit down to note the important details about each item. I write up and photograph about 50 items on Mondays, and then 50 more items on Wednesdays. Economies of scale are very important. Henry Ford did not invent the automobile but he did invent the production line. This is what I am trying to do by streamlining this process—create a production line—and you should do the same. Once this is done, I store my items on my shelves, and then sit at my computer to do my research. I do my research and listing on Tuesdays and Thursdays.

 **Watch Out!**

It is much safer to do your write-ups and measuring away from your computer. You probably don't have much desk space left beside your keyboard, monitor, and printer, and most items are too bulky or fragile to be safely researched in this location.

Cleaning

The first thing I assess when I have everything sitting on my table is whether the item needs cleaning. Most items that have a little bit of dirt or dust on them are fine in that condition (and it may come off in the shipping process, anyway). This type of light dust will not even show up in your photos.

Just to be safe, I often say "needs cleaning" in my listings, even if items are pretty clean. Saying this protects you, the seller, especially if you wrap your items in newspaper, because that can make your items dirty during shipping.

For items that are really dirty and dishwasher safe, I run them through my dishwasher. If they need to be handwashed or cleaned with Windex, I pay my six-year-old daughter to help me. She loves making extra money, and this is something that we can do together. It also teaches her a good work ethic at a young age.

Used toys should be cleaned for health reasons, especially the plastic ones that may have been stored outside. Take a hose and some rags and rinse them off outside.

If you're selling a car or motorcycle, it should also be as clean as possible. It wouldn't hurt to pay for a professional detailing job. The car will show much better in the photos with new wax and carpet shampoo. Also, people may want to come out to see your car (if you say in your listing that this is okay), and you want it to be spic-and-span when they see it in person.

Watch Out!

Be careful when cleaning brass, other metal items, and furniture. I have found that many (if not most) collectors enjoy the patina that is found on older metal work, especially bronzes. In this case, you are better off not cleaning it. The same goes for furniture collectors. Oftentimes, the layers of built-up wax and furniture polish over the years are what add to the value. If in doubt, do not clean! Just say in your listing, "I have decided to leave the cleaning to the eventual buyer to be extra careful." A light dusting, however, is fine.

> ## ☀ Bright Idea
>
> If I have an entire set of silver, and I'm going to sell it one place setting at a time (one dinner knife, one dinner fork, one salad fork, one teaspoon, and one tablespoon), I polish only the place setting I'll be photographing. Then in the listing I say, "your place setting will be shipped requiring polishing." This has never been a problem for me and saves a lot of time!

Polished sterling silver and silver-plated items show much better in eBay listings, so I always polish mine. Polish carefully and gently: Don't scrub so hard that you scratch the surfaces. I use Wrights Silver Polish (found at any grocery store), which comes with a soft sponge. I've used this product since I was a child helping out in my grandmother's store.

In the clothing category, all clothing that's sold on eBay must be cleaned. This is one of eBay's rules. So make sure that your clothing is either brand-new with tags or has been cleaned, and always mention in your listing that the item has been cleaned. If you're going to specialize in clothing, try to work out a deal with your local cleaner for dry-clean-only pieces. If you pay too much for dry cleaning, you may pay more than the item is worth. Another money-saving idea is to buy those dry-cleaning bags that you can throw in your dryer.

Cleaning all types of items is an important part of the process. Your buyer will feel much better about buying a used item that's sparkling clean instead of a new or used item that's dingy. Take the time to make your items presentable.

None of my items from Saturday's sales needed cleaning, but there were some knife marks on the set of the Mikasa dinnerware that I had purchased for $25. (For these, I use Wright's Silver Polish and gently polish the face of the plate. Test this first in a small section on the back side to make sure it won't damage your plate. Most utensil marks are on top of the glaze, so the silver polish just polishes them right off.) I went ahead and polished up the Mikasa set, and it looked as good as new. With everything ready, I now start filling out my I Sell tracking sheets.

Writing up the details

I always sit down with 50 blank I Sell sheets, a pen, a ruler, and a magnifying glass or loupe (a loupe is a small magnifying glass that goes right up against your eye or attaches to your glasses—used a lot by coin dealers and jewelers) to read the small print. These are the details that you use to create your auction title and description (see Chapter 12). The accuracy of your listing is critical to successful sales and repeat business, so study the details carefully.

In Figure 9.2, you can see a copy of my I Sell sheet. I'm going to walk you through how to write up a sheet like this, using a bronze boy playing soccer that I bought on one of the overstock pallets from a high-end retailer.

Name

Although this seems basic, finding a memorable name for your item can make a big difference when you go to pull the item for shipping. So, I call this one, bronze soccer boy. Please see Figure 9.3 to see what this piece looks like.

Size

If you don't include the size in your listings, you'll get hundreds of e-mails (well, maybe not hundreds, but we can hope that that many people are watching our auctions, can't we?), asking you to measure it. The size should be written in inches, and a three-dimensional quote is the best.

If you're selling clothing, state the manufacturer's size but also add some extra measurements. As an example, if it is a dress, give the bust measurement, the length of the arm from the inseam, the length of the skirt from the waist to the hem, and so on. Many manufacturers size differently, and these extra measurements can help your buyers decide to bid. Also, sizes in the past (that is, for vintage clothing) were much smaller than they are now.

I measure my bronze boy, and he is 5⅝" by 2¾" by 2¾", and I note this on my I Sell sheet.

Auction House: _eBay_ Item #: _____

Item: _Bronze Soccer Boy_

NOTES
Size: _5⅝ × 2¾ × 2¾"_

Brand/Artist/Co.: _Malcolm Moran_

Markings: _Malcolm Moran 1951 Carmel CA_

Color: _Brassy Bronze w/hints of black ball w/white blk lines_

Condition: _Brand new in box_

Age or History: _from Gumps_ Quantity: _1_

Photo Info: _____

ACTUAL LISTING

Title: _____

Category: _____

Description: _____
        —Wearing Jersey #13
        —A lot of texture
        —3 Dimensional
        —very sweet face

Figure 9.2. The front top side of one of my I Sell sheets filled out for the bronze soccer boy figurine.

Figure 9.3. Shows the bronze sculpture that I will be describing as I write up my details.

Brand/artist/company

Next, I look for who made this piece. Is there a signature on the base, the side, or anywhere else on the item? Some markings are very hard to find. I look at an item from all sides, because signatures can be on the backs of legs, necks, up inside a chair's frame, or even along the upper edge of a silver sugar bowl. If you miss the brand or the company name, you can be missing a lot of revenue.

For clothing, look at the back of the neck and if there's no tag, check inside, on the side seam. More and more manufacturers are putting informational tags here.

My bronze boy is signed with the maker's name on the base—Malcolm Moran—so I list this on my I Sell sheet.

Markings

Finally, I note any markings word for word. Many items won't have markings, but if they do, your customers want to know exactly what they say. Sometimes, it is helpful to take a picture of the maker's marks (also called the signature) or clothing tag. Different signatures and clothing tags can signify different years of manufacture.

I note all the markings from my item's base, which says, "Malcolm Moran, Moran 1951, and Carmel California." On an expensive item like this, I'll include a photo of the markings in the listing, but it's a good idea to also write the markings down, because those markings may come up in a title and description search. For my statue, I also notice that the jersey is number 13, and I write this down. Who knows—I might sell this to a soccer mom from Upper Saddle River, NJ, whose all-star soccer-playing son wears number 13. Don't overlook anything!

Color

Due to the nature of digital cameras, the Internet, and different monitors, color can get distorted in the process. This is why it's important to describe the color of your item, and do the best that you can in your listing.

Remember that sometimes people search to buy an item because of its color. I redid my bedroom a few years ago and decided I wanted to buy blue and purple pillows for a white couch I had purchased. I went on eBay and searched for "blue pillow" and "purple pillow." If the sellers hadn't put the color in the title, I wouldn't have bought those pillows. But because of savvy sellers, I bought ten pillows on eBay for my couch. Many were handmade crafts, and the color lured me to the auctions.

For my piece, I write that my bronze boy is a brassy bronze with hints of black, and that the soccer ball is white with hand-drawn black lines. I also note in the lower part of the I Sell sheet, under Description, that he has a lot of texture and is very three-dimensional. He has a sweet face, which I also note.

Condition

I cannot stress enough the importance of determining the condition of your items. If you don't put an accurate assessment of the condition in your listings, you'll get a million e-mails asking, "Is it broken?" "Does it work?" or "Is it brand-new?" If you don't describe the condition completely and you leave out a key fact, you will get returns, find yourself with negative feedback, or have to credit a portion of the purchase price back to your buyer. Be smart, thorough, and completely honest in your assessment of any item's condition.

Sometimes you may think, "oh it is just a little tiny nick, no one will notice." Well, you noticed, didn't you? Mentioning it ahead of time in the listing is the smart thing to do. It won't keep people from bidding and you can even say, "I hate to mention such a tiny, tiny speck of missing glaze, but I would rather

---

Moneysaver!

This is really more of a moneymaker than a moneysaver: Think of words to describe your colors that go beyond the bland red, orange, yellow, green, blue, and purple. I often describe my colors very vividly. Some examples include Ralph Lauren red, burnt orange, mottled green, and sky-blue turquoise. You're a salesperson, and you're selling a product that your customer can't see or touch. Also offer some information about the texture or the feel of the item, for example, silky rayon. Go the extra mile.

---

be completely honest in my listings." This way, when your customer gets the piece, he or she already knows about the nick and has come to terms with it. You never want to surprise your buyers, giving them a reason to complain, leave negative feedback, or return an item.

I always give a range of condition in my listings. As an example, if something is in perfect condition, I say "excellent to perfect condition." This way, I'm protecting myself and have a little room for error. Here is a listing of some of the terms and the ranges I use:

- Mint in box, brand new
- Excellent to perfect condition
- Very good to excellent condition
- Good to very good condition
- Okay to good condition
- Poor to okay condition
- As is to okay condition

Oftentimes, I add "with slight wear," or say, "with the usual, slight estate wear." If it's china or pottery that chips easily, like Majolica or Franciscan, I say in the listing, "There are some edge dings, as is very common with this type of pottery." It makes the buyer feel better about the edge dings.

Pottery and china

Let's talk about the types of damage that can be found with china and pottery. There are chips, fleabites, nicks, missing glaze, cracks, crazing, and repair.

- A *chip* is pretty obvious, and you should always measure it for your listing. If it is ½ inch by ¼, inch, say so.

- A *fleabite* or *nick* is a tiny chip that's not worth calling a chip but must be mentioned. If a nick or fleabite has glaze over the top of it, this tells you that the nick was made in the making. The manufacturer felt it wasn't significant and went ahead and glazed it to be sold as a first-quality item.

- *Missing glaze* is also something to note, if there are obvious dots or spots that didn't take the glaze or color.

- A *crack* is self-explanatory. Measure it and note the size. As an example, "this crack is 3 inches long."

- *Crazing* is when the glaze crackles and forms spiderlike veins on the surface. It's different from a crack, because crazing does not go clear through the piece. If you try to feel a craze line on the base of a piece with your fingernail, you won't be able to, because it doesn't go clear through.

- *Repair* is when someone has fixed damage with glue, paste, or other material. Sometimes repairs are so good that they're hard to see with the naked eye. A *black light* (available at most hardware stores) can help identify cracks and repairs, which show up clearly in ultraviolet light.

Please make sure that you note all these flaws. And don't forget about utensil marks on dinnerware that I discussed in the cleaning section.

Glassware

With glassware there can be water marks, chips, fleabites, and cracks (for the last three, see the preceding descriptions for pottery and china). *Water marks* occur when a piece like a vase was used for many years with standing water in it. These can discolor the glass and must be mentioned. Sometimes these can be cleaned. You may also need to mention air bubbles in your piece of glass. Sometimes air bubbles will pop during manufacture and leave an open scar—be sure and mention these also.

Metal items and furniture

Let's talk about the types of damage that can be found with metal items and furniture. Metal objects can bruise or have dents. They can also be tarnished or have, as I like to call tarnish, a "lovely patina" from age.

Furniture also builds up a patina and can have nicks, scrapes, scratches, or pieces missing. With furniture, the damage is usually pretty noticeable, and you should be fine as long as you describe it in detail. Just remember to measure the most pressing flaws, so that buyers know in advance what they're buying.

Toys, electronics, and computers

The damage for toys, electronics, and computers is pretty easy to assess. Basically these items are either new, gently used, used, or as is. And they either work or they don't work. If they don't work, you may want to say in the listing, "selling for parts."

Clothing and fabric goods

With clothing and fabric goods, if it is used, you can say gently worn. If it is new, say "new with tags" (NWT) or "new." Also, make sure you state that it comes from a smoke-free home if it does. This is a huge consideration for some buyers on eBay.

> **Moneysaver!**
>
> It usually doesn't pay to repair an item. I often say in my listings, "this will be a beautiful piece with a little repair work" or "sold as is; needs TLC. (TLC means tender loving care.) If you have to pay someone, say a furniture maker, to cane a chair seat for you, you probably won't get the monetary return on eBay to make it worth your investment. Many eBayers are searching for items that do need work. The vase I paid $10 for sold for over $500 with the following description: "I will let the new owner take care of the repairs, and this piece will look wonderful when professionally redone." Don't waste your money on repair. However, if you can do the work yourself, you enjoy it, and you wouldn't be spending that time otherwise making money, I say go for it.

History and age

Knowing the history of your item can sometimes help to sell it for a higher amount. If you have a great story about your item, by all means, tell it to the buyers in your description. Do you remember the cane that sold on eBay that someone's grandfather's ghost was attached to (they were trying to get rid of the ghost from their house), the famous toasted cheese sandwich that appeared to have an image of the Virgin Mary, or the ice cube that Elvis touched? These all sold for thousands of dollars! Someone was being creative. In the same way, if something was owned by your great uncle who happened to be an early settler of Missouri, by all means write about it. People love a good history, especially for something they're going to purchase.

Provenance is a term used a lot in the antiques and collectible world, and it's worth mentioning here. *Provenance* is proof of ownership or proof of the history of your item. For example, if you're selling a plate that belonged to the Kennedys, and you bought it at a Sotheby auction, use the auction catalog and your receipt of purchase as your provenance. It's best to include these with the purchase and mention them in the description. If you bought more than one item at the auction, go ahead and include a photocopy (color) of the auction page and a regular photocopy of the receipt. I bought the bronze soccer boy on an overstock pallet from an upscale San Francisco retailer. I noted this on my I Sell sheet under age/history.

As far as age is concerned, it is important to try to date your item. People want to know if it's new and, if not, what time period it's from. I make educated guesses in my descriptions and always use a range to protect myself. If I have a vase that I think is 1910s Art Nouveau era, I may say, "I believe this piece is from the 1910s to 1940s and is very Art Nouveau in look and style." This gives me a 30-year window to protect myself.

Table 9.1 presents some important eras to use in your title and description. Note that the 1970s is becoming very collectible now (as well as the 1980s), but no one has really put an era name on it. Often I use "Op Art" in my titles for 1970s items.

Table 9.1. Important Eras to Use in Your Titles and Descriptions*

United States: Common Names of Periods

Shaker/Primitive	1620–1900
Pilgrim	1630–1690
William & Mary	1690–1725
Queen Anne	1725–1750
Chippendale	1750–1780
Federal	1780–1820
Victorian and Renaissance Revival	1837–1901
Eastlake	1870–1890
Anglo-Japanese	1880–1910
Art Nouveau	1895–1910 or 1890–1914
Colonial Revival	1880–1925

Table 9.1. *continued*

United States: Common Names of Periods

Arts & Crafts/Mission	1895–1920
Golden Oak	1890–1930
Art Deco	1910–1930
Eames/Modern/Mid-Century	1945–1969
Op Art	1970s

England: Names of Reigns

Gothic	1000–1600
Elizabethan	1558–1603
Jacobean	1603–1688
William & Mary	1689–1701
Queen Anne	1702–1713
George I	1714–1726
George II	1727–1759
George III	1760–1819
Regency (approximate)	1810–1820
George IV	1820–1830
William IV	1830–1836
Victorian	1837–1901
Edwardian	1901–1919

England: Designer Period Names

Chippendale	1750–1780
Adam	1760–1790

Hepplewhite	1770–1800
Sheraton	1795–1815
France: Names of Reigns	
Louis XIII	1610–1643
Louis XIV	1643–1715
France: Names of Reigns	
Louis XV	1715–1774
Louis XVI	1774–1792
French Country	1790–1940
Directoire	1795–1800
Empire	1800–1815
Louis XVIII and Charles X	1814–1830
Louis Phillipe	1830–1850
Second Empire	1850–1870
Louis XV and Louis XVI Revivals	1870–1930

*All years are approximate.

Please keep in mind that many of these eras cross other into other countries and this is just a guideline. As an example, the Art Nouveau and Art Deco eras were not just American in influence as the Europeans also experienced these effects.

As a very important side note, Eames era items (anything from 1945 to 1969) are very hot right now. When I put "Eames era" in my title, I get double the hits on my auctions. Other terms that describe Eames era are "mid-century modern" and "sleek."

Just the facts

- Always clean and prepare your items prior to selling them.
- Measure your items accurately.
- Note everything you can about condition.
- Look very closely at your item for maker's marks.
- Describe your item's color in vibrant detail.
- Always mention the history, age, and era of your item.

GET THE SCOOP ON...
Finding the perfect spot to photograph ∎
Learning some photography tricks ∎
Editing your photos

Photographing Your Item

Chapter 10

O f everything you do to get top dollar on eBay, I believe that the photo is one of the most important elements. You must have a very good, clear photo, or your item will not sell for as much as it could have. You're trying to sell something to someone who will not be able to touch it, see it, or examine it until it's paid for and delivered. A picture is worth a thousand words. No kidding!

I talk a little bit about photographing in Chapter 6, but in this chapter I will talk about actually setting up your photography area, what props you will need, how to take the best pictures, and how to edit the pictures you have taken.

Setting up your photo studio or area

You should spend some quality time setting up your photo studio as this will save you from not having to retake photos and make you more money in the long run. Invest in a nice background drape, the correct props, and extra lighting sources—if required. Try taking pictures with different combinations of all these variables until you find what works best for you. I can't tell you often enough how important your photos are going to be to your success on eBay.

Lighting

I believe that the best place to take photos is outside in indirect sunlight. The reason that indirect sunlight is the best for taking photos is because of its diffused lighting. The secret to getting a good product photograph is to get control of your lighting. If you get control of your lighting, you shouldn't need a flash.

> **66** I don't recommend using the flash on a digital camera. Your pictures will turn out better if you use a light source separate from the camera, whether that is natural light or another type of light. **99**
>
> Lee Dralle, professional photographer

If you can't take your photos outside, there are some other options for a light source. There are quite a few products on the market to help you with smaller item photography, and some of them are pretty slick. I have used two of these products, and will discuss four commercial kit options so that you can get some ideas:

- **Cloud dome** (www.clouddome.com). It is used for very small jewelry items, stamps, coins, and so on. This product starts at $199 and goes up.

- **Photo Studio** (www.americanrecorder.com). This sells for $119.95. I have actually tried this product and for the price it is pretty neat. It doesn't take up much space and works well for small to medium items.

- **Cube Lite** (www.cubelite.com). Options vary from 2' to 6.5.' I have tried this product and—while quite large—it does a great job. These are not sold as a kit but in individual pieces and can get quite spendy. This is a very professional system.

- **Lowel ego light** (www.lowel.com). This alternative source of light from an industry leader in location lighting sells for $125.00.

Any of these systems can be used inside your home to take better pictures. You want to investigate them thoroughly prior to purchasing. Also, before you buy, consider whether you can set up something similar on your own.

Background

If you aren't using a commercial kit (anything similar to those listed above) to take photos, make sure you have a nice drape background for your photos. I recommend an off-white or beige color for your background drape—something neutral without being a stark white or black. Buyers don't want to see your house, your spouse, your dog, or your kids. Would you want to buy something from someone when you get too close of a personal look at his or her life? I have seen photos on eBay that show people's kitchen counters, their dining rooms, and their pets. Not a good idea from the buyer's point of view and not safe for the seller.

 Watch Out!

Some people try to get really fancy with their photos on eBay. They place a plant or flower next to the item, put it on a lace doily, or use some wild fabric underneath it. I have also seen people actually put fruit in a fruit bowl. Do *not* do this. It distracts from the item. Your photo should be plain and simple and focus on what you're trying to sell.

Props

In your photo area, you want to have some props handy. I have two plate stands that I use to display many different items. I have a small wooden box and a beige drape that I use if I need to lean a large item up for the photo. I even have a hook from the ceiling for hanging lamps and a clothing mannequin for clothes. I also have a black velvet pad that I use for some jewelry.

A clothing mannequin can be a great investment. As I mention in Chapter 3, I bought an adult half-hanging mannequin and a child half-hanging mannequin to display my clothing on. They were very reasonably priced (on eBay, of course!). If you're going to be specializing in clothing, you may want to buy a life-size mannequin that stands on the floor. Your customer doesn't want to see the clothing modeled on any person (unless it is Christy Turlington), so if you don't want to spring for the mannequin, at least fold it nicely and display it neatly for your photo. It's a good idea to iron clothing before photographing it, because wrinkles will show up and hurt your sales price.

Transporting your items to your studio

To get all my items to my outdoor photo studio, I put them all in plastic bins, with I Sell sheets (see Chapter 3 and the appendix) next to each one. Then, when I've taken the photos, I put my I Sell sheets in the same order, and when I go to my computer to edit the pictures, the sheets are in the same order as the photos, and I can quickly write down the name of the finished picture on the correct sheet. It makes picture taking a breeze!

Quality and features

Photos for eBay don't have to be saved at the highest resolution. In fact, they shouldn't be. Image files used on the Internet can be much smaller resolution (and, therefore, much smaller size) than files used for printing, and they will still look great. Use the lowest quality setting on your camera that has acceptable picture quality. All cameras are not created equal, so you will need to play around with your camera to find out what is the lowest setting that you can get away with and still have awesome photos! My camera has a three-star system, with three stars being the highest quality and one star being the lowest. I take eBay pictures with only one star. That way, my camera can hold about 90 pictures before I have to dump the memory.

The basic features that you will want to familiarize yourself with are the following:

- Quality level
- Flash (to turn it off)
- Viewfinder (video display)
- Zoom

When I start taking pictures, I check two things. First, I make sure that my quality level is at one star. Then I scroll through my options and press the button that turns off my flash. That is all! I'm ready to point and shoot. I always turn on the video display (viewfinder) on the back of my camera. This feature is invaluable. It lets me see what the final picture is going to look like, and I can decide whether I need to keep shooting or what adjustments I need to make—to my lighting, the positioning, or the angle.

For really tiny items, like jewelry and coins, I use my zoom feature. The farther away I stand and hold the camera really steady (or mount it on a tripod), the better the zoom works for me. Some cameras have a macro feature for close-up photos. In many cases the symbol is a small flower but check your owner's manual to be certain. This feature can be an important consideration when purchasing a camera if you will be photographing small items that require fine detail.

Photography tricks

From my years of taking pictures for eBay, I have learned so much. I finally feel that my pictures are at the level that they need to be for selling successfully. I have learned by trial and error—or by fire—as some would say. In this section, I will share my tips and tricks.

Shoot two to three pictures

When you're taking your photos, always shoot two to three pictures of each item. After the first photo, check the viewfinder on the back of your camera to decide whether you need to take one or two more. This saves time if your original shot isn't as good as you thought, because you don't have to find the item (once it is stored) and take it back to the studio to shoot again. This also saves money, because you won't be settling on a so-so photo just to be done with it. You will have your choice of two to three photos, so that you can pick the best one!

If your item is going to sell for $100 or more, I recommend taking at least six photos. Take your six photos from every possible angle and shoot any significant markings. Do a close-up and get some great detail for your listing.

Pixels

Photos on eBay need to fit into a 400 × 400 pixel area. *Pixel* is short for picture element. It means the tiny dots that make up a picture. My camera in its lowest quality setting takes my pictures

---

Moneysaver

eBay has a feature that you can click on and pay for (when you're listing your item) called a *picture pack*. The basic picture pack costs $1 and you get six supersized photos and the gallery included. The gallery typically costs 25¢, and each photo (after the first free one) costs 15¢. Supersized photos are an extra 75¢, so this is $1.75 worth of features for only $1. So, if I'm going to use six pictures and the gallery ($1.05), I may as well use the picture pack and get the supersized feature and slide show because it is going to cost me less.

> **🚗 Watch Out!**
>
> Don't make your pictures too large. I would say 800 × 800 maximum (if you pay for supersize and have used a higher quality than one star on your camera) because, remember, not everyone has DSL or cable, and big photos take big time to download with dial-up. Don't lose customers by turning them off before they even get to see your listing. Keep your photos in the eBay basic range, 400 × 400 (which eBay will automatically size them to) and keep your customers coming back for more.

at 640 × 480 pixels. You could spend your time sizing it to eBay's 400 × 400 specifications, but you, don't have to, because eBay will size it for you. Why waste your time? Also, eBay offers a supersized feature for 75 cents, in which case your photos can go from 500 × 500 pixels up to 800 × 800 pixels. If you have an expensive item, you may want to supersize the photo.

If you don't want to let eBay host your photos, you can get your own Web space, and then you can make your photos as large as you want and use as many as you want for no extra fee. You would just be paying the Web service that hosts your photo storage site. This is beyond the scope of this book, but I wanted to mention that there are other options.

White and reflective items

If you're taking a photo of a white item, I have a trick for you. White items can be the hardest to photograph, because they can fool the exposure meter on your camera. When taking a photo of a white item, try pushing the button halfway down while focusing on something that's not white but is at the same distance from the camera as your item. Keeping the same distance is very important, or your picture will be out of focus. Keep the button pushed halfway down as you move the camera from pointing at the non-white item to pointing at your item. By doing this, you'll set your exposure at the appropriate level so that when you move your camera to shoot the white item, it will be properly exposed.

When taking a photo of anything that reflects, be aware of what is shown in the reflections. Do not let yourself be shown in the photo. That is a big no-no. Stay out of the way! When I shoot mirrors, I generally have them point up to the sky so that all you see is wonderful blue and white clouds. For stainless items, I try to hide behind a box or chair.

Saving your photos to your hard drive

Once you've taken your pictures, you need to get the photos from your digital camera and onto the hard drive of your computer so that you can edit them. Your camera may have come with a memory card or a cable that hooks into your computer. My camera came with a USB cable that plugs right into my laptop. My camera also came with an editing program called Photo Impact, and this is what I use for editing.

Editing programs are similar enough that I will walk you through the screens of Photo Impact, and you should be able to apply this knowledge to your program. However, keep in mind that there may be some differences, so you may need to play around with your editing program to find the same settings.

Once I plug my camera in to my computer and turn it on, the back side of my camera says **Connected to computer**, and a screen on my computer comes up that says **Copy pictures to a folder on my computer using Microsoft Scanner and Camera Wizard**. Your program will probably say something different. Just remember that you want to get those pictures copied onto your computer and click the button that will do that. If you get stuck, pull out the manual that came with your camera or go to your camera maker's Web site. Don't get frustrated; once you get this mastered, you will be on your way.

I click on **OK** and it asks me to choose which photos I want to copy to my hard drive. I choose all of them. Next, I'm asked to choose a file folder to save the photos in. It's important to take note of where you will be saving each batch. I have files set up for every month and year. This way, it's easy for me to find pictures when I need them. Once I have chosen the file, I click **Next**, and my pictures are all copied to my hard drive. It then asks me if I want to work with them now or be finished. I choose to exit, because I know that they are all successfully placed on my hard drive.

Editing

Now it is time to edit your photos to make them ready for eBay. Look at every single picture, and then compare them all and choose those with the brightest, most in focus, and best angles to edit. In the old days, we used to have to do a lot to our pictures. Not anymore. Most digital cameras do such a good job that not much editing is needed. I discuss the basics here, which includes the following:

- Rotating
- Cropping for size and outside interference
- Adjusting brightness and color contrast

Rotating

If you take your photos horizontally, you'll have no need to rotate. However, if you take a vertical photo of a tall, skinny item, you need to know how to rotate. Here is a photo of a vase that I took vertically. All I need to do to rotate this is to go into **Edit/Rotate & Flip**, and then **Rotate Right 90°**, and my vase that was lying down is now standing right-side-up (see Figure 10.1). How handy.

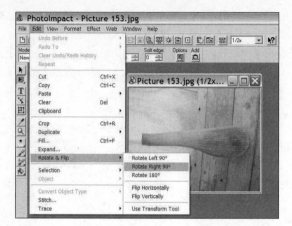

Figure 10.1. This computer screen shows the steps you take to rotate a picture taken vertically so that it becomes horizontal.

Cropping and sizing

The next thing that you need to know how to do is crop. It is best to always crop your pictures close to the actual item so that the item takes up most of the picture. Also, if you have outside interference—something in the background that you don't want to show (for example, part of your swimming pool, your hand, or a section of your desk)—you can crop it out. To crop, choose the selection tool or the dotted line arrow from your tool bar. Then take the arrow and use it to draw around your object where you want it to be cropped. Then go to **Edit** and choose **Crop** (see Figure 10.2). It automatically cuts off the background and the wasted space.

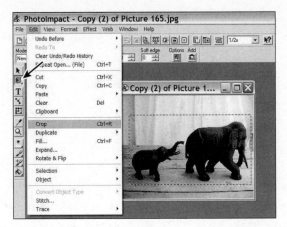

Figure 10.2. This figure shows the dotted line crop tool and where you find it in the menu bar.

Adjusting brightness and color contrast

I hardly ever do anything to the color or the brightness/contrast of my photos. The reason that I don't have to do this is because I have my lighting under control, so my pictures look great without this adjustment. If you do have some issues with your lighting and/or you want to doctor your photo after the fact, there is a great tool to use for this. Most of the photo programs have it, and it is called Auto Process. Choose Format from your dropdown menu, and under Format should be a button called **Auto Process**. Click on this. Once you click on **Auto Process**, you will be able to choose each option individually (like brightness or contrast) or you can choose to play with all of them at once. I recommend choosing all of them at once and this is called **Batch**. So choose **Batch**, and up will come a screen that looks like the one in Figure 10.3.

Watch Out!

Messing around with some of the Auto Process Batch options to see how they can help your photo can be a lot of fun, but don't spend much time doing it. Although the options are interesting, if you're taking your pictures correctly to begin with, you shouldn't need to use most of them.

You will have lots of fun ways to play with and work with your images. The options available for my photo program are **Straighten**, **Crop**, **Remove Moire**, **Focus**, **Brightness**, **Contrast**, and **Balance**. The only three I've used on a consistent basis deal with color and light. These are **Brightness**, **Contrast**, and **Balance**. You can click on each of them individually or together, and then preview how your photo is going to look.

Figure 10.3. A picture showing the **Auto Process/Batch** function in most photo programs.

Save and name

After you have your picture rotated, cropped, and ready to go, it's time to save it somewhere that you can easily find it again. This is a serious issue. You can spend hours looking for your photo when you're doing your listings if you didn't save it and name it something that you can find easily. Once I've done all the editing work to my photo, I save it in the folder named for the current month and year, and then I write the name of the photo on my I Sell tracking sheet. This way, when I go to do my listing from my I Sell sheets, the photo name is right there where I can find it.

Always save your photo file in jpg or gif format. The eBay system can only handle jpg and gif files, and jpg is preferred. To save as a jpg, choose **Save As** from the file menu and choose jpg from the dropdown menu that appears below your photo name.

Picture Manager

eBay also has a service called Picture Manager, where they will charge you by the month to store photos. If you own an eBay store, you get a discount on the Picture Manager fees. Table 10.1 gives you the current rate chart, and I have estimated the number of photos for the storage space based upon an average picture that is 400 × 400 pixels (eBay's default setting for a regular photo). One thousand pictures may sound like a lot, but I have 2,000 items in my store, plus another 500 or so each month at auction. That's probably 3,000 photos each month that I have on eBay.

Table 10.1. Picture Manager Fees

Storage Space	Approx. Number of Photos	Per Month	Per Month for eBay Store Owner
50 MG	1,000	$9.99	$4.99
125 MG	2,500	$19.99	$14.99
300 MG	6,000	$39.99	$34.99

The monthly charge for Picture Manager is based on how much storage space you need, but regardless, you pay one monthly fee for all your photos instead of paying eBay 15¢ for every additional photo (after the first free one) or paying an extra fee for each individual listing to supersize your photos. The down side is the monthly fee, plus Picture Manager can take a lot of your time just trying to keep it clean by deleting photos you don't use anymore. I choose not to use Picture Manager, and I manage my photo costs by using just one photo per listing. I use multiple pictures only on very expensive items.

If you do use eBay's Picture Manager, once you have stored your photos, eBay offers a program so that you can edit your photos. You can rotate, crop, and do any color correction.

Just the facts

- Spend time getting your photo studio set up perfectly for your requirements.

- Purchase the props you will need—plate stands, mannequins, and background drapes.

- Mess around with all the variables: lighting, backgrounds, camera, and props until they work perfectly for you.

- Take two to three photos of each item so that you have plenty to choose from when you get to the editing phase.

- Use multiple photos when you are selling expensive items—I recommend six to twelve.

- Crop your photo closely so that buyers see only what they are going to buy.

- If any of this is confusing for you or you can't make it work, hire a computer/camera expert to come in and get you up and running. Don't be afraid to ask for help!

GET THE SCOOP ON...
▪ What is this item? ▪ What is it worth? ▪
Where do you start? ▪ How do you
get the help you need?

Doing Your Research

One of the most important ways you can earn top dollar on eBay is to be a great researcher. You need to know exactly what each item is and how to describe it, or it either won't sell or it'll sell for less than it's worth.

Even for brand-new items, researching your competition is important. Being able to outdo your competitors with your service, extra features, or just the way you position your listing can bring you top dollar.

Research is one of my favorite aspects of selling on eBay. It's like a treasure hunt, and the treasure is something you own. You will be extra motivated to find out all you can, because this information will put money in your pocket (not your boss's pocket!). Spend some time checking out all the tips and tricks I discuss in this chapter.

Identify your item

To help you do your research, I'm going to walk you through several examples in this chapter. First, let's take a look at the brand-new bronze soccer boy that we have been discussing, and I will research him on eBay and the Internet. I'll also take a look at a few pieces that are harder to research and identify, including a flatware set and a piece of Early American Pattern Glass. I will show you some great Web sites for researching these types of items.

Use eBay to do research

The first place that I go to do my research is on eBay. Why not? You want to sell your item on eBay, and there's no better site to test the waters than the site you're going to sell it on. When you research for identification purposes, you will most always use the completed auction research tool that I discuss in Chapter 3.

The bronze soccer boy was signed Malcolm Moran, so I'll begin searching using his name. (Remember to type in as few words as possible.) Click on the **Advanced Search** link next to the regular search field located on every page. On the Advanced Search page that appears, type in "Malcom Moran," and check the box next to **Completed listings only**. Then press the **Search** button (or hit **Enter** on your keyboard). If you need a refresher as to what this screen looks like, flip to Chapter 3 and look at Figure 3.3. Nothing comes up, and guess why? I spelled Malcolm wrong. Do you see how critical the proper spelling is on eBay? Next I try the correct spelling for "Malcolm Moran," and two items come up that were sold or listed in the past two weeks on eBay. See Figure 11.1 for a copy of these auctions. Very interesting.

 Watch Out!

Never use current auction searches to do your research. So many times, people make this mistake and just type their search terms into the search boxes on every page. Do *not* do this. Current auctions give you no indication of what the items will really sell for and only give you a snapshot in time. You want completed auction research, because that information shows you two weeks worth of history, and you get to see what items actually sold for. Many people don't bid until the very last seconds, which makes a current auction search not a true indication of prices. You use current auction research only when you want to check out your competition.

Figure 11.1. The completed auction research on eBay showing two auctions with Malcolm Moran in the title. Notice that a similar sculpture to mine sold for over $150. This is great news!

I was happy to see that eBay was not flooded with Malcolm Moran bronzes and that there was definitely interest in them when offered for sale. These pieces actually sell when priced right! This is good information, so I note some of the details of these completed auctions in the Auction Comparison section of my I Sell sheet (see the Appendix for a blank sheet). I wrote down that one had sold for $152.50. I also took the time to write down the date I purchased it, the price I paid ($78.87), where I bought it from (a wholesale lot on eBay), and the market value. The market value was given to me as the suggested retail price from the upscale San Francisco retailer who sold it to me on a pallet of overstocks—$342.90. I will use all of these figures to determine my starting bid price.

Finally, while on eBay, I take a look at what category the seller of the other bronze statue used. This saves me time when I have to choose a category and category number. If you see a

---

☼   **Bright Idea**

To find the category number, look up to the address bar on your computer screen. For this auction, here is what is listed in this area: http://cgi.ebay. com/Malcolm-Moran-Bronze-Sculpture-Boy-Flying-a-Kite_W0QQitem Z5416283276QQcategoryZ553QQssPageNameZWDVWQQrdZ1QQcmdZViewItem. After the item number it says category and there is a number with letters before and after it, Z553QQS. 553 is the category number for Art→Sculpture, Carvings, so I note this on my I Sell sheet. eBay has recently added these letters to confuse hackers. Look carefully to find the category number that you want to use.

---

category early on that looks perfect, note it on your I Sell sheet so that you have it in front of you when you do your listing. The seller had used Art→ Sculpture, Carvings, and this sounded great to me.

I'd like to research a few more items on eBay so that you can get the hang of it. First, I am going to look at something that will be a little bit trickier than the bronze statue, because although it has maker's marks on it, there is no pattern name. (It is very important to know the name of your china, flatware, or crystal pattern if you're going to be selling it on eBay. Not knowing this can cost you money.) I bought a stainless flatware set at a garage sale last weekend. It was an interesting, Southwest-style pattern, but the only markings on it were "Supreme by Towle 18/8 Korea." So I got on eBay and typed in "Towle stainless southwest" in the completed auctions search box. (Note that "supreme" is a quality designation, like "deluxe" would be, and as such, is not a helpful search term.) Nothing came up with that search. Then I tried "Towle stainless," and I searched by highest price first. More than 100 items came up, and I looked at all the thumbnail pictures on the left-hand side of the listings. I didn't see my pattern anywhere. Still, don't give up. There is still another place to check—the Internet—and I talk about that in the following section.

Next, I researched a glass item (a butter dish) with absolutely no maker's marks. This was tough, let me tell you. The first thing I did was to realize that it was probably antique, 1900s or so, and was not blown glass (there was no pontil mark and I could see the seam marks in the sides of the glass), so I knew that it was pressed glass. Blown glass will have a rough or polished pontil mark on the base where it was broken off of the glassblower's rod. For more information on glass, please read my book *How to Sell Antiques and Collectibles on eBay....and Make a Fortune* (McGraw Hill, 2005). It was most likely EAPG (Early American Pattern Glass); see Figure 11.2. I searched on eBay under completed auctions for EAPG butter dish, and 56 items came up (see Figure 11.3). The most expensive was $146.34. Wow!

Figure 11.2. The Early American Pattern Glass butter dish that I am trying to research and identify.

Figure 11.3. Completed auction research on eBay for EAPG butter dish.

Even though I couldn't find my exact butter dish, I did find plenty of information. I'll try one more idea for tracking down information on this butter dish in the "Ask for help" section later in this chapter.

Bright Idea

Make sure you're sorting by highest price first when you do your completed auction research. You want to learn from people who are doing this right, not from the guy who only got $1 for his butter dish. Read all the descriptions and titles from the sellers who got top dollar. Jot down notes on your I Sell sheet about what key words are used in the titles, what history or information sellers include in the description, and how much sellers charge for shipping. You can learn a lot from other sellers, but always keep in mind that they may not be experts—take everything you read with a grain of salt. Verify the information before you put it in your own listings.

Google leads you to Web sites

The next place I check for any information is on Google (www.google.com), a search tool for finding resources on the Web. It was started at Stanford University and it is currently the number one search engine on the Internet.

Once on Google's site, I typed in "Malcolm Moran." I found that too many items come up for this search, and most of them were related to sports. Turns out, there's a Malcolm Moran who is a basketball sports writer, and another who is an actor. To narrow my search, I typed in Malcolm Moran sculpture, and this time, I got lucky. About five hits down, I found his official home page (see Figure 11.4).

Figure 11.4. Google search for Malcolm Moran sculpture that brought up his official Web site about halfway down the page. There is valuable information on this site.

The prices on his Web site substantiate the market value and the data I have already collected. The bronzes range in price from $125 to $1,600 for larger works. The best piece of information I found is his biography. I took notes from this (in my own words) and used this in my actual auction listing that I go over in Chapter 12.

Malcolm Moran. Born on Bainbridge Island in the Puget sound. Studied at the Cornish Art School in Seattle, the University of Washington, the Kobe Union in Japan, the Art Center School in Los Angeles, and Cranbrook Academy, Birmingham, Michigan. Refined technical skills working on advanced styling concepts for General Motors, Ford, and Boeing. Appointed Art Director of the Seattle World's Fair. In 1963, settled in Carmel, California, to open gallery and studio with longtime friend/partner, Donald Buby. In that environment, Moran became leader of the contemporary bronze sculpture movement. Innovator of dozens of techniques in bronze used today.

It is so important to have background information on the company or artist who made your item, and where it came from. I discuss this in the provenance section of Chapter 10. Your research phase is the time to get all this background information gathered together. Print it out if it's easier for you, but make sure you have it.

Getting back to that stainless flatware, I use the Replacements, Ltd. Web site for all of my china, crystal, and silver research.

To use this Web site to do my research, I clicked on the tab at the top of the home page that says **Silver**. "Silver," to Replacements, means any type of stainless steel, sterling silver, silver plate, or hollowware. Once the list of manufacturers of silver appeared, I clicked on the **T** at the top of the page, so that all the manufacturers that start with T come up. Next, I clicked on **Towle**, and that took me to a page that lists all the patterns with bars running down the left-hand side.

☀   **Bright Idea**

Replacements, Ltd. has a wealth of research information. I use it about four times a day. Replacements stocks over 200,000 china, flatware, and crystal patterns and has photos of most of them. There is a handy thumbnail photo page that allows you to quickly scroll through hundreds of photos of your manufacturer's patterns until you find yours. It is a huge time-saver!

The bars have the text **Click here for Image Gallery.** If you click on these bars, thumbnail photos will come up for your perusal. A thumbnail image is simply a smaller version of a larger photo so that many of these can be displayed on one page. If you decide you want to look at the image in more detail, just click on the thumbnail.

For a long time, I didn't know about this feature and used to spend hours clicking on each of the pattern names. My very smart father found this feature for me, and I am grateful every day!

I scrolled through the thumbnails until I got to the page with the Ms, and there was my pattern. It is called Mesa. By clicking on the **Mesa** icon, I was taken to a page that showed all the different pieces available and the prices. Replacements' prices are quite high, and I typically can get about 30 percent of their prices on eBay. I paid $5 for this flatware set at a garage sale and got 45 pieces. I added up Replacements' prices, and I had $426 worth of flatware at their prices. I hoped to get about $125 for these pieces on eBay. That was a fantastic return on my investment. However, I wouldn't have a chance to get that much if I hadn't found the pattern name.

Use reference books

When I can't find anything quickly on the Internet or on eBay, the next place I go is to my reference books. I own quite a few reference books about antiques and collectibles. Likewise, you want to invest in books that go into detail about your niche. You

Watch Out!

The price quotes in printed guides are garnered from retail establishments, shows, and live auctions from around the country. These suggested prices vary considerably from the actual amount you may receive on eBay, because eBay is a global marketplace and can level out the playing field. You may receive more or less than the price guide quotes due to many factors—not just the impact of the regions from which a price guide quote was gathered, but also time of year, timing of your auction, and your title (to name a few).

can never read enough or learn enough about your topic of interest. Doing so keeps you at the top of your game.

Some books that I own in my library and recommend are:

- *Antique Trader Antiques & Collectibles Price Guide,* Krause Publications, $17.99

- *Kovels' Antiques and Collectibles Price List,* Random House, $16.95

- *Schroeder's Antiques Price Guide,* Collectors Books, $14.95

- *Warmans' Antiques & Collectibles Price Guide,* Krause Publications, $19.99

The antiques and collectibles business is constantly changing and so are the prices. By the time reference books—such as those I just mentioned—finally get to print, some values may be outdated. Still, the information about each company, their different maker's marks, the different patterns they produced, and overall general information is quite valuable. Leaf through reference books and read them consistently so that you can identify treasures when you're out hunting.

Remember that the condition of your item is very important when valuing and identifying your item (see Chapter 9).

Ask for help

As a last resort, I will place a question mark and/or the word "Help" in my listing title and ask fellow eBayers to help me out with identification. This works extremely well. If the item is worth a lot of money, I also consider paying for an appraisal (see the following section for more information on this).

I e-mailed a photo of the butter dish (Figure 11.2) to a good friend of mine, Elaine Henderson, who is an expert on EAPG. I met Elaine when I was writing my antiques and collectibles book, and her Web site is wonderful (www.patternglass.com). She e-mailed me back that it was a copy of a cut glass pattern and she didn't know the name, but that it was 1900s. Based on her knowledge, I knew that my butter dish wasn't one of the really rare ones I saw in the completed auction research. It wasn't Vaseline glass or a fancy color, just plain, clear Early American Pattern Glass.

Based on the help I received from Elaine, I decided to put it on eBay with a question mark and "Help" in the title. I used the following as the title "EAPG Butter Dish Clear Gold Cut Glass Wonderful Help?" I think that sometimes using "Help" and "?" in the title can get more people to actually look at your auction, because they think that they may be getting a bargain. This auction, after five days, had 70 people looking at it. That's a lot of people! I started the bidding at $9.99, because I had nothing to lose. I had paid only $2 for this item.

If this item was something that I had thought was worth a ton of money, I would have put a huge reserve on it, say $999, and then waited to hear what it actually was. Once it had been identified for me, I then would have done some research, found the real value, and lowered the reserve to a reasonable price. (eBay refunds your extra funds for the super-high price when you lower it, as long as there haven't been any bids).

The reason I would put such a high price on a rare item is so that no one would have bid on it. If someone bids on it, you can't revise your title; you can only add to the listing. I would have wanted to change the title if it had been a very special piece.

Bright Idea

Make friends and pursue relationships with people in your field. My grandmother always said that the antiques and collectibles business is full of friendly and helpful people. She was right. Use these friendships when you get stuck. Your friends won't mind helping you out with their area of expertise, as long as you're happy to reciprocate when your friends need your help.

Within one day of my listing this item, I got an e-mail from Joni of Washington State, and she said, "Your butter dish is Northwood #12 circa 1906 and should have an N in the bottom and the top. Regards, Joni." Wow! I e-mailed her back and said, "You are so right! I found the signature in the base. Thanks so much, Lynn." I couldn't believe I missed a signature! Me, who grew up in the business and turns over every item when I visit friends or eat in restaurants, missed the signature. I just never expect EAPG to be signed. But with Joni's help, I was able to post all that on my listing, and the bid is up to $15.49, with two full days left to go.

Pay an expert to identify your item

If you have an item that may be worth a lot of money and you can't be certain, you may want to pay an expert to identify it for you. I strongly recommend getting appraisals and authentications in this situation. My grandmother was a well-known appraiser and she always said, "You wouldn't let just anybody work on your teeth, why would you not pay for an expert opinion on an item of value?"

You want to pay for an appraisal, grading, or authentication only if the item is going to be worth more than you pay for the service. This can get tricky, as I have learned firsthand. (See Chapter 3 for an example with a Ken Griffey, Jr. baseball card.)

Appraisals and appraisers

There are three types of appraisals, and these are sorted by the price value. The lowest value will be given if you needed to sell it tomorrow—also known as the *street value*. What could you get in cold hard cash for this item on eBay tomorrow? The next value will be a *realistic market price*. This is what it's worth if you have the time to search for the perfect collector. Finally, the highest value is that of *replacement or insurance valuation*. Sometimes, these can be way too high, and a lot of dealers don't even bother asking what this value is.

If you take your item in to a dealer and pay for a written appraisal, make sure you send the appraisal with your item when you sell it. Show the appraisal or link to your item and then say, "This appraisal will be shipped with your item. It will be very important for you to keep for investment and insurance purposes." This can help get your buyers in the investment mode, and they may bid higher.

There are many wonderful registered appraisers around the country. Try to find an appraiser that specializes in what you have and find one close to you. It is always best for the appraiser to see the item in person. To point you in the right direction, here are a couple of Web sites of appraisal organizations that may be able to help you find one in your neck of the woods and/or in your specialty:

- www.appraisers.org (American Society of Appraisers)
- www.isa-appraisers.org (International Society of Appraisers)

Some companies also offer online valuations and appraisals. One that I will be testing this year is Instappraisal.com. I really like its home page (www.instappraisal.com). The site gives great free advice and even has a handy listing of silver hallmarks. Its basic appraisal service starts at only $17.95 per item.

Authentication and grading

Authentication and grading services are used for items like autographs and Beanie Babies to let your customer know that the item is not a fake. Grading is used to put a standard condition rating on something like a baseball card or a gold coin. eBay recommends several companies for this; see Figure 11.5.

Figure 11.5. eBay's page where they recommend companies for opinions, authentications, and grading.

Generally speaking, people at these companies are highly trained, practiced, and tested in their areas of expertise. Using these services can help you garner more money on eBay. I personally wouldn't sell any expensive item like a gold coin or baseball card without getting it graded.

Bright Idea

eBay has already done some of the legwork for sellers. If you click on the **Sell** link at the very top of the eBay home page, then click **See all. . .** under the "Best Practices" header in the "Selling Resources" section at the bottom of the page, this takes you to a "Resources" page; in the "Third Party Services" section, look for the **Opinions, Authentication, and Grading** link. Finally, eBay takes you to a page that looks like Figure 11.5. eBay recommends companies to perform authentication and grading for many different items, including Beanie Babies, books, coins, comics, jewelry, Native American artifacts, political memorabilia, stamps, general items, trading cards, and sports autographs and memorabilia.

As an example, my grandmother had 50 expensive gold coins to sell. We shipped them off to NGC (National Guaranty Corporation) to have them graded. We paid about $12 each in grading fees. They came back from NGC in about two weeks encased in plastic for safekeeping with the grades written on the front side, making them much easier to sell. I sold the coins for over $12,000, and this more than covered the $600 we paid to have them graded. Grading protects you as a seller and also lets your buyers know exactly what they are getting. They can then bid with confidence, and a confident bid is a higher bid.

Researching the competition

Before you decide to list your item on eBay, take some time to see what else is out there right now being sold on the site. If there are 100 similar items being sold by a wholesaler in Japan who is practically giving them away, wait a few weeks to put your item up for sale. As you're scoping out the competition, also look closely at the starting bid price, shipping charges, and which titles and descriptions are getting the most action.

Timing

Timing is very important, and not only time of year and time of day, but also timing in relation to your competition.

Time of year

November and December have always been my strongest months and will probably continue to be, because a lot of money gets spent during the holiday season. Typically, the summer months are very slow for me. I always thought people were outside enjoying the nice weather and not stuck inside at their computers.

However, this summer has been exceptionally great for me. This July was one of my best summer months ever. So, it really depends on how hard you work at it and what great stuff you're selling. I am finding that more and more people are checking eBay year-round and a lot of the buyers are doing their eBay searches while at work, so the nice weather isn't hurting me.

Another thing to note about time of year is that you don't want to be selling Halloween costumes in January or swimsuits in February. You typically do the best if you sell close to your season. Don't forget though, that as eBay becomes more and more of an international marketplace, it is always summer in some part of the world.

Time of day and week

Next let's talk about day of the week and time of day. Studies show that auctions ending on a weekend typically do best. One famous study took similar gold coins and found that the coins that ended on a weekend sold for 2 percent more than those that ended during the week.

From my experience, the day of the week doesn't matter as much as the time that the auction ends. When you list something on eBay, it ends 1, 3, 5, 7, or 10 days from that exact time that you list it. Remember that eBay is on Pacific time, so if you start an auction on the West Coast at 10 p.m., it will be ending at 1 a.m. on the East Coast. This is probably a little too late to snag any New York bidders. I have found that the best times for me to list my auctions are between 7 a.m. and 7 p.m. Pacific time. That way, it is neither too early out here nor too late on the East Coast.

Competition

Always research your competition's timing. To do a current auction search, just type in your keywords in any of the search boxes on any page. When I do a current auction search on eBay for Malcolm Moran, no other bronzes are currently listed. Perfect! The timing is right.

Price and terms

If you have an item that is a *commodity* (that is, it's very similar to—if not exactly like—other goods being offered), keep an eye on your competitors' pricing and terms. If they're offering the exact same item at a very low starting price, note this in your research. Also, what are they charging for shipping? This can make or break your deal, too.

As an example, let's take a look at an ESPN Sports Center Game Station that I bought on one of the overstock pallets on eBay. I did my pricing research by checking completed and current auctions. Please see Figure 11.6 to see what I found.

- The games that started at a lower price, say $49.99 or even as low as $9.99, tended to go higher and get closer to the $100 level.

- The seller who went above $49.99 and started his game at $59.95 got only $59.95. The seller who wanted $120.00 as a Buy It Now did not sell his item.

- Those sellers who charged only $35 for shipping got more money for their items.

- The seller who wanted $50 for shipping got a high bid of only $76.

I used all of this data to decide that my item should start at $49.99 and I would charge only $35 shipping/handling/insurance. I sold it for $102.50. My competition research paid off, and I got top dollar for my item.

Figure 11.6. Completed auction research for the ESPN Game Station. Note how the shipping charges quoted by the different sellers show up on this page. This is very good information to have.

Just the facts

- Research is the most important component to everything that you will do as a seller on eBay.

- You must be able to correctly identify your item using eBay, Google, or other Web sites.

- Use reference books and ask for "help?" in your title if you get stumped.

- Pay for an appraisal, authentication, or grading if you have a valuable item. It will help you get a higher selling price.

- Research your competition and know what their timing, prices, and terms are.

GET THE SCOOP ON...
■ Knowing how to categorize your item ■
Determining a great title ■ Writing a
killer description

Listing Your Item

In this chapter, you find out how to list your items. How exciting, but a bit intimidating, right? Fear not, because in this chapter, I walk you through the process in detail.

If you've read the last several chapters in this book, you've already done so much of the background work that your first listing is going to be a breeze.

Making eBay a daily routine

The first thing you must do each morning or day when you start your eBay work is sign in. eBay will keep you signed in for one day and does not automatically log you off for inactivity. You may be asked to sign in again on certain sections of the site—if you bid, go to post on the boards, or want to change your information. But you don't want to have to input your password every single time you change basic pages on eBay. Instead, use the sign-in feature, and eBay will keep you logged in and remember your password for one day. To activate this handy feature, go to the eBay home page and click on the small

Sign In hyperlink at the top center. On the sign-in page, you will be asked for your user ID and your password. Before you hit the **Sign In Securely** button, be sure to check the box that says, "Keep me signed in on this computer unless I sign out." (See Figure 12.1 for a look at this page.)

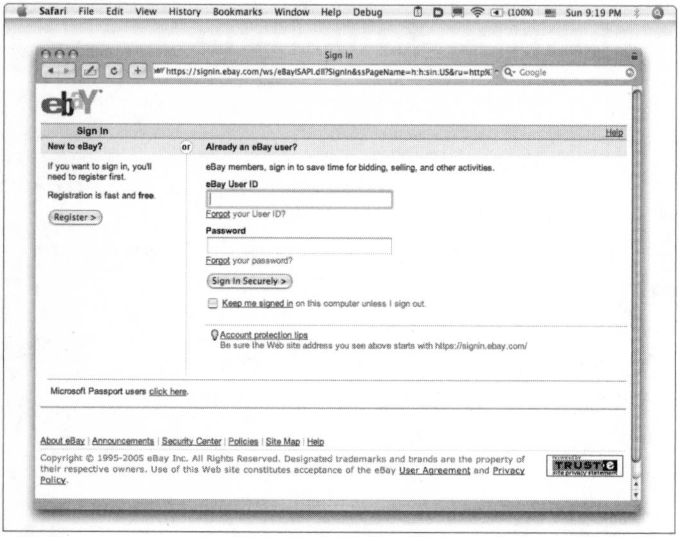

Figure 12.1. The eBay sign-in page, where you need to sign in each morning so that eBay remembers your info. This is the start to your eBay day!

Starting a new listing

After you've signed in, click the **Sell** tab found in the menu at the top of each page. On the Sell page that displays, click the **Start a New Listing** button, and a page that looks like Figure 12.2 appears. This page asks you to choose your selling format. You currently have four options: sell at online auction, sell with fixed price, sell in your store inventory, and advertise your real estate. Choose the **Sell at online auction** button. (I discuss selling in your store inventory in Chapter 17.) Click the **Continue** button at the bottom of the screen, and you will be taken to the category page.

Watch Out!

If you use a shared network or public computer, never ask the system to save your user ID and password. Also, make sure you click the **Sign out** button at the top of every eBay page when you leave. Protect yourself from identity theft.

Figure 12.2. Once you click on the **Sell** tab, you're directed to a page that looks like this. Here is where you choose your selling format.

Categorizing your item

There are currently three ways to identify and choose the best category for your item. eBay may tell you differently, but I believe that in addition to the navigational and organizational purposes they serve, these categories serve an eBay internal tracking purpose. eBay wants to know which categories are hot, what is selling, and which items are selling for the highest prices.

Knowing how eBay categories are used

eBay says that its categories are like the aisle signs in a grocery store. They guide buyers to the specific department, aisle, and shelf where an item is located. I believe that this is true maybe 30 percent of the time. The rest of the time, it's a crapshoot.

I have made serious mistakes with my categories in the past. For example, I have been listing numerous items quickly and have forgotten to change the category number. I listed a Prego Ride-On Tractor toy in the Majolica #453 category (a type of pottery), and it still sold for close to $200, which was way over my estimate. I just don't think categories matter that much, so don't spend too much time or worry on this issue. However, it's still in your best interest to choose the best category for each item so that interested buyers can find it easily.

Here is more information from eBay: "Each category begins with a top-level description, such as "Home & Garden," and continues with up to five more levels. For example, you might find a decorative basket listed in: "Home & Garden → Home Decor → Baskets."

Choosing a category from your research

If you found your category number from doing research (see chapters 9 and 11), you input the number in the category choice box (it comes up automatically at the bottom of the Select Category page), and then click **Continue**.

Most eBay buyers don't search by category, however. They search with a title search. In certain cases, buyers do search by category, but only if the category is super specific. As an example, my mother collects Blenko glass, so she searches by category. She sits and watches her category (eBay category #18874: Pottery & Glass → Glass → Art Glass → North American → Blenko) as the auctions are ending and tries to pick off bargains. As I write this, 677 items are up for sale in that category. On the other hand, a category that I use a lot is eBay category #25: Pottery & Glass → Pottery & China → China, Dinnerware → Other. This category is so broad that it probably doesn't get a lot of people shopping and watching it specifically. Currently, there are 19,474 items listed for sale in this category. You see how the Blenko category is much more specific.

Choosing a category by entering keywords

You may also choose your category by entering keywords. You simply enter descriptive words about your item, and then click the **Search** button (see Figure 12.3).

Figure 12.3. This is the eBay page that asks you to choose your category, filled out to search for a category using keywords.

In a new window, eBay shows suggested categories based on the percentage of listings with those words in the title that listed with that category (See Figure 12.4).

As an example, I will use a keyword search to find a category for the same bronze soccer boy. I type in "Bronze boy" for my

keywords in the example shown in figures 12.3 and 12.4. I recommend not getting too specific or too vague. When I get too
specific, like "bronze Malcolm Moran soccer boy," I get confusing results or none at all. I've found from experience that you
should choose the two or three most important search words
and use only those. If you choose four or more, you may get
nothing. Notice in Figure 12.4 that there are several good
options to choose for this category. I decide against choosing
the second one, Antiques → Decorative Arts → Metalware →
Bronze, at 22 percent. I don't feel comfortable using this category, because the boy is not antique, and I try to never mislead
my customers. There is not a category on eBay for collectible
bronzes (which is a shame). Because of this, I choose the first
category, Art → Sculpture, Carvings, which is #553 and the exact
category I chose in Chapter 11. Great!

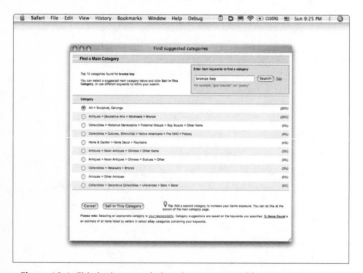

Figure 12.4. This is the new window that opens up with your category
choices from eBay, along with the percentage of times they were used.
Choose the one that means the most to your listing.

> ### ☼ Bright Idea
>
> When the category number comes up (using any of the three different methods), make a note of it. All too often, I do this research and get the information, but something happens with eBay or my Internet connection, and I lose everything I inputted. If I have taken great notes (like writing down the category number), I can quickly fix the problem or start over with the listing.

After I check the radio button next to the Art → Sculpture, Carvings category, I click the **Sell in this category** button at the bottom of the page. It takes me back to the Select Category page, but now the string for the category will show, and I'll have a category number (in this case, #553) at the bottom of the page. See Figure 12.5 for what this page looks like. *Note:* Because I already had this category number from prior research, I could have just typed it in the box and saved a step.

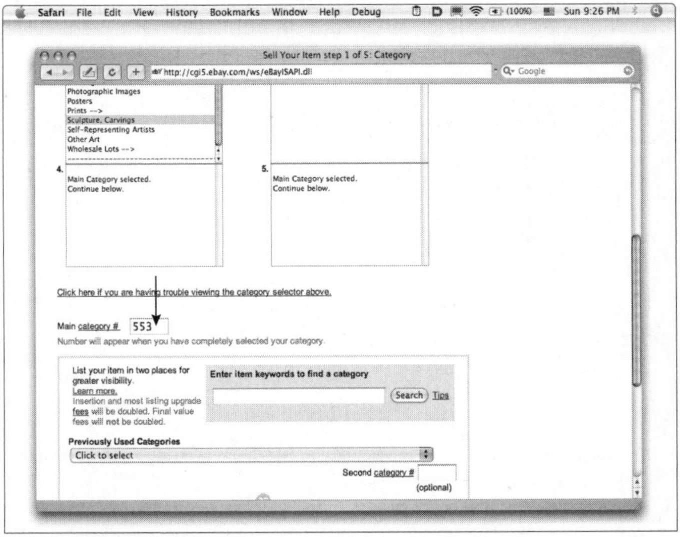

Figure 12.5. This page on eBay shows up after you've chosen your category using the percentages. Scroll down to Main category #.

> ### 🚗 Watch Out!
>
> Don't feel obligated to use the category with the highest percentage as your choice. I choose the top one only about half the time, because sometimes, the category with the highest percentage has nothing to do with your item. Just remember that choosing a category is not the most important part of your listing. In fact, of everything I talk about in this chapter, your title is what you should spend your time on. Get really quick at choosing categories—it just doesn't matter that much!

Choosing a category by browsing the category directory

The other way (at this stage) to choose your category is by browsing through eBay's entire category directory. This category directory comes up when you open the Select Category page (refer to Figure 12.3). I do not recommend using this feature, however. It is far too time consuming, and you can get lost in there! Think about browsing through the aisles of a department store that has 40,000 divisions. Yikes! If you must do it this way, click in each box from left to right until you get a list of suitable choices. Once the string has led you to the category you desire, check the box (note the number in your notes), and then click **Continue**.

Doubling up on categories

eBay gives you the opportunity (at an added expense) to use two categories to list an item. eBay often quotes statistics saying that listing in double categories will increase your sales price, but I haven't found this to be true. I recommend using only one category unless your item is very expensive (because your insertion

---

☼ **Bright Idea**

There are certain categories that I use all the time. I have made a cheat spread sheet in Microsoft Excel. I have about 50 of the categories alphabetically listed that I use the most. This way, I can quickly access the category numbers without lengthy research or a time-consuming category search.

---

fees and certain listing upgrade fees will double) and unless both categories are super specific. An example of when I used two categories was when I had a Vienna bronze inkwell that I knew was going to sell for over $500. I listed it in both the Antique bronze category and the Inkwell category. This made sense for me. However, I've sold close to 50,000 items on eBay, and I've used double categories less than 25 times. Use your best judgment, do your research, and choose the best category in the least amount of time.

Writing a good title for your listing

Your title is super important—I cannot reiterate this enough. The majority of buyers search for what they want to buy using a title search only. Sometimes, a buyer will search by title and description, but these searches can bring back too many unrelated items, so most buyers search by title only. The title is one of the most important parts of your listing.

After you have chosen your category and click the **Continue** button, the next page that comes up asks for title and description. You're now entering the Title and Description portion of the eBay listing/selling form. It is Step #2, as you can see at the top of the page in Figure 12.6.

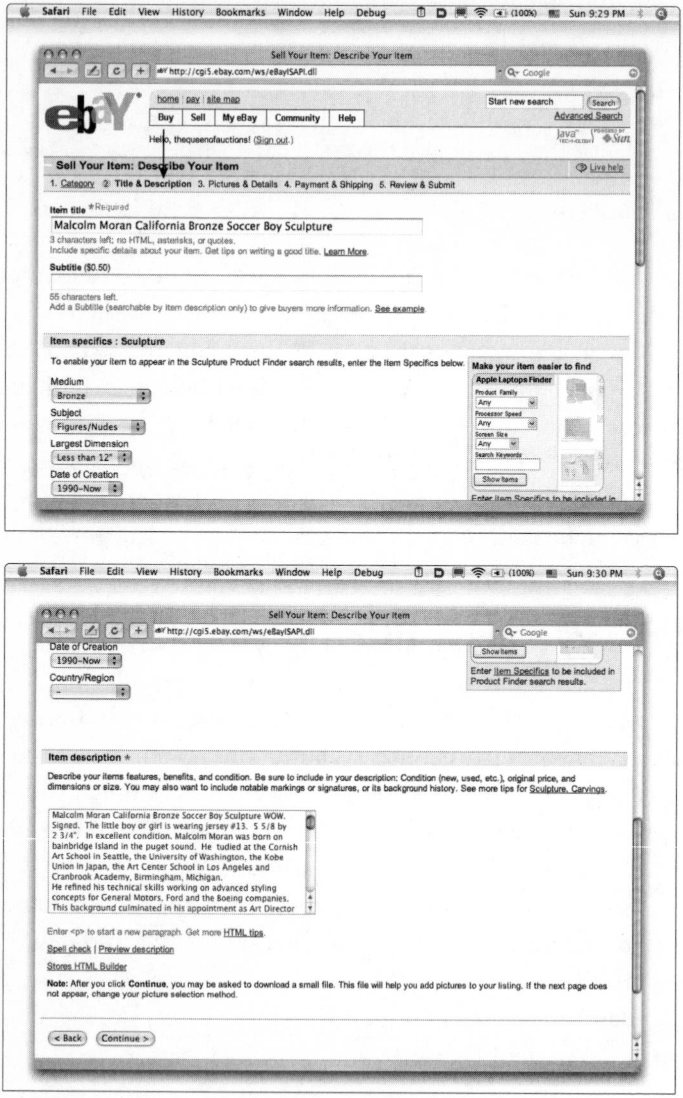

Figure 12.6. Here is the page on eBay that asks you to input your title and description. This page has been filled out for my bronze soccer boy.

Use as many characters in your title as you can

You have 55 characters and spaces to work with, and it's in your best interest to use them all. Please leave out punctuation in your title. Punctuation wastes valuable space and, according to eBay, messes with the search engines. Start to think in 55-character sentences; I can almost do this in my sleep! I type in the description, and then find that I only have one character or space left. I get that close. It is scary weird!

For example, you may have a pair of new men's socks to sell. Think first about all the ways you can describe them: color, condition, age, brand name, size, fabric, and then a great finishing adjective. It is easy to use all the characters when you think this way. An example of a bad title would be "Men Socks." A much better title would be "Ralph Lauren Black Men's Socks New Size 9-12 NWT Super!" Notice that I used all 55 characters/spaces. Your title gets buyers to your auction—whether through keyword searches or with an eye-catching and intriguing title. Always try to use the entire 55 characters/spaces available to you.

To get as much out of your title as possible, use well-known TLAs (two- to four-letter acronyms), as follows:

- BIN: Buy It Now
- FE: First Edition
- HTF: Hard To Find
- LE: Limited Edition
- LN: Like New
- MIB: Mint in Box
- MWMT: Mint with Mint Tags
- MWT: Mint with Tags
- NIB: New in Box
- NR: No Reserve
- NWT: New with Tags
- OEM: Original Equipment Manufacturer

Other considerations

In the title, try to include information like the maker, era, shape (round/square, big/small), origin, year, best feature, color, and size. Think hard about your item from your potential buyer's point of view. You may also want to include an adjective like "wonderful" at the end. Why? If 100 items come up in the buyer's title search, you want yours to stand out. If you don't believe the item is wonderful, unique, or rare, why will anyone else?

Spelling is super important. You wouldn't believe how many errors are made in speelling (oops—just kidding). If you spell the title wrong, the item will not come up in a buyer's search. As an example, I've sold a lot of Schafer & Vater, an early German porcelain that my grandmother loved to collect. I had hundreds of pieces and could never seem to get the spelling right in my listings. When I have spelled it right, the items sell for a lot more than when I misspell it. Right now on eBay there are 64 completed auctions for "Schafer & Vater" and only two for "Schaefer & Vater." You get the point. *Note:* If you're a savvy buyer, you can find some bargains by searching for misspellings!

Here's a sample title based on all the background work I did for the bronze boy in Chapter 9. From my I Sell sheet (see Chapter 5), I take the keywords and use these to form my 55-character/space title. I choose the artist, the part of the country, the medium, the form, and the sport. My title looks like this: "Malcolm Moran California Bronze Soccer Boy Sculpture." I have three characters left and could have used NR for no reserve. However, I did have a reserve, so I have to be happy

---

Moneysaver

eBay offers the option of using a subtitle, which costs 50¢. This is not cheap. Use this feature only when you're selling an expensive item and you can't tell your story in 55 characters/spaces. The subtitle will not be searchable in a title search; it is searchable only as part of the description. The benefit to the subtitle is that when buyers are skimming through auction titles, the subtitle may catch their eye and tell additional valuable information.

with just using 52 of the 55 characters and spaces. Other words I considered putting in the title were mint, darling, unique, and figurine. However, I thought the words I chose were most likely to be pulled up in a search.

Using item specifics to search

Only certain categories on eBay request further input on the item's specifics. eBay believes that these item specifics make it easier for buyers to search. See Figure 12.6 for this form—it comes up right after the title. In the Art → Sculpture, Carvings category from our example, there are several drop-down menus from which I was required to make selections.

- The first selection was Medium. My choices were Bronze, Ceramic/Porcelain, Glass, Jade, Metal, Paper, Stone/ Marble, or Other. This was an easy choice for me; I clicked **Bronze**.

- Next it asked for Subject and the choices were Abstract, Animals, Figures/Nudes, Masks, Religious Statues, Others. This was also quite easy and I chose **Figures/Nudes**.

- The third item-specific category was Size: less than 12 inches, 12 to 24 inches, 2 to 5 feet, and over 5 feet. I knew that this sculpture was only 5⅝ inches tall, so I quickly chose the category of **less than 12 inches**.

- The fourth item specific was Date of Creation. I could choose from pre-1900, 1900 to 1949, 1950 to 1969, 1970 to 1989, and 1990 to present. I knew this was a newer piece, so I clicked on **1990 to present**.

- The final item-specific category was Country/Region, and the choices were Africa, Asia, Canada, Europe, Latin America, US (yes, this is just US on the eBay site), unknown, and other. This was another easy choice, so I clicked on **US**.

The jury is out over whether these item specifics help drive up sale prices. I figure it can't hurt, especially if I fill out the forms quickly. If I don't fill out these forms, my auction will not display for potential bidders who use the Category Finder feature (displayed to the left of auctions in these specific categories). In my experience, few buyers use the Category Feature and my auction still shows up for buyers who search using regular title searches. Sometimes, when I have a $10 item that has no chance of going for more, I skip this step, because it may be a time waster, and a key to selling successfully on eBay is keeping your time per item to a minimum. The more items you can list well in a short amount of time, the more money you make.

Writing a good description

Your description is another of the most important keys to selling your item. You want to be thorough and accurate in your listing. If you don't list all the information required, you'll get a lot of e-mails requesting more information, and answering the same questions over and over can be time consuming. Time is money. If you make sure to include all the information in the original description, you won't be answering unnecessary e-mails.

Knowing what details to include

Here are the most important details to include in your description. (See Chapter 11 about researching and noting this information when you first sit down and look over your item):

- **Size:** Height, width, and length, plus a description, such as small, medium, or large.
- **Brand:** Artist, company, manufacturer, designer, and so on.
- **Markings:** What is the signature? style number? edition? issue? Where is it located?
- **Color:** Sometimes, the Web can alter the color, so describe it as best you can.
- **Condition:** Note all flaws, chips, cracks, stains, tears, discoloration, and so on.
- **Age:** What is your best guess as to the item's age? Is it new, vintage, old, antique? Give a range.

■ **History:** Where did you get it? Was it bought new and used a few times? Did it belong to a relative?

If you include all this information in your description, your listing will be very informative. Information helps sell items. Sometimes, the item's history (also known as *provenance*), is more interesting to the buyer than the item itself.

Avoiding returns

Remember that if you don't describe all the damages and defects accurately, you'll get returns, and customers will be tempted to leave negative feedback. I was so busy closing my grandmother's retail location in 2002 that my descriptions got a little simple. I forgot to list important information, and I found myself writing a lot of refund checks. I do *not* like to do this, and neither will you.

Here are a few examples of the missing important points in my descriptions. I sold an antique level that had belonged to my grandfather, an architect. It sold for $17.29, and I asked for $7 shipping, handling, and insurance. The man who bought it also purchased a rosewood matrix tool from me for $65. He e-mailed to say that the rosewood tool was great but that the level was missing the liquid in the two side measures and the listing description had not reflected this damage. He was right. I had said that the liquid was perfect in the center section, but since I don't really deal in tools, I didn't think to check the side vials. He wanted a refund, and I agreed. Instead of having him send the level back to me, which would have cost me an additional $7 in shipping (and who knows whether I could have resold it), I just refunded him his $24.29 and told him to keep the item. It was a painful lesson learned the hard way!

Another good repeat customer had purchased a strand of genuine ruby beads from me for $79.99, plus $8 shipping, handling, and insurance. She e-mailed to say that they were lovely but that my description had stated 12½ inches, and she assumed that the string was double this, or 25 inches around. I should have said 12½ inches "in circumference." She felt that we were both to blame and offered to pay the shipping both ways. I thought this was fair and sent her a refund check for $79.99 when I received the beads back in the mail.

Just remember, the more accurate your description, the fewer returns you will receive. You will also save time by not having to answer extra questions and re-list items.

Filling out the description

When you get to the auction description section of the Title & Description page, note that there are two tabs: **Standard** and **Enter your own HTML**. Unless you're a die-hard Web designer, choose the **Standard** tab (which is the default). It allows you to enter and format your text the same way you would in a typical word processing program; in other words, you no longer have to know even basic HTML to make your description look good. (The only formatting I use is a paragraph break <p>. I think this is important so that your listing doesn't run on forever and ever without any breaks.)

Be warned, however: some people go overboard with colors, fancy fonts, and even sound. I don't think that this is necessary and, in fact, I think it can hurt your business. When I'm shopping on eBay, if I run across a Web page with too much going on, that's too pretty, and that has too many extraneous details or music (which scares the dickens out of me), I tend to pass on that auction. Also, more and more people are surfing eBay while at work, and a listing with sound can get employees in trouble and also cause them to click away from your auction as fast as possible. I've

---

☼ Bright Idea

You have seen this one before, but it is so important that I want to remind you that there's a little yellow question mark on every eBay page with live help waiting at the click of a hyperlink. If you get stuck, don't beat yourself up or waste time trying to figure it out. Click on that hyperlink, and, usually within two to three minutes, there's a live person waiting to correspond by e-mail.

been doing basic text in my auctions since 1998 and have been very successful. The best eBay sellers are trying to sell an item with a title, a description, and a photo, not with graphics skills.

Looking at a sample description

Let's take a look at the bronze soccer boy and see what I included in the description. I had done the preliminary write-up and research (described in chapters 9 and 11), so this is what I used from all that.

Malcolm Moran California Bronze Soccer Boy Sculpture WOW. Signed. The little boy or girl is wearing jersey #13. 5 ⅝ x 2 ¾ inches. In excellent condition.

<P>Malcolm Moran. Born on Bainbridge Island in the Puget Sound. Studied at the Cornish Art School in Seattle, the University of Washington, the Kobe Union in Japan, the Art Center School in Los Angeles, and Cranbrook Academy, Birmingham, Michigan. Refined technical skills working on advanced styling concepts for General Motors, Ford, and Boeing. Appointed Art Director of the Seattle World's Fair. In 1963, settled in Carmel, California, to open gallery and studio with longtime friend/partner, Donald Buby. In that environment, Moran became leader of the contemporary bronze sculpture movement. Innovator of dozens of techniques in bronze used today.

<P>I have lots and lots of new-in-box gift items up for sale from World Famous Gumps (San Francisco). These are all very high-quality items and all have never been used. Please check all of our auctions for more wonderful items from Gumps. Gumps carries only the finest items.

<P>Good luck bidding! We owned Cheryl Leaf Antiques & Gifts in Bellingham, Washington. Our Grandmother was Cheryl Leaf, and she owned and operated her store for 51 years and was highly respected in the antiques and collectibles business. She was a charter member of the National Association of Dealers in Antiques and wrote many articles for its journal.

<P>Buyer to pay $8 for UPS shipping, handling, and insurance in the continental USA. California residents to pay 7.75 percent sales tax. Thanks for looking & bidding! We take all major credit cards also:

☀ **Bright Idea**

Once you have a great auction insert or tag to use in all your auction descriptions (and you want to list more items), you can choose one of your auctions that has the correct shipping and terms and just search by that auction item number. Once the screen comes up, there's a button that says **Sell similar**, and you need to click on this. Once you do that, all of that previous auction's information will come up. All you may need to change is the category, title, photo, price, and description. This is a huge time-saver.

Visa, MC, AMEX, and Discover. Please e-mail with any questions. <A href="http://www.ebay.com/powersellers.html">

At the end of each auction description I always use the same information (my tag or insert) which includes talking about my grandmother and her business. I also thank potential buyers for looking and bidding and let them know that I also accept all major credit cards. At the end of my tag you see the HTML for my PowerSeller logo. You should consider writing a tag or insert to use at the end of all your auctions.

Start thinking about what you want to tell your customers in every listing. Details you might consider include your background, some of your most important sales terms, and whether or not you collect sales tax. I discuss sales tax in Chapter 13.

Just the facts

- Choose a category quickly using one of the three ways I discuss.

- Spend some time making your title eye-catching and use great keywords.

- Always try and utilize all 55 characters/spaces in your title.

- Write a description that answers all of your buyers' questions before they are asked.

- Don't leave out key items like size and condition in your description or you will be bombarded with questions and possible returns.

GET THE SCOOP ON...

■ Choosing your starting price ■ Knowing
what features you should use ■ Making
shipping decisions

Listing Your Item and Making Decisions

Another of your most important decisions when selling on eBay is where to start the price for your item. You can do everything else perfectly: your title can be motivating, your pictures professional, and your description just like a short funny story. But if you don't price the item correctly, it just plain isn't going to sell.

In this chapter, you'll be going through Step 3 "Pictures and Details" (see Figure 13.1), Step 4 "Payment and Shipping," and Step 5 "Review and Submit" on the eBay Sell Your Item form, using the same bronze boy as an example.

Calculating your auction starting price

The research you do before you list an item (see Chapter 11) prepares you for this step. To recap what I found out about the bronze boy, a similar figurine sold on eBay for $152.50, and the bronze statues on the sculptor's Web site list at anywhere from $125 for small pieces to $1,600 for larger ones. I also

Chapter 13

noted on my I Sell sheet that I had paid $78.87, and I wrote down the market value at the retail store where I bought the overstocks ($342.90). See Figure 13.2 for all of this data. This is the kind of information that's critical to determining your price.

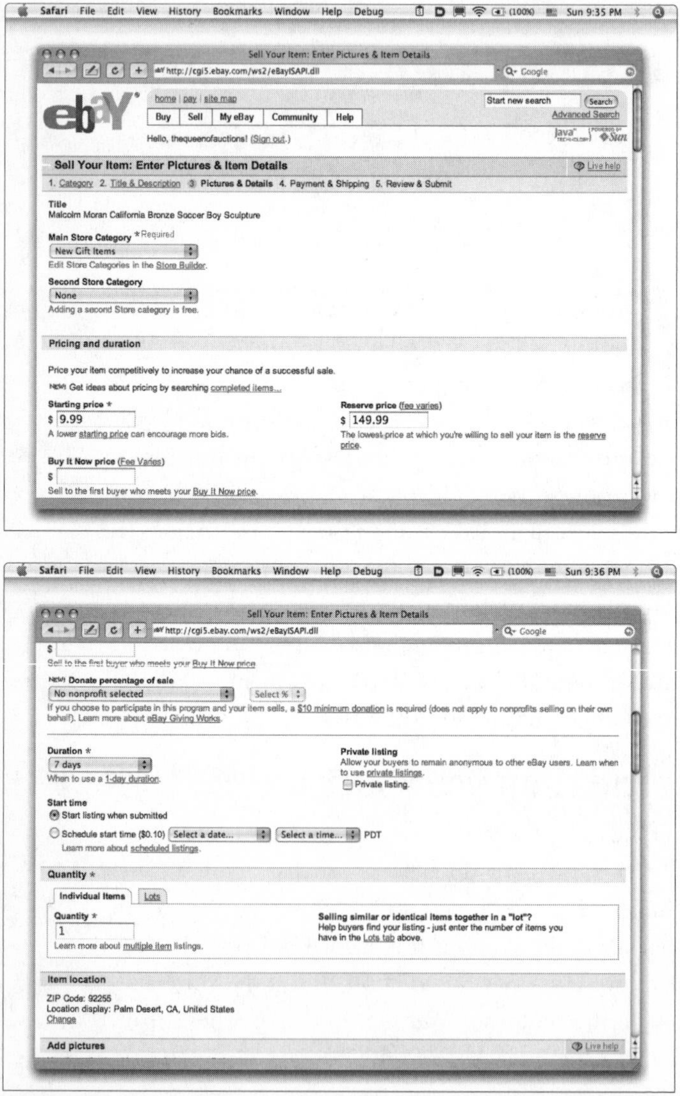

Figure 13.1. The first thing you are asked in Step 3 is for pricing and duration information.

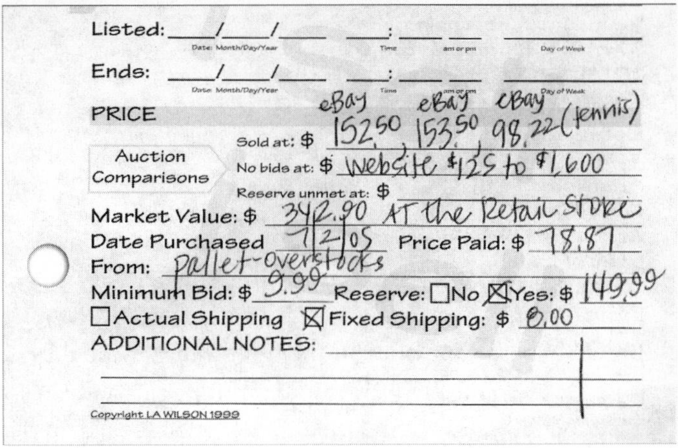
Listed: ____/____/____ ____:____ ____ ________
Date: Month/Day/Year Time am or pm Day of Week
Ends: ____/____/____ ____:____ ____ ________
Date: Month/Day/Year Time am or pm Day of Week
PRICE eBay eBay eBay
Auction Comparisons
Sold at: $ 152.50, 153.50, 98.22 (tennis)
No bids at: $ Website $125 to $1,600
Reserve unmet at: $
Market Value: $ 342.90 AT the Retail Store
Date Purchased 7/2/05 Price Paid: $ 78.87
From: Pallet-Overstocks
Minimum Bid: $ 9.99 Reserve: ☐No ☒Yes: $ 149.99
☐Actual Shipping ☒ Fixed Shipping: $ 8.00
ADDITIONAL NOTES:

Copyright LA WILSON 1999

Figure 13.2. Shows the lower portion of my I Sell sheet filled out for the soccer boy sculpture. You can see how important it is to take good notes when you're researching a potential price.

There is one more place that I go to do both price and identification research for antiques and collectibles—a great site called PriceMiner (www.priceminer.com). PriceMiner's data is kept on file for years—data gathered from eBay, Tias.com, and Go Antiques. I type in Malcolm Moran (the sculptor's name), and five items come up, including a similar bronze that sold for $153.50 on eBay. There is also a statue of a child playing tennis that sold for $98.22 at online auction (eBay, I assume). I take notes on all of my findings.

Considerations when pricing: too low and too high are equally bad

Pricing for a garage sale, an antiques store, a department store chain, and even for eBay is a delicate science. I often used to second-guess myself in the antiques store: "Am I pricing this too cheaply? What if I am giving away an item worth tens of thousands of dollars?" It was nerve-wracking.

> **Moneysaver**
>
> Do not be naïve and just guess on price. It just doesn't work this way, and you will waste a ton of money on failed listings. The listing fees can eat you alive if you aren't selling the majority of your items the first time you list them. It's important to analyze the data you collect and make an educated decision.

The beauty of eBay is that if you do price an item too cheaply, but you have titled it and positioned it correctly, the marketplace will probably raise your price to the level where it should be. I love this about eBay (and all auctions)! But pricing too cheaply is not a good idea anyway, and pricing your item too expensively can be downright dangerous.

There are many important considerations to think about when choosing a price.

- How rare is your item?
- How in demand is your item?
- How many substitutes are there for your item on eBay (or elsewhere)?

These can be hard questions to answer until you actually put something up for sale on eBay and see what happens. If you're selling a collector's plate that's very common (say, 50,000 were made) and you ask more than the going rate, it will not sell. However, if you have a rare handmade piece of Native American art that's distinctly unique, you can almost name your price (within reason, of course).

Another important consideration with antiques and other expensive items (like electronics, cars, and clothing) is its *perceived value*. If you price something too cheaply, the buyers may think your item is no good. They may say to themselves, "if she thinks it's worth only $10, why should I pay $100?" On the flip side, if it is overpriced, customers may walk away and not give any of your auctions a second look, because they may believe you overprice everything. It's a fine line.

Pricing strategies

I've gone through many pricing strategies in my eBay career. In the beginning, when I was selling my grandmother's personal collections, I would price items where I thought they should be selling. If I had a Baccarat vase and my research told me they were selling for $99, I would set the starting bid price at $99. This protected me from giving anything away, but it also limited the auction dynamics. As a result, I rarely got any bidding wars going that may have driven the price even higher.

The next strategy I tried was to start every auction at 99¢. I did this when I was closing the shop and moving back to California, and I had to sell a ton of merchandise in a relatively quick time. I thought that by starting the auctions so low, the auction dynamic would kick in, and items would sell for a lot of money. I was wrong, and found that I was selling far too many items at that starting price of 99¢. For most of these items, I could have at least gotten $9.99 at auction and maybe even more if I had put them into my eBay store. It is a pain to ship an item for 99¢! I lost a lot of money using this pricing technique. I do not recommend this strategy.

I now start most of my auctions at $9.99. If the item doesn't sell, I drop the price to $2.99, $3.99, or $4.99 and list it again. If it doesn't sell the second time at auction, I move the item into my eBay store (see Chapter 17). If the item is more valuable than $9.99 or I have a sentimental attachment or paid more for it, I start the auction at one of the eBay tiered pricing rates.

Moneysaver

Start your items as low as possible to save money on listing fees. I start most of my auctions at $9.99, and this costs me 35¢ in basic listing fees. If I were to start them at $99.99, the basic listing fee would be $2.40. That may not sound like a lot of money, but consider this: I list about 400 items each month and 400 items multiplied by $2.05 per item (the difference between $2.40 and 35¢) is $820! That's a lot of money and a lot of incentive to keep your prices low.

If the item I'm pricing is valuable but is worth less than $100, I start the item at $24.99, $49.99, or $99.99. If it's worth over $100, I consider using a hidden reserve, which I discuss in the "Reserve price" section.

A price example

I would really like to double my money on the bronze statue. This means that I need to get close to $150 for it. I think this is a reasonable figure, especially based on the data collected from eBay and PriceMiner. Also, this price is in the range for a new piece (which this one is) from the sculptor's Web site. I can't expect to get full retail on eBay (that would be the $342.90 that the store from which I bought the pallet was asking). In fact, many items on eBay are selling close to manufacturer's wholesale, but the wholesale price is right in that same range of $150. I decide to go for the $150, but I'll call it $149.99 instead (because it sounds slightly cheaper).

Reserve price

A reserve price auction is a great option to protect your investment. Although it will cost you more in listing fees, it's definitely worthwhile for certain items.

A *reserve price* means that you won't sell the item for less than this price. This way, you ensure that you get at least the reserve price, or you don't sell it. The $1 to $2 extra charge for a reserve price auction is refunded if your auction reaches the reserve price and sells.

Every reserve price on eBay is hidden from the bidders. They will not be able to tell how much your reserve price is. If you think your piece is worth over $100, consider using a reserve, combined with a low starting price, to get the auction dynamic going. But do keep in mind that your insertion (listing) fee is based on the reserve price and not on the starting bid price.

For the bronze soccer boy, I decide that I want a reserve price of $149.99, but I don't want to start the auction at $149.99 and scare buyers away. I also don't want to start it at $9.99 with no reserve, because if only one person bids the $9.99, I would

Watch Out!

Another point to consider is that some eBayers believe that if you set a reserve, the market will not bid the item up much more than the reserve price. I have seen this happen and also not happen. Often, my items will sell for the fixed reserve. Other times, the price will go slightly higher. It really just depends upon the market dynamics, but some eBayers claim that you are, in effect, just setting a fixed price when you set a reserve price (even though the price can and often does go higher).

be obligated to sell it at that price. I think a $9.99 starting bid with a $149.99 hidden reserve would get some interest. My listing fees are based on $2.40 for the $149.99 price, plus a $2 reserve fee, so the basic listing fees for this item so far will cost me $4.40. If it sells for the $149.99, the $2 reserve fee will be refunded. eBay does this to encourage you to set realistic reserve prices—ones that will be reached. Notice in Figure 13.1 that I have input $9.99 as my starting price, with $149.99 for my reserve price. If this were a nonreserve auction, there would be nothing in the reserve price box.

Some buyers don't like reserve price auctions and won't bid on them. They feel that you're taking away the entire auction dynamic, and they won't get involved. Other buyers may e-mail you and ask what your hidden reserve price is. If they ask nicely enough, I usually tell them. Most of the time, they just want to know whether the auction is worth their time. I don't think it can hurt to tell in most cases.

Typically, you want to set your starting price at a fraction of the reserve price. Several years ago, eBay said that it would allow starting prices of reserve auctions to be no less than 10 percent of the reserve price. This would mean that my soccer boy would have started at $14.99. There was such an outcry, though, that eBay pulled back on that ruling. However, 10 to 25 percent of your reserve price is a good range for the opening bid price.

Buy-It-Now (BIN) price

The buy-it-now (BIN) price feature lets you specify a price that you will accept for your item and sell immediately. The BIN feature used all by itself allows the first buyer willing to pay your price to get your item. This works just like a fixed-price sale.

If you use the BIN option in conjunction with an auction style listing, a buyer can agree to the BIN price only before anyone else bids. The BIN price is higher than your starting bid price, and once a bid has been placed, the BIN option disappears. BIN fees vary by the price you choose for the BIN (see Table 13.1).

Table 13.1. Buy-It-Now (BIN) Fees	
Buy-It-Now Price (US$)	**Fee (US$)**
US $0.01–US $9.99	US $0.05
US $10.00–US $24.99	US $0.10
US $25.00–US $49.99	US $0.20
US $50.00 or more	US $0.25

Many buyers like the BIN feature, because it allows for immediate gratification. They know that they're going to be able to purchase your items instead of waiting several days to see whether they win the auction. As a seller, however, I don't like to use the BIN feature, unless it's for an item that I have multiples of and know exactly what I hope to receive for it. I would much rather use the auction format and let the marketplace bid up my item higher and higher. Also, instead of using the BIN feature in the auction format, it's a lot cheaper to do a fixed-price listing in your eBay store (see Chapter 17).

Donate a percentage of sale

On eBay, you have the option of donating a portion of your sales price to charity. This is a really neat feature that eBay added around the time of the tsunami in late 2004. I did this when I donated 10 percent of a painting's proceeds to the Marine Toys For Tots charity. There are literally thousands of charities to choose from. Keep in mind, however, that the minimum donation is $10. So even though I donated 10 percent and my painting sold for $85, I was obligated to donate $10 instead of $8.50.

To use this feature, choose your charity, and you will be asked to sign up with Mission Fish, the company that runs this service for eBay. Next, choose your percentage to donate, and these range from 10 percent and go up in increments of 5 percent, all the way to 100 percent.

If you use this feature, a banner shows up in your listing that says a percentage will be donated to the charity you've chosen. I don't know whether this helps you get more money for an item; I suppose it depends upon who is doing the bidding. However, it is a great way to give back to the community.

Duration

The next part of the eBay Sell form to decide on is the duration. There is great debate over how long you should have your auctions run. The choices are one, three, five, seven, or ten days, and I highly recommend choosing seven days. This way, if a customer checks eBay only every Monday from the office, he will see your auction. I think that ten days is too long, and eBay also charges an extra 40¢ for a ten-day auction. That may not sound like a lot, but 40¢ times 400 items a month is an additional $160 that goes to eBay.

☼ Bright Idea

A private listing allows your bidders' IDs to be hidden. This is a great feature when you're selling a wholesale lot (that will probably be resold on eBay), selling something very expensive, and/or are carrying approved pharmaceutical products. This feature does not cost any extra, and you just need to click on the **Change to private listing** button to use this feature.

Knowing when shorter is better

You may want to use a shorter auction format, say a one- or three-day auction, if you have items that have expiration dates, like sporting event tickets or food. You may also want to use these shorter durations if you're a high-volume seller who lists a lot of identical items. Currently eBay allows you to list only ten identical items at the same time (on the same day), so by using a one-day selling format, you'd be able to list seventy of these per week instead of only ten per week with a seven-day listing. Shorter auctions are also good to use during the holiday season, when shoppers are in a real hurry. Also, if you're in a hurry for cash, a three- or five-day auction could be just what you need. I do all my auctions as seven-day auctions, however, so this is what I choose for the bronze figurine (see Figure 3.1 again).

Choosing your start time

Your next decision on the eBay Sell form (Figure 3.1) is the start time—another area of debate. Your auction starts and ends at the exact same time that you list it (but one, three, five, seven, or ten days later). This means that if you're listing on a Sunday at 5 p.m. eastern time, and you choose a seven-day auction, your auction will end at 2 p.m. Pacific time (5 p.m. eastern time) the following Sunday.

 Watch Out!

Even with the auction sniping software, I have found from experience that the best times to list items are between 7 a.m. and 7 p.m. Pacific time. By doing this, your auctions end between 10 a.m. and 10 p.m. eastern time and between 7 a.m. and 7 p.m. Pacific time. That's not too early and not too late for those people that live across the United States. About 80 percent of my sales go to the United States and Canada, so it makes sense to think in terms of North American time zones. You don't want to be listing in the middle of the night and possibly miss that one bidder (who doesn't know about the sniping software) who was going to make a difference in your final bid price.

With all the auction sniping software (see Chapter 1), bidders don't need to be at their computers so much anymore when the auction ends. This means that starting times/days and ending times/days aren't as critical as they used to be.

You can also choose to schedule your listings to start on different days and at different times. This is a great feature to use when you're going on vacation or if you have to list at odd hours, like in the middle of the night. It costs 10¢, and you can choose a day 21 days out and time increments that go around the clock in 15-minute increments. I used this feature when I went on a three-week vacation to Spain in 2003. I was able to schedule 100 auctions to start each week that I was away. It was really cool! I staggered each auction to start (and, therefore, end) 15 minutes after the last one.

I don't like to schedule my auctions with eBay's software (Selling Manager Pro and Turbo Lister), because unless you want to pay the extra 10¢ to delay the start times, your auctions will all be uploaded at the exact same time. Instead, I like to stagger my ending times, so that if someone is bidding on multiple items, he or she has a chance to bid on all the auctions. I believe that if all my auctions end at the exact same time, I will lose bidders. By going the traditional route, my auctions are all automatically staggered about two to four minutes apart, because this is how long it takes me to type in each listing.

I listed the bronze soccer boy on a Friday night, July 15th, at 7:30 p.m. Pacific time, so my auction would end seven days later on Friday night, July 22, at 7:30 p.m. You can see that sometimes I can't even follow my own advice. I do push the 7 p.m. time suggestion to 7:30 and even 8 p.m. sometimes. This is only 11 p.m. eastern time, so I think it's okay. If the world were perfect (and I weren't a single working mom), I would have tried to have all auctions end before 7 p.m. Pacific time.

Quantity

You need to decide about the quantity. I talk about Dutch auctions in Chapter 1, and if you're going to be doing these, I recommend clicking on the blue button that says **Multiple Listing** right below the **Quantity** button. For the purposes of this book, I assume you'll usually have a quantity of one. Because this quantity is what automatically comes up, you don't need to do anything else here.

Item location

The final portion of the Sell form in Figure 13.1 shows your Zip code, city, and state. This information automatically pulls from all the data you input when you registered to sell on eBay, so you don't need to do anything here except check that it's correct. This is great information to have in your listing, because eBay has a feature in which buyers can search for items in their geographic areas.

Add pictures

If you want to add pictures to your listing, you do that during this step of the listing process (see Figure 13.3). See Chapter 10 for details on taking and including photographs, but here's my advice in a nutshell: if your item is worth less than $100, one to two pictures should be sufficient. Remember that your first photo is free, and each one after that costs 15¢. If your item is worth over $100, you may want to go for the picture pack that eBay offers, and include six to twelve photos.

There are three ways to put your photos on eBay: enhanced picture service, basic picture service, and using your own Web hosting service.

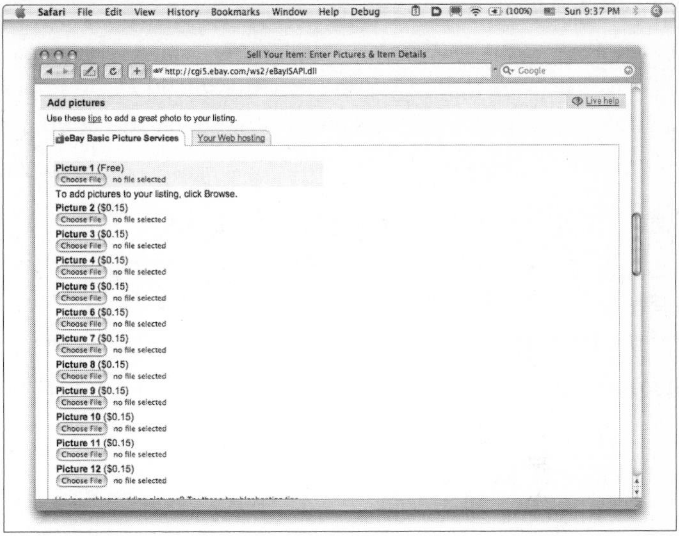

Figure 13.3. This is where eBay uploads your photos to its Web space, and is a continuation of Figure 13.1.

Enhanced picture service

The first is eBay's enhanced picture services, which is a free service from eBay that allows you to preview, crop, rotate, and color-correct your pictures, in case you didn't already do this. It doesn't allow you to do advanced color correcting or save the photos with a name that you choose. I find that the program that came with my camera works much better than the one eBay offers, so I don't use this feature. But you may like it!

Basic picture service

The next way is with eBay's basic picture services, and this is what I generally use. I click the **Browse** or **Choose File** button for my first picture, and up comes a box that shows the contents of my computer hard drive. I find the file folder called My Documents, and then July 2005. I type in the name of my first photo, which happens to be MM1. I click on the **open** button, and the URL for my photo is now in the picture #1 box. I have decided to use five photos for this item (given that it's fairly expensive), so I go to picture #2, find my next photo (MM2), and repeat this process.

This process is very easy, and eBay will upload all these photos to its Web space when you click **Continue** at the bottom of your computer screen.

Your own Web hosting for pictures

If you have your photos stored on Web space other than eBay's, click on the **Your Web hosting** button and enter the address or URL where your photo(s) is located.

Picture options

You're given more options, which are lumped together in a category called Picture options.

Automatically, you're given the standard photo size of 400 × 400 pixels. This is what you'll use for almost all of your auctions. But because I'm using five pictures, I've decided to choose the picture pack for up to six photos, because this costs me only $1 for the five photos, the option to supersize, the picture show, and the gallery. The *gallery* is the tiny picture that will show up to the left of your auction listing title when someone does a search. (Please see Figure 7.1 to see what these tiny pictures look like under the heading for "Picture Gallery.") Remember from Chapter 10 that if you don't use the picture pack and still want to *supersize* (up to 800 × 800 pixels) your photos, you will see that this is available for 75¢. Supersize photos are great for unique items with a lot of detail like fabric and art. They are not necessary for commodity items like sports equipment and CDs.

The *picture show* option is available for 25¢. This feature has your multiple photos appearing in a slideshow player at the top of your listing. You don't want to choose this option for only one photo; it really works best with at least three photos.

Choosing extra features

eBay breaks down the next features that it tries to sell us (although some are actually free) into several sections: listing designer, increase your items' visibility, promote your listing on eBay, gift services, and page counter.

Listing designer

Listing designer is free, and it puts a colorful decorative border around your listing. I don't use this feature, but I know a lot of sellers who do. I choose not to use it, because I think that there is already so much going on in my listings: my store banner, my text, and my photos. My thinking is, the simpler the better. Of course, this is your decision, and you may have some fun playing around with all the options.

If you do decide to use this feature, you need to choose a theme category (new, special events, category specific, patterns/textures, holiday/seasonal, eBay stores, and miscellaneous). Once you choose the category, you're taken to more specific options, such as borders made up of baby-rattles and books. There are over 220 to choose from, and some of them are really quite nice.

Increase your item's visibility

In the big, black outlined box, eBay shows you what an example with gallery looks like, shows you your actual listing with a box where the photo will go if you choose the gallery, and also show you how text will look with bold.

Gallery

I always use a gallery photo for my first auction listing on eBay. It costs 35¢, and this is not cheap, but I use this feature because I think it really does enhance my listing. Many buyers have told me that they search only for items that have the gallery. If my item doesn't sell the first time, I take the gallery option off and lower the price. So you can see in Figure 13.4 that I checked the gallery box.

> **Moneysaver**
>
> Of all the extra features, the gallery is the most important one, and the only one I recommend spending your money on as you begin your eBay business. If you want to try some of the others at a later date, when you know more about eBay and have a feel for the site, I encourage you to try them. But in the beginning, save yourself as much money on your listings as you can. Remember that these little fees all add up!

X this box

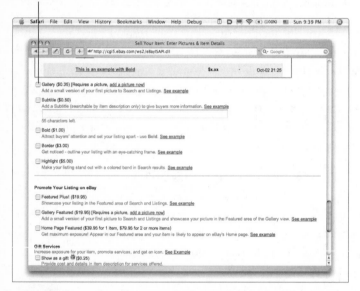

Figure 13.4. Here are some of the extra features eBay offers. This is a continuation of figures 13.1 and 13.3.

Subtitle

The next option is subtitle. See Chapter 12 for a discussion of whether a subtitle is worthwhile or whether it's just eBay's way of hitting you one more time with additional fees. This one costs 50¢. I only recommend using a subtitle in rare instances.

Bolding, framing, and highlighting your title

The next features (see Figure 13.4) are all ones I don't use, but you should know about them. These all relate to the 55-character title that will show up in an auction search. They have nothing to do with the actual listing.

- To bold your title costs you $1.

- A border outlines your listing title with an eye-catching frame, and this costs $3.

- Finally, you can highlight: for $5, eBay will put a colored band across your listing title.

Promote your listing on eBay

I recommend using these promotional options (Featured Plus!, Gallery Featured, Home Page Featured) only if you have a really expensive item and/or want to drive traffic to your other auctions. A man in one of my classes uses the Featured Plus! at Christmastime, because he owns a Christmas ornament business. If he uses Featured Plus! for one of his many auctions, he finds that it drives a lot of traffic to his other auctions and to his eBay store. I encourage you to try these only for very special circumstances, however.

Featured Plus!

Featured Plus! is for words only and costs $19.95. It puts your title listing in bold at the top of certain search and listings pages.

Gallery Featured

Gallery Featured is also $19.95 and is for photos and title. It puts a small version of your first picture on certain search and listings pages and also showcases your picture in the featured area of the gallery view. These positions are rotated among other sellers who have also paid for gallery featured, and eBay doesn't guarantee how many times your item will be featured.

Home Page Featured

The last option is Home Page Featured, and this costs $39.95 for one item or $79.95 for two items. This is for text only (no photos) and it offers your item a *chance* to be on the eBay home page. This is not guaranteed, however. Your listing will also have a chance to be featured on the eBay Buy Hub page (to get to the hub page just click on the **Buy** tab at the top of most eBay pages—this page allows buyers to surf the site easily), but it's not guaranteed, either. The only guarantee is that your listing will be shown in the eBay featured-items section.

There are a lot of rules and regulations that you need to read before you sign up for any of these expensive features. Click on each link to learn what they are. I have used only Featured Plus set!—one time for a very expensive item.

Gift services

The second-to-last choice in this section is whether to show your item as a gift. This costs 25¢, and a gift icon will be placed by your title. I don't recommend using this option. It is pretty common knowledge that anything you buy on eBay can be a gift and that most sellers will ship it to the gift recipient instead of directly to you. Bottom line: this is a waste of money. I used it once by mistake, and when I tried to modify my listing to get rid of it and get my money back, I couldn't.

If you do decide to use it, click on all the services you provide and tell potential buyers what they cost: gift wrap and card, express shipping, shipping directly to a gift recipient. These extra add-on services could make you some extra money, but I suggest advertising them in your listing without paying the 25¢ fee.

Page counter

The last feature is a page counter that shows how many people have visited your auction page. It's free, and I use it all the time. This counter can be hidden (so that only you have access to it), or it can be shown to everyone on eBay. I say go ahead and show it. If you have a really hot item and your counter shows that a lot of people have looked at it (like 500 hits), it can encourage bidders to place higher bids and to bid early.

This feature gives me great information. As an example, if I have 40 or more people look at an auction, and it doesn't sell for $9.99, my price is probably too high. If only three people look at it, there may be something wrong with the title, or it could be an item that's never going to sell at auction. (There may just not be a demand for it, and it may be better off being listed in my eBay store.)

Payment and shipping

The Payment & Shipping section of the eBay Sell form (see Figure 13.5) is the last section before you review and submit your listing.

Keep in mind that eBay remembers all of your payment and shipping information for each specific auction, so when you go to list additional items, you can use the **Sell similar** button to list other items, thus skipping this section in the future. Just make sure that the auction you choose to do a "sell similar" from has the correct method and price for shipping. As an example, I have different auctions with my UPS shipping priced at $7, $8, $9, $12, and $15. I also have auctions with USPS priority flat rate at $5. I will want to make sure that the auction I use as my template matches the item's shipping requirements that I am listing.

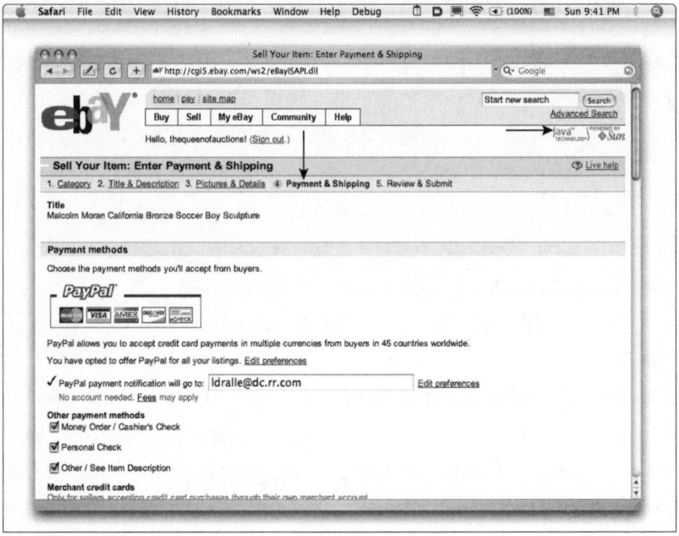

Figure 13.5. Shows the eBay Sell Your Item form with the payment methods portion of the payment and shipping section.

Payment methods

I discuss payment methods in great detail in Chapter 7, so I will go quickly through the Sell form here.

- The first option is for PayPal. Remember that PayPal is an eBay company and is one of the best ways to collect funds. Check this box, and then input the e-mail address where you want the payments to go. Buyers can pay with credit cards through PayPal.

- Next, you're asked for other payment methods. You probably want to check the box for money orders and cashier's checks and for personal checks, if you've decided to accept these payment methods. If you check the **Other** button, this means that you want bidders to read your item description for more options.

- There is a merchant credit card section if you have your own merchant account. I do (because I ran an antiques store for many years), so I check the Visa/MC, Discover, and AMEX boxes. You probably don't have a merchant account already set up, so you will not check these.

- There are some buyer financing options offered through Paypal. Paypal will hold the loan, and you will be paid right away in full. I see no reason not to offer this service. There is really no downside. Your buyer is the one who will get stuck with the extra interest payments, not you as the seller. Go ahead and click that you will offer this option.

Shipping and sales tax

In the shipping section (see Figure 13.6), the first required field is your ship-to locations. eBay's first option is Will ship to the U.S., and then you have the option to choose to which other areas you will deliver goods. I choose the Worldwide box. I see no reason to cut out the extra business that comes from overseas. But again, this is your decision, and you need to do what you feel the most comfortable with. Just be very careful if you're selling expensive items overseas and do your research on the buyer (see details in Chapter 8 and in the following section). There is one last option here and it is Will not ship—local pickup only. This is a great feature for furniture and other large items.

Research your buyer

I sold an expensive gold coin to a buyer in Sri Lanka, and he paid with a credit card through an e-mail. Luckily, my assistant was behind in her shipping duties, and the coin sat around for a week and had not been shipped when I got a disturbing phone call. The call was from a police officer in Ohio who wanted to know why I had charged his credit card for over $300. It turned out that this buyer in Sri Lanka had signed up for eBay two days before my auction ended, had no feedback, and was using stolen credit cards. Check out your buyer's feedback and history before shipping expensive items overseas.

⚠ Watch Out!

Keep in mind that even if you check the box for pickup only, buyers will still invariably e-mail and ask you to ship heavy, bulky, and large items. Be ready to quote shipping charges using Greyhound and other freight companies because believe me, they will ask! Check Chapter 8 if you need more information on shipping.

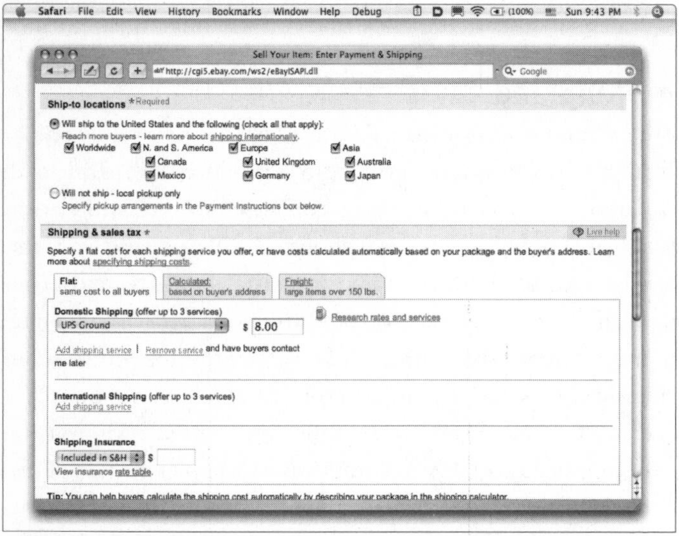

Figure 13.6. This figure shows the shipping portion of the payment and shipping section of eBay's Sell form.

Flat rate or calculated

In the shipping and sales tax area, you input your shipping fees. I choose the *flat rate* option, because that's how I've chosen to run my business. For domestic shipping, you can use the scroll down bar and choose from many different options: UPS, DHL, FedEx, and USPS, all with various options within each. There are also some generic options like Other and Standard Flat Rate Shipping. Choose the one you want, and then input the price. I click on UPS ground and input that it will cost the buyer $8 for shipping and handling.

If you're going to do *calculated* shipping costs, go ahead and click on that button. eBay will ask you for the weight, type of package, whether insurance is included or extra, the shipping company, and if you want to add a handling fee (and how much that will be). This is the eBay shipping calculator and it is a very handy feature. It will take your Zip code and the buyer's Zip code and figure the cost plus insurance and handling (if you have specified this). The shipping calculator will show up in your auction and calculate the cost for each unique buyer.

International shipping

Next is the international shipping section. Here, you can take the time to quote what type of international service you offer, by using either the flat rate or the calculated rate. You can quote three different options. I don't take the time to fill this out, because there are so many different factors involved, and I send only about 20 percent of my business overseas. The different factors are the following:

- Weight
- Size of package (once a package is over 36 inches in length and girth, the prices increase dramatically)
- Country

I would much rather quote overseas shipping on a shipment-by-shipment basis. But do what works best for you. If you're always shipping the same item(s) and know exactly what it costs to go to Europe, for example, you may want to have this showing up on all your listings.

Shipping insurance

It's a good idea to offer shipping insurance, so I've picked the drop-down box under Shipping Insurance that says "Included in S&H" and $0.00 for the cost, because I use UPS, and UPS automatically insures for up to $100. If my item happens to sell for more than $100, I am more than happy to cover the insurance. And UPS's insurance rates are very reasonable. You'll find the same with DHL and FedEx (see Figure 13.6).

The four options for you to use in the Shipping Insurance section are Not Offered, Optional, Required, and Included in S&H (Shipping and Handling). If you choose the middle two, a box will pop up for you to input the amount that the insurance will cost.

Sales tax

Finally, you may need to give information about sales tax. I have filled out the form that says if my buyers are in California, I will be charging 7.75 percent sales tax. Be sure to check with your accountant so that you can fill in this section also. Just pick your state and then fill in the rate, if your state requires you to charge sales tax. And note that I just charge sales tax on the item price, not on the total including shipping and handling.

Returns, payments, and buyer requirements

In this area of the eBay Sell Your Item page, you may choose a return policy, decide whether you offer a discount on multiple purchases, and determine whether you will sell only to buyers who have a certain feedback rating.

Returns

I don't list a specific return policy, because I have found that some eBay purchases can turn into buyer's remorse. People get caught up in the frenzy of the bidding and lose their heads. Then they receive the goods, and although they are just what you described, they want to return them. This is unacceptable to me as a seller, and I usually take back goods only when I have messed up in my description or misrepresented the item in some way. For this reason, I don't spell out a return policy.

If someone is extremely unhappy with a purchase and it honestly wasn't your fault, I recommend taking it back if the customer pays the shipping both ways. I don't want any unhappy customers, and this policy tends to ensure a return customer for life. Use your own judgment, but remember that eBay fortunes can be made and lost on the customer base you build.

In the payment instructions, I say "We want our customers to be completely satisfied and stand behind all our merchandise."

You may consider saying something similar to show that you're a reputable dealer. This is also the area where you may want to say that you hold personal checks for two weeks, say that you expect payment within a certain number of days (specify how many), and tell buyers how often you do your shipping. If you're selling part-time, be sure to clarify in this section. As an example, you can say, "We ship only once a week, on Tuesdays" or "We go to the post office on Tuesdays and Thursdays." By telling your customers this information up front and in all your listings, you'll have a much better chance of keeping your feed-back all positive!

Offering discounts for multiple purchases

You may want to specify a shipping discount for multiple pur-chases, but try to steer clear of specifying what the rate will be. If you click on the blue button that says **Offering a shipping dis-count,** you will be shown to a page with many different options. I click on the link that says, **Yes, allow buyers to combine pur-chases within [x] days and send a single payment.** I allow buyers to shop for 30 days, but you have much shorter options. Then I click on the button that says I will specify shipping discounts later. I do this so that I have control over the shipping totals. Shipping costs are so varied that I couldn't possibly set a price without knowing what the individual items are that the person purchased.

As an example, I also say within my listings, "Save on shipping with multiple purchases. This is usually the base s/h/i price for the first item, and $1 to $2 for each additional item, depending upon size and destination." This way, my buyers get an idea of the costs, but it also leaves it open to my judgment. If someone buys a large vase and the shipping is $25, and then buys an addi-tional large vase with the same $25 shipping, I don't get stuck paying $50 for shipping but collecting only $26 or $27.

Buyer requirements

This is the final section in Step 4, "Payment and Shipping". eBay says that "buyer requirements can help reduce your exposure to buyers who might make transactions more difficult or expensive." But eBay also says that you should "select your requirements carefully, as they may reduce your selling success."

I have no buyer requirements set, but you have many to choose from. You can block buyers from countries to which you don't want to ship, and you may also block buyers with negative feedback scores of –1, –2, and –3.

You may block buyers with unpaid strikes against them, and buyers who won one of your items and never paid. Finally, you may block buyers without a PayPal account.

Once you have chosen your requirements in this section, click **Continue** or **Go to Review**. All you have to do now is check the review and submit section of the Sell Your Item form.

Review and submit your listing

The review and submit process is Step 5 of the eBay Sell Your Item form.

At this stage, you double-check your work. I recommend doing this thoroughly and diligently the first 20 to 100 listings you write. After you get comfortable with what you're doing, reviewing and submitting becomes a formality. (I don't check anything anymore except for my photos. I still mess up on those occasionally, and this is the only step that you will see them.) After you have verified that everything is perfect, you see the fees that eBay is charging for your listing. Make a note of these

---

Moneysaver

Most of my auctions cost 70¢ to list: 35¢ for the insertion fee (based on $9.99 starting bid and no reserve) and 35¢ for the gallery. Shoot for this price range for most of your auctions. If you have to pay more for some, that's okay, but this is a good price range to be in.

on a spreadsheet or an I Sell sheet (see Appendix). These fees figure quite heavily into your profit and loss.

For the bronze figurine, I was charged a $2.40 insertion fee (based on a price of $149.99), a $2 fee for the reserve price auction, and $1 for the picture pack. This added up to a grand total of $5.40, which I consider to be a lot of money.

The final step is to click on the **Submit Listing**. I tell you, this is the best feeling in the whole world—you are actually going to have something up for sale on eBay. What a thrill! Once you click on that button, up comes a screen that says Congratulations and gives you the eBay item number. Remember to write down the item number and get ready for the fun to begin.

Just the facts

- Make sure you pick the best starting price for your auction.

- Use reserve price auctions for expensive items and things you don't want to sell for less than a certain amount.

- Seven-day auctions are the best choice for most sellers.

- Try to start your auctions between 7 a.m. and 7 p.m. Pacific time so that you don't cut out any East Coast buyers.

- Make sure you use at least one photo in your listing.

- Use the gallery feature when you list an item for the first time on eBay.

- Page counters are free and a great tool to see how well you have written your auction listing.

- Quote a flat rate shipping price or use the shipping calculator in your listings.

- Accept as many payment methods as you feel comfortable with—the more the better.

During the Auction

Congratulations! You have some items up for sale at auction, and this is the *beginning* of your profitable venture. However, you may think that after the item is listed, you can turn off your computer, walk away for the seven days, and check back at the auction end to see how much money you made. Not!

Selling items on eBay is an ongoing process. You must be available during the auction to monitor the process, answer questions, make revisions, and post additional information. This chapter shows you how.

Keeping a close eye on your auctions

Keep a constant watch on your auctions. Check the counter, check the questions, and check the bid price frequently.

To monitor questions, you need to access both your e-mail account and the Internet (to check My eBay.) Potential bidders frequently ask questions during a current auction, and such questions show up as a question to answer in My eBay and as an e-mail in your inbox. Bidders who have won an item can also

> **Moneysaver**
>
> eBayers who are serious about buying want their questions answered immediately so that they can make a buying decision. Plan to check both My eBay and your e-mails every single day, at least once. (I check first thing in the morning and also in the evening.) It is amazing to me how many bidders e-mail back after I have answered a question to thank me. They tell me that most sellers don't even bother to answer questions, much less to do it so quickly. Set yourself apart from everyone else and give great service before the auction has ended. This will translate into money in your pocket.

ask questions through the completed auction page, but in this case, the question will show up in your e-mail in-box and in your "my messages" on eBay.

Check both My eBay and e-mail constantly—daily or even several times per day. I am very serious about this in my eBay business. I've found that if I take a day off and come back to my computer, a potential bidder has already asked a question twice, because I have not answered it yet.

Answering questions through My eBay and e-mail

My eBay is a great resource to check throughout the day. I check it for my dollar totals, questions, and for buyers who have combinable shipments and/or need invoices. (I talk about sending invoices in Chapter 15.) Note: My eBay will look slightly different for you if you have not paid for Selling Manager or Selling Manager Pro.

My eBay is a really handy feature. In Figure 14.1, you see that I have 2,196 active listings, and that the total for what is definitely going to sell is $225.63. Also see that I have four items with questions.

When a buyer asks you a question through a current auction by clicking on **Ask Seller a Question,** the question shows up in My eBay and is also sent to your e-mail in-box. The person asking the question must choose between four subjects:

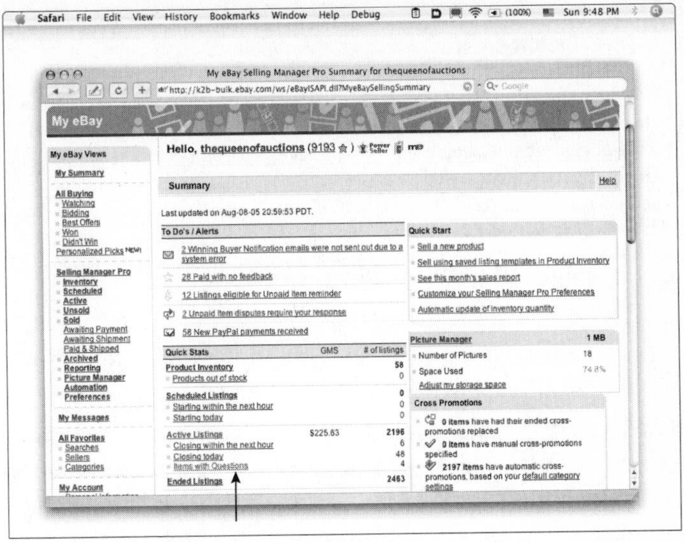

Figure 14.1. My eBay page for TheQueenofAuctions.

- **General:** Anything not covered with the shipping and payment options. Some examples could be size, condition, era, or even the item's history. Even though you may have noted all of these in your description, some buyers will miss reading about it and send a question.

- **Shipping:** A buyer may ask you to quote some different shipping options. Usually it is a foreign buyer asking for a shipping price to his or her country.

- **How to pay:** Again, you may have listed all the payment options in your listing, but the potential buyer missed seeing them. He may ask if you accept PayPal or inquire to see if cash is acceptable.

- **Combined shipping:** When potential bidders ask about combined shipping, they want to know if you offer a break on shipping charges if they purchase more than one item. Even though I spell this out in all of my listings, we still get this question quite a bit. They may ask, "If it is $9 to ship one plate and I win two of your auctions for two plates, how much for two to Zip code 98225?"

I like to answer the question both on the eBay site and from my own e-mail account. By answering twice, I get a few benefits. First, I know that the buyer will have two chances to see the answer. Second, if I answer from my own e-mail account, my signature with all my information gets to the potential bidder, and that person may feel more comfortable making a bid if she knows my name, address (PO Box), and telephone number. You may not want to make all of this information available. However, I have been doing this since 1998 and have never had a problem. Third, it makes it easier for bidders to e-mail me back since they don't have to access me through the eBay auction page; they have my e-mail address in their in-box. And if I answer through eBay, I can then post the question and my response on the auction page, which helps all bidders get additional information.

To answer a question through My eBay, click on **My eBay** at the top of the page. After it comes up, click on **Items with Questions.** A screen appears, showing all of your active auctions and the questions for each one. Click the **Respond** hyperlink, and this will take you to the question screen (see Figure 14.2).

The question in Figure 14.2 is about combined shipping, so I answer her, and then check the box that allows me to post this question and response in my listing. This is valuable information for all bidders, so I feel comfortable posting it. Keep in mind, however, that once an answer is posted, it cannot be edited.

After I answer a question in My eBay, I copy my response, paste it into the e-mail that came from this potential bidder, and hit **Send**.

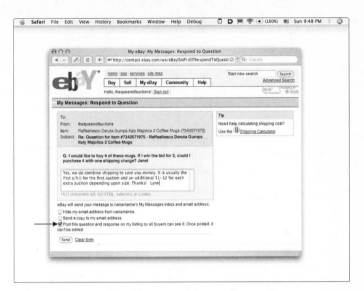

Figure 14.2. A question with an answer, for one of my auctions.

If a bidder asks a question through an auction that has ended (inactive auction), the message will show up *only* in your e-mail in-box. The subject line will be "Message from eBay Member," and you should answer these through your e-mail. It will also show up in "my messages" and it's a good idea to answer it there also.

If you're getting a lot of questions or comments about an auction and there are no bids, you may want to revise your listing or change your title. If there are a lot of questions or comments about an auction and there are bids, you may want to add to your listing. The following section discusses how to do both.

 Watch Out!

You may get some questions that are very personal in nature. For example, I had a woman e-mail a question about combined shipping for a dish set, but she also went into great detail about the pattern, saying that her grandparents had owned this set, so she was going to bid as high as possible to win the auction. It is not a good idea to post these types of questions on the auction page for all bidders to see. Use your best judgment and err on the conservative side. You don't want to make any bidder angry.

Fixing a mistake in your listing

If you make a mistake in your listing or forget some important details, you may revise your listing, add to your description, or even end it early (if it was that bad of a mistake!). The following sections look at an example of each.

Revising your listing

Use the Revise Your Item feature if your item has no bids, the auction has more than 12 hours left, and you realize you've made a mistake. You can change your title, change your description, and even change the price if you need to do so. In Figure 14.3, look at the arrow that points to **Revise Your Item.** These options will show up only on your screen, because you're signed in as the seller of this item. No one else can see this screen.

Figure 14.3. One of my auctions with more than 12 hours left to go.

To use the Revise Your Item feature, make sure that you are signed on to eBay and pull up the auction page by using the auction item number. If for some reason you are not signed on to eBay, the **Revise Your Item** button will not appear and it can be frustrating trying to figure out why it isn't. When that page comes up, all you have to do is click on the **Revise Your Item** button on the upper left-hand side, and then change what you need to change. If you want to change the title and description, click on **edit title** or **edit description.** You can also change the category by clicking on **edit main category**. To change the price, click on **edit price and details.**

Adding to your listing

After your item has bids, you're not allowed to revise the title or description, but you can add to your listing. As an example, suppose you list a serving dish, but you didn't include the measurements. Two buyers e-mail you with this question, and although you answer both questions and post the responses on the listing, a third person e-mails you with the same question. The best thing to do is add to your listing description.

To do this, make sure you are still signed on to eBay and pull up the auction page, using the eBay item number. In the upper left-hand corner, click on **Revise Your Listing.** On the screen that comes up, click on the link that says **Add to Your Description.** A text box appears that allows you to add whatever you like. You may write something like, "Oops! I forgot the dimensions. This piece is 12" by 14" by 8."

Ending your auction early

If you're too late to change the title or description and an addition to the description will not be sufficient, you may need to end your listing early and start over.

Here's an example. A friend of mine who sells on eBay e-mailed me to say that she had listed a very expensive violin and had received a bid for $300, when she noticed that it had a serious crack in it. She asked for my advice, and I told her that adding to the description was not sufficient—she would need to let every bidder know about the damage, and the best way to do this was to end the auction early and start over.

> ### Watch Out!
>
> When a bidder gets a notice from eBay that his bid was cancelled, he may be very upset. To keep my bidders from getting angry, I e-mail the bidders myself, apologize for the inconvenience, and explain the situation. Also, if it is an item that I will be relisting, I give all bidders the new auction number. This helps to keep everyone happy, and it also increases the chances that the bidders will bid on the new revised and corrected listing.

There are other cases where you may need to end your auction early. Some of these have happened to me! I broke a piece while it was up for sale, made a mistake in counting pieces, listed something that I didn't have to sell, and lost an item. All of these situations qualify as reasons to end an auction early.

To end an auction early, go to My eBay and look to the lower part of the page under the heading "Managing your auctions," then click on the link that says **End my auction early.** Next, input the eBay item number. If there are any bids, eBay asks you to cancel all the bids. You then need to choose the reason for ending the auction early. There are four to choose from:

- The item is no longer available for sale.
- There was an error in the starting price or reserve amount.
- There was an error in the listing.
- The item was lost or broken.

Click **Continue,** and your listing will be ended and no longer show up on eBay. Bidders will be notified through eBay that the listing ended early and that their bids were canceled.

Deciding not to end your auction early (or add a Buy It Now)

If you have something rare up for sale and a bidder notices that you're relatively new to selling on eBay, she may try to make you an offer by asking you to end the auction early and sell it to her. (She may also ask you to add a Buy It Now.)

Do *not* do this. The bidder will have all sorts of excuses, like "It's my mother's birthday tomorrow" or, "I had one of these when I was a kid." Blah, blah, blah. All I say to such bidders is, "Thank you for the inquiry. I hope you win the bid, but it is my policy to never end auctions early. Too many people have already expressed an interest in this item." Enough said.

Bidders like this are usually trying to take you for a ride and get a great bargain. It can be tempting, especially if the offer is for a lot of money, but let the auction play itself out. In the majority of cases, you'll get more money by staying the course.

Quoting overseas shipping costs

One more important thing to stay on top of is quoting shipping charges to international addresses and to Alaska and Hawaii. If I have 200 auction items up for sale during any one week, I can expect to answer about ten e-mails with tricky or unique shipping questions. There is no possible way to plan ahead and have every single option in your listing. In fact, you can think you have it covered, and then someone wants a quote by boat with insurance to Croatia. What?

There are just too many variables with international options, so just make sure that you answer these questions quickly and post the responses on your listing. That way, if the international bidder does win the auction, it is very easy for you to remember what you quoted that bidder for shipping charges.

Make sure that when you quote an international shipping charge, you tell the potential buyer that the price is for shipping *and* handling. I always round up the weight on international shipments and add an extra couple of bucks, but I've had several buyers e-mail after they received a package and say "You charged me $8.00 but I can see right here on the box that the postage was only $5.40. I want a refund." I always e-mail right back and say that the difference is the handling fee I quoted. I tell them that I have to pay an employee to go and stand in line at the post office with all foreign shipments, and $2.60 was cheap for that! One problem with the postal service (USPS) is that the postage you pay is right on the box, so that everyone can see it. With UPS or FedEx, no one knows but you. However, I typically use USPS for foreign shipments, because its rates are the most competitive.

Just the facts

- Always keep a close eye on your auctions.

- Answer questions quickly through both My eBay and your own e-mail account.

- Be prepared to quote international shipping.

- Know how to revise or add to your listing in case of an error.

- Know how to end your auction early in case of a major mistake.

How to Make Your Transaction a Successful One

PART IV

GET THE SCOOP ON...
■ Notifying your winner ■ Collecting money ■
Shipping the item ■ Getting and giving feedback

Chapter 15

Completing the Sale

When bidding has ended on items you have up for auction, it's time to check all your auctions and see what has sold in the past day. It's also time to notify the winning bidders, a task that can be set up automatically so that eBay sends out notices. If you have a buyer with combinable shipments, you need to send him a new invoice, with cheaper shipping rates. You also want to make sure that you collect the money *before* you ship. (Never ship until you're paid!) You then want to ship the item quickly and let your buyer know the tracking number and/or the day the package was sent. Finally, you want to set up your feedback automatically to save you time. This chapter shows you how to do all that and more!

Find out what sold and to whom

When your auctions end, the way to check your sales is to click on the **Advanced Search** hyperlink, and then click on the link on the far left-hand side called **Items by Seller.** You'll see a page that looks like the one in Figure 15.1. Note in Figure 15.1 that I have input my seller ID, asked for completed auctions for the last day, and asked for the bidder's e-mail addresses. I have unchecked the box that says "Show close and exact User ID matches," which is checked by default.

Figure 15.1. The screen that comes up when you click on **Items by Seller.**

Your choices for completed listings are for last day, last 2 days, last week, last 2 weeks, and last 30 days. Try to monitor your completed auctions on a daily basis, so that you need to look only at what closed in the past day.

Don't click the box that asks for close matches, because if you do this, it will bring up anyone with a user ID close to yours, and then to get to your own information, you have to click another button on the far right-hand side that says **View Seller's Items.** This just adds another step and doesn't add any relevant information.

When you click **Search,** everything that you sold in the past day comes up. See Figure 15.2 to see what this screen looks like. If an item sold at auction, the screen will show the buyer's user ID and e-mail address. If it was sold out of my store (see Chapter 17), the screen will give me the option to **See Buyers.**

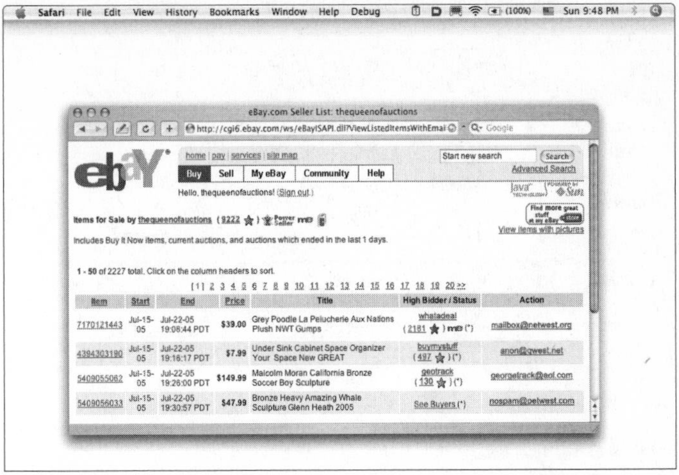

Figure 15.2. The eBay Sales page that shows everything that I sold in the past day with the buyers' user IDs and e-mail addresses.

I use the back of my I Sell sheets (see appendix) to write down this information and keep it all in one place. See Figure 15.3 to see an example of what I wrote down for a bronze soccer figurine. You may, instead, want to keep track of this information on a ledger or in a spreadsheet. Whatever method you choose, it's handy to have this information at your fingertips in case of problems or if you need to e-mail your buyer.

I also write down how many feedback points the buyer has. This is helpful information later on if the buyer doesn't pay. If a non-paying bidder has fewer than five feedback points, it is probably a good bet that the transaction will never be completed. (See the glossary in Chapter 1 for more on feedback points.) There is also a place on my sheet for me to note when I e-mail the buyer.

Always keep good records, because eBay periodically purges its records. They purge by seller information after 30 days. If you wrote down the item number, you can look up the information their system for 90 days. After that, you are out of luck.

Auction House: _____ Item #: 5409055062

Item: _____Moran Bronze Soccer Boy_____

BUYER INFO

Date Ended: 1/22/5   # of Bids: 20   Winning Bid: $ 149.99

User ID: _____GEOTRACK (130)_____

Email Address: George Track @ aol.com

Name: _____ Phone:( )_____

Address: _____7615 N. 30th St._____

City: _Miami_ State: FL Zip: 33185

_____ Email: __/__/__ Reply: __/__/__

_____ Email: __/__/__ Reply: __/__/__

SHIPPING INFO

Package Weight: __2__ ☒Ground ☐Air ☐

Shipping Charges: $ 6.3 Date Shipped: 1/25/5

How Shipped: ☒UPS ☐USPS ☐FEDEX ☐_____

Tracking #: _____

_____ Email: 1/25/5 Reply: __/__/__

PAYMENT METHOD

☐Money Order ☐Cashier's Check ☐Personal Check
☐Visa ☐MC ☐Amex ☐Discover ☐Escrow ☒ PP

Credit Card #:_____ Exp. //

$ Amount for Item:	$ 149.99	Sales Tax
$ Amount for Shipping:	$	
$ Amount for Insurance:	$ 8.00	
TOTAL RECEIVED-Date 1/23/6	$ 157.99	$

PROFIT/LOSS   LESS:

Listing Fee:	$	5.40
5.25% × 25 + 2.75% × 124⁹⁹ Selling Fee:	$	4.74
Additional _Refund Reserve_ Fees:	$	<2.00>
Credit Card Fee 4 %:	$	6.32
Actual Shipping Charges:	$	6.37
Cost of Item:	$	78.87
TOTAL PAID OUT:	$	99.70
Profit/(Loss):	$	58.29

FEEDBACK	Date	Positive	Negative	Neutral
I Sent:	1/26/5	☒	☐	☐
I Received:	__/__/__	☐	☐	☐

Copyright LA WILSON 1999

Figure 15.3. The back side of my I Sell sheet, filled out with the buyer's important information including user ID, e-mail, and address.

Watch Out!

After about two weeks, you can no longer get your buyer's e-mail directly from eBay. They change this listed information to say Contact Member, and you have to e-mail the buyer through the eBay system. So be sure to write down all contact information so that you have it if you need it later.

After I have written down all of my buyer's information on the I Sell sheet, I file these in my Waiting for Money book. (I love when my Waiting for Money book is very thick. This means I'm having a great month!) You can do the same thing, using a ledger sheet or a system of your own. After checking in all the sold items, I make a pile of the sheets for the auctions that didn't sell—see Chapter 17 to know what to do with those items.

The next step is to make sure that you have a system in place for notifying your winners. This is discussed in the following section.

Notifying the winning bidder

The bronze soccer boy that I had up for auction and we have been discussing throughout this book, reached the reserve price of $149.99. Yippee! That was fun!

Still, at this point, there's work to do. In the old days, before PayPal and eBay automation, sellers actually had to type out each winning bidder's e-mail. Can you believe that? It was definitely the Stone Age, and if you weren't right at your computer to send out an e-mail within seconds of the auction ending, boy would you hear about it from your buyers. eBay shoppers want to pay quickly, some within minutes of the auction end, and they can't do that without knowing the total required.

Today, the best way to automate this feature is through Selling Manager or Selling Manager Pro, which are covered in this section. You also find out how to send invoices of all types.

Automation preferences

Selling Manager and Selling Manger Pro are programs that eBay offers for a monthly fee on their site: Selling Manager is $4.99 per month, and Selling Manager Pro is $15.99 per month. These programs allow you to keep templates for inventory items, archive auctions, get reports, and track what was paid and shipped. The most important feature of both programs, however, is that they allow you to set automated preferences. This is the only feature I use them for, and it's worth the monthly fee. Start by going to My eBay and clicking on the **Automation Preferences** link shown in Figure 15.4.

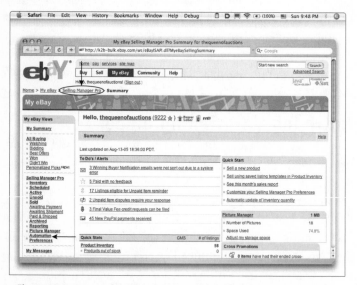

Figure 15.4. A copy of the My eBay page with Selling Manager Pro circled and an arrow showing the **Automation Preferences** link.

Once you click on **Automation Preferences** there are boxes to check for automatically sending the following:

- Automatically send a Winning Buyer Notification e-mail to your winning buyer(s) after item has sold.

- Automatically send a Payment Reminder e-mail after a listing has closed and the item remains unpaid.

- Automatically send Payment Received e-mail when payment has been received.

- Automatically send Item Shipped email when I mark a sold listing as shipped.

- Automatically send a Feedback Reminder e-mail if feedback has not been received.

Of all of the available options, I only use the winning buyer notification and the feedback reminder, but I discuss all of the automation options in the following sections.

Winning buyer notification

Winning buyer notification works like this: once an auction has ended, eBay sends an e-mail to the winning bidder with the eBay item number and title, your payment instructions, the auction ending price added to the shipping charge (if you specified the shipping price in the listing—please refer back to Chapter 8), and a **Pay Now** button that takes the buyer right to PayPal (discussed in Chapter 7). You can also include your own content. I have chosen to include my eBay store logo in the e-mail, along with a custom message giving my terms, my mailing address for checks, and my telephone number.

Payment reminder

This automated feature sends buyers a payment reminder. I tried this for a few weeks and found that it created more work for me than it saved in time. The biggest drawback is that the

---

Moneysaver

I highly suggest that you utilize the winning buyer notification feature. Just think how much time you'd spend if you had to send out all those e-mails by hand. I sell about 100 items a week, so multiply this by about 3 minutes to fill in all the personalized information for each auction, and this would add an additional 300 minutes (or five hours) to my work week. This is worth the $4.99 to $15.99 monthly fee for Selling Manager in time saved alone.

people who had sent checks would get all freaked out by these payment reminders and e-mail me frantically, explaining that they had sent the payment and that the mail must be slow, etc., etc., etc. They would ask me to see whether the check had arrived, so I would spend extra time doing research.

I don't recommend this feature. I find it better to send unpaid e-mail notices on a case-by-case basis. I talk more about this approach in Chapter 16.

Payment received

This feature automatically sends an e-mail when payment is received. If your buyer pays with PayPal, eBay will know that he has paid and will send out a message. This is a nice feature, and you may want to use it, but since PayPal also sends out a separate "Your payment has been sent" e-mail, sending a "Your payment has been received" e-mail is somewhat redundant and increases the risk that you'll irritate your buyers with gratuitous e-mails. If your customer pays by check, you can pull up your eBay item screen using the eBay auction item number, mark the item as paid, and eBay will automatically send the payment-received e-mail.

I don't use this feature, because I see it as just another e-mail in someone's in-box, when they already get too many e-mails from eBay. If you used all these automated features, your poor buyer could get five different e-mails for one winning transaction! That's too many, so I try to limit the ones I send to a winning buyer notification, plus an e-mail when the item ships.

Item shipped

This automatic feature lets your customer know when his item has shipped. It's not really very automated, because you have to go into your listings and mark the "shipped" box for each listing, and then eBay will send each buyer a generic e-mail.

Instead of using this feature, I have UPS automatically e-mail my customers the tracking number. DHL and FedEx also offer this feature and you can read more about it in Chapter 8.

Feedback reminder

The last feature is to automatically send a feedback reminder if feedback has not been received. You can choose how many days after shipping to send the feedback reminder. I use this feature, but the downside is that if I don't take the time to pull up the eBay auction (using the eBay item number) and mark that the item was shipped, eBay won't know that they were shipped and, therefore, will not send the feedback reminder e-mail. See the "Leaving feedback" section at the end of this chapter for additional information on leaving feedback.

Sending an invoice

If your auction sale was very straightforward—one item to one buyer in the United States—you don't have to do anything, because eBay automatically sends the winner an e-mail with the total. However, if the purchase was not so straightforward, was made by a foreign buyer, or involves multiple items, you need to go to the actual item number to send an invoice or into My eBay for combinable purchases.

Sending an invoice

To send an invoice, once you type in the eBay item number, the listing will come up, along with a large button on the upper left-hand side that says **Send Invoice.** Click on this button, and it takes you to a screen similar to the one in Figure 15.5. Change the shipping amount, then specify how the item is going to be shipped. eBay will also ask you whether insurance is Not Offered, Optional, Required, or Included in S&H (Shipping and Handling). Choose the correct option, and then note if you are collecting sales tax. Finally, click on the button at the base that says **Send Invoice,** and you're done!

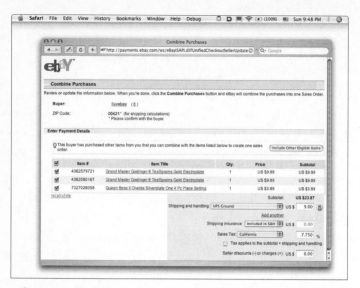

Figure 15.5. The Send Invoice page from eBay. This example happens to be for multiple purchases but looks just like the one you would use for a single item.

Sending a foreign invoice

To send an invoice for a foreign purchase with the correct shipping information, you need to pull up the item, by item number. Foreign sales can get tricky at this point. When you make a note of who purchased your item (if you use I Sell sheets [see the appendix], there is a place for this on the back side), if you see .ca, .de, .it, or anything like that at the end of the e-mail address, it's a good bet that your buyer is from a foreign country.

Many times, these buyers will get the automated e-mail from eBay and assume that the same shipping and handling costs that are quoted for the United States apply to them. They will then go ahead and pay with PayPal, and when you see their physical address in the PayPal screen, you realize that they owe you more shipping money. It gets tricky and difficult to collect at this time. Instead of taking the automated approach, send an invoice as soon as you see that a buyer is from a foreign country. Often, the more savvy foreign buyers will e-mail you and ask for a new, corrected invoice. This is very helpful.

Sending a combined shipping invoice

If your buyer makes multiple purchases from you, you will see a link on the My eBay page that says **Buyers with Combinable Purchases,** with a number. This link only shows up if you have buyers with multiple purchases. Click on the link, and it takes you to a screen listing all the buyers, the quantity of auctions won, and the total amount (without shipping). Click on the buyer's ID that you want to send an invoice to, and up will come a screen that looks like Figure 15.5.

Once you are on this screen, check each item that you want to send the invoice for, and then adjust the shipping rate. Make sure that you have chosen the correct shipping method, shipping insurance, and sales tax, just like you do for a foreign invoice. Finally, click the **Send Invoice** button, and you're finished. These invoices make life as an eBay seller very easy. Please be sure to use them.

Collecting the money

Now that automated e-mails and the invoices are out of the way, it is time to collect the money. This is really the best part of the entire process! Because 80 percent (or more) of your payments will come through PayPal, I spend most of this section talking about that service.

Every day, I go into my PayPal account twice (once in the morning and once in the evening) to check in and see who paid for what. To see what the PayPal front screen looks like, take a look at Figure 15.6. If you click on each person's transaction, it takes you to a page that shows the item, item number, how much the person paid, the shipping address where they want it shipped, and whether they have a confirmed address.

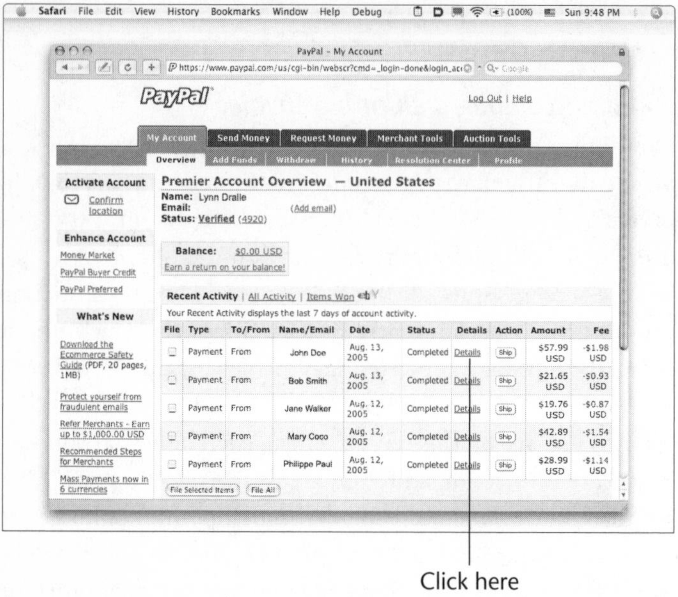

Click here

Figure 15.6. The front page of the PayPal screen, once I have logged in.

A confirmed address means that the shipping address that you are shipping to is also an address where that person gets a credit card bill. Now this gets tricky because some people do not have credit card bills sent to home addresses anymore—people use a PO Box, because mail fraud is so prevalent. This means that about 40 percent of the items I ship out go to unconfirmed addresses. However, I do check to make sure that the user ID, the e-mail address, and the name on the shipping label all have something in common.

Here is one way that you can protect yourself when shipping to an unconfirmed address. As an example, if the buyer's ID is "bobthegreat," his e-mail is bobjones@hotmail.com, and I am shipping to Bob Jones, I feel pretty confident that this is the owner of this PayPal account. However, if I see a buyer with user ID "Susan55" and an e-mail of SusanHayworth@aol.com, and she asks me to ship it to Yolanda Brown, I take an extra step. My

> ### Watch Out!
>
> PayPal will not protect you as a seller if you ship to an unconfirmed address. What this means is that if the PayPal account that your buyer used to purchase your item is fraudulent or a stolen account, and the address that you ship to says "Unconfirmed," PayPal can go in and request documentation from you for an inquiry. If it does turn out to be a fraudulent transaction, PayPal can take the payment back from your account. I know this sounds drastic and it is. It happened twice to me in 2000 before PayPal instituted an inquiry system.

assistant, Maureen, is great at watching for these discrepancies. If she finds one, I e-mail the person at the PayPal e-mail address on file and say, "We are concerned that this eBay shipment is going to a name that does not match your e-mail address. To protect both you and ourselves from fraudulent activity, can you please verify the ship-to name and address?" I usually hear right back from the buyer, who is happy that I am taking these extra precautionary steps. The buyer may say, "I am sending it to my mother because it is her birthday." By taking this extra step, we have not had any PayPal chargebacks (resulting from an inquiry that turned out to be fraudulent) in over five years.

To check on money through PayPal, the first thing I do is sign in. Once I have signed in I go to the front page also known as My Account. Next, I click on the **details** button by each buyer's name (see Figure 15.6). Once in the detail screen, I note all the buyer's information and make sure the buyer has paid the correct amount by double-checking it against my completed I Sell sheet. After I have marked the I Sell sheet as paid, I go ahead and file the buyer's information from the front screen. It does happen (quite a bit) that buyers pay twice by mistake. When I find this, I always refund one of the payments immediately.

If someone pays through a checking account instead of by credit card through PayPal, the payment can show up on your front screen as Uncleared. Wait until the status changes to Cleared (this can take 7 to 10 days) before shipping. Also, as the money in your PayPal account grows to large amounts, make sure you take the time to click on the **Withdraw** button and transfer the money into your checking or savings account. Otherwise, guess who is making interest on your money? Not you—PayPal!

When checks come in the mail, I sit down with my Waiting for Money book and check in all the information in the same way that I go through the PayPal payments. Once I have a stack of paid I Sell sheets, it's time to pull the items and get shipping (see the following section).

Shipping the item

When you pull items for shipping, it is always a good idea to take your I Sell sheet or ledger and pull up each item by its item number on the eBay screen. I have to do this, because I have over 2,000 items listed in my store and usually another 200 at online auction, and if I only go by my notes, I can get confused. Instead, double-check each and every item with the auction photo on the eBay site—before you ship it out. This can save costly shipping mistakes.

After I have the item(s) packed, with my newspaper article and order form tucked inside, I close up the box and write the buyer's name on the outside. Then I weigh the box and write the weight on the I Sell sheet. I repeat this until I get through my stack of I Sell Sheets, and then sit at the computer and input my labels into the UPS online system. After the labels print out, I go and find the correct boxes and place the labels on them. Refer to Chapter 8 for more information on how to ship.

You can also ship and print labels directly from PayPal. (PayPal used to charge for this, but now it doesn't.) You can print labels for USPS and UPS. Keep in mind that the UPS rates will be higher through PayPal than if you have a UPS account and go directly through UPS. Also, UPS will not pick up from you if you go through PayPal, which means you have to flag down a driver or drive your packages to a UPS drop-off location.

> **Moneysaver**
>
> To refund money through PayPal, make sure that you go into the item detail screen for the transaction and click on the **Refund** button at the bottom of the page. You can make partial refunds (in case someone has overpaid for shipping) or total refunds. Make sure you always do it this way instead of just sending money through PayPal. If you don't use the **Refund** button, your original PayPal fee will not be refunded and these fees can add up!

This is not very handy if you're shipping a lot of items. However, using PayPal labels can be a great way to start your business.

E-mailing tracking numbers

You can e-mail tracking numbers through PayPal. To do this, go to the item detail page for your transaction, and then click on the feature that says **Tracking Info ADD**, input all the details, and PayPal will send an e-mail to the buyer.

UPS is my carrier of choice and it automatically sends an e-mail with tracking numbers to your buyers. FedEx and other companies also offer this service. When I ship with USPS Priority (which I rarely do) I don't e-mail tracking numbers because it costs 40 cents extra for the tracking number, and also because the items usually get to their destinations quickly. I do try to e-mail foreign buyers when their items ship, because those shipments can take from one to eight weeks.

Figure out which system works best for you, but do let your buyers know that their items have shipped. It keeps the lines of communication open and can allay the fears of new eBay users, who may be very skeptical. Good communication leads to positive feedback, which is discussed in the following section.

Leaving feedback

It is common courtesy to leave positive feedback for your buyers on a timely basis, and you can automate this feature (it used to take hours!), as discussed in the "Automation preferences" section earlier in this chapter. This section discusses your options.

> ☼ **Bright Idea**
>
> Save yourself a lot of wasted time and make sure (no matter what shipping
> system you are using) that after the box is packed, you either write the
> buyer's name or the eBay item number on the outside of the box. Do you know
> how much time it takes to open 15 already-packed boxes, looking for a
> Noritake plate because you didn't write any information on your boxes? Scary!

You can leave feedback after the buyer has paid for your
item or after the buyer has paid for the item *and* has left you
positive feedback. The second option protects you a little bit, so
that if a buyer pays, gets the item, and leaves you negative feedback without contacting you, you still have an edge, because you
could leave reciprocal negative feedback. I don't play these
games. Negative feedback is a fact of life on eBay and will happen no matter how hard you try. (I have 17 negative out of over
12,000 positive responses!) So, I opt to leave the positive feedback as soon as the buyer has paid. This has really paid off for
me recently, as I have gotten a lot more reciprocal positive feedback, and it has come more quickly than before.

You also have a choice to write your own glowing feedback
or just let eBay randomly leave some of their stored comments.
Click on the **Edit stored comments** link to add to what eBay recommends or to write your own comment. This link is found on
the Automated Preferences page, next to the **Automatically
leave the following positive feedback** heading.

If you choose to not use the automated system, you can still
leave feedback by going to the My eBay page and clicking on the
feedback link on the lower left-hand side under My Account.
The eBay feedback system keeps eBay an honest and safe place
to trade. Take the time to leave feedback for your customers.

Just the facts

- Use automated e-mails to notify your winners—what a time-saver!

- Make sure you know how to send a simple invoice, a foreign invoice, and a combined shipping invoice.

- Collect your money and note what has been paid.

- Ship your items and e-mail the tracking numbers to your clients.

- Leave feedback. It's very important and helps to keep eBay self-regulated.

GET THE SCOOP ON...
Dealing with nonpaying customers
■ Working with unhappy customers ■
Addressing shipping problems

Chapter 16

Troubleshooting

When running an eBay business, it is important to know how to put out fires when they occur. And believe me, they occur on a consistent basis. With eBay, anything can happen . . . and it does! Some customers never pay, some customers are unhappy with their purchases, some items never arrive at their destinations, some items arrive damaged, and some customers leave you negative feedback. Now, some of that you can blame on the customer or the delivery service, but there are times when you, as a seller, make mistakes. It happens. In this chapter, I talk about how best to deal with each of these situations while always remembering the mantra, "the customer is always right."

Your customer doesn't pay

I sell about 400 items a month on eBay and each month, I have a hard time collecting for about eight items (or 2 percent). I usually give the customer two weeks to pay (yes, I know that this is very generous), and then I start sending reminder e-mails through eBay. You may want to send the reminder at one week instead of two. That decision is up to you.

Using the eBay reminder system (as opposed to simply sending an e-mail from Outlook or some other e-mail program) is great and tends to look more serious than if you just e-mail the customer on your own. Non-paying bidders can be intimidated when they get a "You did not pay" e-mail from eBay.

To send a reminder-to-pay e-mail through eBay, go to the My eBay screen and in the lower right portion is a section that says **Dispute Console**. The first line says **Eligible for Unpaid Item Reminder.** All the auctions with payments still pending will show up. Check on the box on the left side of the item for which you want to send a reminder, and a screen pops up that looks like the one in Figure 16.1.

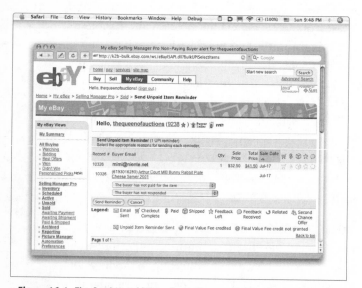

Figure 16.1. The Send Unpaid Item Reminder screen through eBay. Notice that you must choose two reasons.

eBay asks you to choose two reasons. The first box that appears has two choices only and they are:

- The buyer has not paid for the item.

- We have both agreed to not complete the transaction.

I usually choose the first one—the buyer has not paid for the item. The next box that appears has quite a few more options and they are as follows:

- The buyer has not responded.

- The buyer has refused to pay.

- The buyer wants shipment to a country that I don't ship to.

- The buyer wants shipment to an unconfirmed address.

- The buyer wants a payment method I don't accept.

- The buyer is no longer a registered user.

- Other reason.

I usually choose the first option here also. After you have checked a reason in both boxes, go ahead and click the **Send Reminder** button. This automatically opens an unpaid item dispute with your buyer. The buyer has the opportunity to respond to you through the eBay system, and these responses will be listed right below the **Eligible for Unpaid Reminder** button on the My eBay page. About half the time, the buyer will pay, and the other half, I end up having to relist the item (see Chapter 17). Legitimate negative feedback is just as important to eBay's feedback system

---

Moneysaver

The beauty of using the eBay system to open these disputes is that if the buyer doesn't follow through and pay, you can automatically click on a button to request a refund of your selling fees (not the listing fee, but the final value auction fee—see Chapter 1 for more info about fees). If the buyer doesn't respond in 7 days, you can request a refund, and this will show up as a credit on your eBay account. In the past, it was very hard to request these refunds, but this system helps you get your money back faster and easier.

as positive feedback is, but there is a high risk that a non-paying bidder will leave retaliatory negative feedback. When possible, I wait until the last day of eBay's 90-day data retention period before leaving a negative. This reduces the chances that I'll receive a negative in return.

Your customer is unhappy with the purchase

Your customer may be unhappy with the purchase for a number of reasons. Just when I think I've heard everything from customers, something new springs up.

If the customer is unhappy because I made an error in the listing, I take the item back for a full refund, and I pay the shipping costs both ways. Some of the errors I've made when listing include the wrong dimensions, the wrong color description, the wrong estimate of the item's condition, or the fact that I think it is antique and the buyer disagrees. As you can see, a lot of these reasons are subject to interpretation. I tend to err on the side of "the customer is always right," and this has paid off very well for me. Even though I've made an error, I can end up keeping a customer for life.

If the customer is just unhappy or has buyer's remorse, I try to work with her. If nothing can be agreed upon, I take the item back, but I ask the buyer to pay the shipping costs both ways, and then I just relist the item, as discussed in Chapter 17.

☼ **Bright Idea**

Before I agree to take any item back, I always ask the buyer what would make her happy. This way, the ball is in her court. As an example, if a piece has more damage than I described, I ask her whether a partial refund would make her happy and how much she would expect. The answer is usually much less than I would have offered, and I don't have to pay for the return shipping. This saves me money.

Your shipment never arrives

Sometimes your item never gets to your buyer. This happens most often with shipments overseas, although this past Christmas, I had three UPS packages that never reached domestic destinations.

Most foreign buyers don't want insurance, and so when a package goes missing, it's up to you to decide what to do about it. When I ship airmail overseas, it should normally take about seven days, while surface shipping can take six to eight weeks. However, on packages that have gone missing, I ask the international buyers to please wait a minimum of four to six weeks (if not two months), because more often than not, the package will eventually show up. The challenge with these shipments is that once they leave the United States Postal Service (USPS), the responsibility lies with each foreign government's postal service, and some are not very good. For this reason, if you're shipping expensive items overseas, use a carrier like Airborne Express (now called DHL) or FedEx that actually has employees in those countries.

Some international buyers expect a full refund (even though they didn't pay for insurance), and some will just say "no worries." It really depends on the buyer, so make sure you're following through and answering all e-mails. I normally refund the purchase price if an international item goes missing. It happens rarely—maybe ten times in the past seven years.

If you did purchase insurance through USPS or are using a carrier like DHL, FedEx, or UPS, file a claim with the company. USPS claims can't be filed until six weeks after the shipment date, which can get frustrating for both you and your buyer. However, when I file a missing package claim with UPS, the company is very good about following through. Usually within seven days, I have the claim paperwork and once it's filled out, I get a check within another seven days. This is another reason why I enjoy working with UPS. The three packages that went

> **Moneysaver**
>
> Once I know that my shipper (usually UPS) has approved the claim, I go ahead and refund the money to my buyer, even though I have not yet been paid by UPS. Your buyer will really appreciate this. With UPS, I know that the check will arrive quickly. And if the customer paid with PayPal, remember to go into the PayPal system to do the refund, so that your PayPal fees will be credited back to you. See Chapter 7 for more on PayPal.

missing this past Christmas were all left on people's porches and weren't signed for. UPS investigated quickly and paid the claim money for all three.

Your shipment arrives damaged

No matter how carefully you pack your items, something at some point is going to get broken. Make sure that you immediately answer a customer's e-mail about any damage, telling the buyer that you're very sorry. This is a tough situation, especially if it's an item your buyer had been searching for. The buyer may be very unhappy. Usually, if you packed it really well, the buyer won't blame you but will put the blame on the shipping company. However, if your buyer thinks you packed the item poorly, he or she will likely be very vocal about it. Keep a cool head and apologize again and again. It is better not to make excuses and blame others. Just say you're very sorry.

If your buyer paid for insurance or you required it, go ahead and file a claim with your carrier. Most carriers want the customer to hold onto the merchandise for a week, in case the carrier wants to pick it up for inspection. I have found that UPS picks up for inspection only items that are over $100 in value. However, this may be because I have been shipping with them for many years; it may be different with new accounts.

I had a gravy boat break several days ago, and I just filed the claim today. It was valued at $14.99, and UPS automatically approved it without even looking at the box. I just got the faxed paperwork saying it was approved. Even though the refund is

Watch Out!

If you don't pack your item correctly (according to your shipper's rules) your claim will not be paid. As an example, UPS asks for bubble wrap or double boxing, and then 2" of packing peanuts on all sides. I learned this lesson the hard way. I shipped a $500 glass Victorian Dome without double boxing it. It was a very tricky item to ship. It arrived broken, and UPS picked up the item and denied the claim. Ouch! Luckily, when UPS went to return the damaged item to me, it got lost. They ended up paying the claim anyway. My lucky day!

approved, however, you still need to provide substantiating documents. UPS asked me to fill out a form that includes the cost of the item and the shipping charges (they actually refund these, too), and then send proof of the value. For this, I faxed a copy of the eBay page showing the winning bid. The whole process took only about 15 minutes, and was definitely worth $20.00.

For claims with the USPS, you actually have to go in and wait in line to file them. It's a lot of bureaucracy and wasted time. If the item I shipped with USPS was relatively inexpensive, sometimes I just refund the purchase price without filing the paperwork. An hour of my time (and your time) is worth much more than $12.99.

You ship the wrong item

Shipping the wrong item happens far too often and can get complicated. It's a scary feeling when you realize that you have sent the wrong item. Here are some examples.

- I shipped 4 salad forks instead of 4 dinner forks.
- I shipped a 2005 Royal Copenhagen plate instead of a 2005 Bing and Grondahl plate.
- I shipped a biscuit barrel to one lady, and her perfume bottle to the biscuit barrel lady.

There are two places for error. The first is when you pull the item. Make sure you've picked the right item and double-check your listing, comparing the photo to the item in your hand. This is the first place you can make a mistake. For this reason, I like to have one person pull items to be shipped and a second person double-check the work. The second place is when you're shipping, especially if you mix up the paperwork or forget to write the customer's name on the box. Be very careful when shipping and placing labels on boxes.

What to do when an error is made? If you figure it out ahead of time, by all means, let everyone involved know about it. The best defense is a good offense. If you let your customer know about the problem before the package arrives, he or she is usually much easier to work with. When a customer alerts you to the problem, try to resolve it quickly.

In the case of salad forks being shipped instead of dinner forks, I opted to just send the extra dinner forks and told her to keep the salad forks. The salad forks had not sold, and it would have cost me more money in shipping both ways. The customer was very happy with this solution. In the case of mixed-up shipments, I asked each buyer to forward the package to the correct buyer and offered to pay for their time and shipping costs. Of course, the buyers were both so nice that they asked only to be reimbursed for their shipping costs and not their time. eBayers, on the whole, are an awesome bunch, and if you keep them informed about what is going on, they are great to work with.

Your customer leaves you negative feedback

Any of these reasons discussed in this chapter could be a reason for your customer leaving you negative feedback. Just remember that as long as you're keeping the lines of communication open with your buyer, you have a good chance of keeping your feedback all positive. Answer e-mails quickly and work diligently to find a solution that makes everyone happy.

However, negative feedback is a fact of life. I was two years into selling on eBay when I received my first one. I was devastated and couldn't get over it. I had bent over backward to make

> ### ☼ Bright Idea
>
> If you find yourself in a situation where you must leave negative feedback and are afraid of negative feedback retribution, leave the feedback as late as possible on the 90th day. Once the 90th day has passed, no one will be able to pull up that item number, much less leave negative feedback for you. eBay purges its items by item number after 90 days.

a fussy customer happy, and when it was all finished and she was happy, she still left me my first big negative. That hurt. There was nothing more that I could have done. She was new to eBay and wasn't happy that UPS took so long to deliver, that the package got rerouted, blah, blah, blah. Her complaints were endless.

So remember, just do your best and don't be upset if you get a few negatives. Look at the bright side and see how many wonderful positive comments you have. I just got a negative today (and I hadn't had any for a year), and I started to get upset, but then remembered that I had received 12,500 positives. Now, that is something to smile about!

Just the facts

- Be on top of your slow and non-paying bidders and file Unpaid reminders with eBay.

- Answer and read e-mails on a daily basis so that your buyers know that you are on top of things.

- Solve problems quickly.

- Remember that the customer is always right.

- File lost and damaged claims with your carrier as soon as you are notified about the problem.

- Refund your buyer's money as soon as you can.

GET THE SCOOP ON...
Relisting an item ▪ Setting up an eBay store
▪ Donating unsold items to charity

Chapter 17

What to Do if Your Item Doesn't Sell

J ust because your item doesn't sell the first time you put it up for sale on eBay doesn't mean your item will *never* sell. Quite honestly, putting an item up for sale for one week really doesn't give it the exposure it may need. If someone has been looking for an item for years, what are the chances that he or she looks at eBay that very week that you have listed it?

In this chapter, I show you how to relist your item and give it another week's exposure. If that still doesn't work, don't be discouraged: your item may need more than two weeks' exposure before it will sell. An eBay store gives your items a lot more exposure for a reasonable price. This chapter shows you how to set up an eBay store and discusses the different bells and whistles available. Finally, for those few items that will never sell on eBay (not at auction and not in your store), this chapter discusses your options for disposing of them.

Relisting items at auction

Suppose you listed your first ten items, but nothing sold. Don't be discouraged. eBay is a numbers game: it's all about getting as many items listed on the site as you possibly can. This means listing—and then relisting—your items at auction.

Keep in mind that once you have listed an item at auction, much of your most time-consuming work is done. To list an item for the first time takes work: you have to prepare the item, photograph it, and actually list it. After all that, you'd be crazy to give up and not keep going. eBay encourages relisting by offering to refund your second set of insertion fees (see Chapter 1) if it sells the second time.

Consider what this means in monetary terms. Say you paid 60¢ for the insertion fee (your starting price was $24.99), and another 35¢ for the gallery (see Chapter 1), for a total of 95¢ the first time out. Your item doesn't sell, so you relist it for $9.99. This costs you 35¢ for the insertion fee, and 35¢ for the gallery—a total of 70¢. If the item sells the second time around, eBay credits you the second insertion fee, or 35¢. It doesn't credit you any money for extra features, however, nor does it offer any incentives to list an item for a third or fourth time. (This tells me that eBay recommends listing an item only twice, then moving it to your eBay store. This is exactly what I do—see the following section.)

Watch Out!

If you wait more than 90 days to relist your item, it will have been purged from the eBay system, which means you lose all of your listing information. Make sure you either move an unsold item into your eBay store or relist it at auction before the 90 days are up. You don't want to lose all that information or have to input it again! eBay also states that your item must be relisted within 90 days of the closing date of the original listing, or you will not be eligible for the relisting credit if it sells the second time.

Knowing how to relist

To relist an item on eBay is really quite simple. Just go to the auction page by typing the item number into any search box. There are search boxes on almost all of eBay's pages. Once you are on your item's auction page, a big grey button shows up on the left-hand side that says **Relist.** Just click on this button, and you will be taken to a page that looks like Figure 17.1.

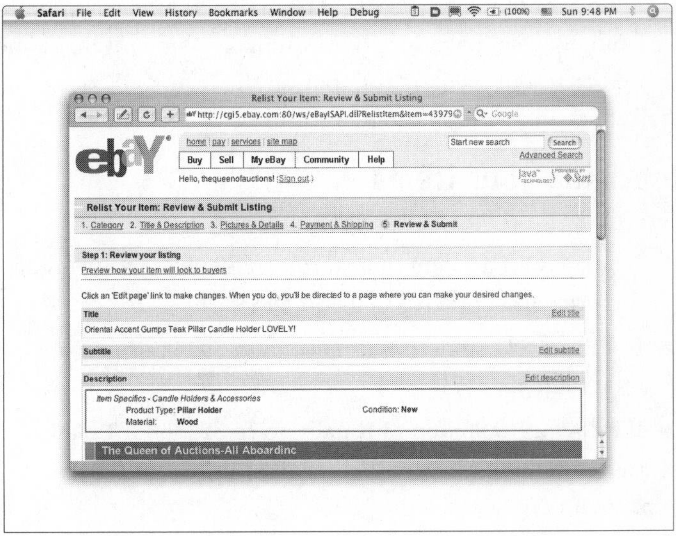

Figure 17.1. What the Relist your Item page looks like on eBay.

Just as you do when listing an item (see chapters 12 and 13), you see five hyperlinks across the top of your screen. Simply click on the area you want to change. If you want to work on your title, click on the second link, and up comes your title and description for you to change. If you want to change your price (and this is usually all I change), click on the third link, and up comes your pricing information. I also get rid of the gallery and delete any extra photos. If my listing price has to go down, one photo has to do! When you finish making your changes, click the **Go to Review** button at the bottom of the screen.

> **☼ Bright Idea**
>
> When I go to relist an item, I always check my counter first. Did 100 people look at my auction? Or did only five? If 100 people looked at it, the title was great, and I need to adjust my price. If only five people looked at it, my title could use some work.

After reviewing your listing, click the **Submit Listing** button at the bottom of the page. You'll be assigned a new item number from eBay, so make sure that you make a note of this somewhere. I cross out the item number on the front and back of my I Sell sheet and write in the new one.

Repricing your items

Here's how I reprice my listings:

- When I relist an item that started at $9.99, I always lower the price to between $1.99 and $4.99.

- If it was a $24.99 item, I usually go to $9.99, or perhaps a little higher.

- If it was a $49.99 item, I usually go to $24.99. If I really think the item is worth the $49.99, I may even relist it at the same price.

Although I follow these guidelines, I decide on each price on a case-by-case basis, and you will need to do the same. I also get rid of any extra features for the relist.

Timing your relistings

You may be asking about timing; that is, when should you relist it? Should you wait a week, a month, or list it closer to the holidays? Those are all great questions. I typically try to relist my items as soon as possible, so that I get the benefit of another week's exposure right away. Then, if the item still doesn't sell, I put it right into my store. The more items I have up for sale at any one time, the better. If I hold onto the listing and wait a month, no one will see it at all.

Opening an eBay store

Suppose your item has been up for sale at auction for two weeks, and you have had no bites. It's time to move your item into your eBay store. There is a monthly fee for an eBay store that you don't have when auctioning items and selling fees are higher. However, in an eBay store, items are cheaper to list. There are three levels of eBay stores: basic, featured, and anchor.

A basic eBay store

The basic eBay store is $15.95 per month, and this is where you probably want to start out. A basic store doesn't have the bells and whistles that the more advanced stores have (see the two following sections). I had the basic store for three years, and it worked just fine for me. I suggest that you get the basic store and try it out. For $15.95, what do you have to lose?

A featured eBay store

The next level is the featured store, and it's priced at $49.95 a month. This is the type of store I have now, and the reason I upgraded from a basic store is because a featured store gives you more exposure on eBay. When buyers do searches, a featured or anchor store comes up before a basic store.

Also, the featured store gives you Selling Manager Pro (see Chapter 15) for free, and I was paying $15.95 a month for this software, so the featured store really only costs me $34 a month. I upgraded about three months ago, and I have seen a dramatic increase in my store sales!

An anchor eBay store

The last option is an anchor store, which costs a whopping $499.95 per month. It's not for me—yet, anyway! It does, however, give you a lot more exposure on the eBay searches. Oh yeah, your first 30 days are free for any of these three options.

eBay store fees

Here are the insertion fees, also called listing fees (see Table 17.1), for all three eBay stores.

Table 17.1. Listing Fees

Duration	Insertion Fee	Surcharge	Total
30 days	$0.02	NA	$0.02
60 days	$0.02	$0.02	$0.04
90 days	$0.02	$0.04	$0.06
120 days	$0.02	$0.06	$0.08
Good until Cancelled	$0.02 for every 30 days	NA	$0.02 for every 30 days

So, it basically costs 2¢ per month to list any item at any price. The Gallery feature is an additionl 1¢ and I recommend using this. This is a great deal. I started out doing the 30- or 60-day duration, but then I was having to relist each item every 30 or 60 days when it didn't sell. Now, I list my store items as Good until Cancelled. My listings automatically renew every 30 days, and I'm charged 3¢ (2¢ listing plus 1¢ Gallery) every 30 days.

In Table 17.2 I list the store final value fees (also called selling fees).

Table 17.2. Selling Fees

Closing Price	Final Value Fee
Item not sold	No Fee
$0.01–$25.00	8% of the closing price
$25.01–$1,000.00	8% of the first $25, plus 5% of the price over $25
Over $1,000.01	8% of the first $25, plus 5% of the price between $25.01 and $1,000.00, plus 3% of the price over $1,000.00

Consider this example. If I sell something in my eBay store for $49.99, it cost me the listing fee shown in Table 17.1 (2¢ plus 1¢ for the gallery per month), plus the selling fee shown in

> **Moneysaver**
>
> All the same features offered with eBay auctions are offered in the eBay store. Extra photos (after the first free one) cost 15¢ each month, and this can add up. For this reason, I only use one photo in my store. If buyers want to see more photos, they can e-mail me. The gallery is only 1¢ a month, So I use this in all my store listings. (See Chapter 10 for information on photos and the gallery.)

Table 17.2. Suppose it was in my store for 6 months before selling, which means this item cost me 18¢ in listing fees. Compare this to listing the item at auction, which would cost $1.55 ($1.20 listing fee plus 35¢ gallery fee), and that's for only one week's worth of exposure!

The final value fee in the store would be $25 × 8 percent ($2.00), plus $24.99 × 5 percent ($1.25), for a total selling fee of $3.25. Including the listing fee, the total fees are $3.43. Not bad. Compare that to the fees if it had sold at auction. The selling fees would be $25 × 5.25 percent (that's $1.31), plus $24.99 × 2.75 percent ($0.68), plus the $1.55 listing fee, which is a total of $3.54. It would cost more to sell at online auction than it would to have six months exposure in the store. Wild!

Improved store search feature

One of the biggest benefits to having a store is that eBay has added a new search feature. In the old days, if someone searched for an item at auction and nothing came up, eBay wouldn't show the buyer what was available in the stores. This has now changed: if 1 to 30 items come up in a search, eBay will show additional items from the stores. If no items come up, eBay will show up to 30 store items. eBay chooses the store items to show based on first going with anchor store items, then featured store items, and finally basic store items. Since I upgraded to a featured store and eBay added this great search option, I've seen a dramatic positive effect on my business.

Setting up a store

It is relatively easy to set up an eBay store. There are a few simple requirements before you can open your store.

- You must have an eBay Seller's account (see Chapter 7).

- You must have a credit card on file with eBay.

- You must have a feedback score of 20 *or* be ID Verified (which costs $5 through eBay) *or* have a PayPal account (see Chapter 7).

Click on any of the free store trial buttons that you see on the eBay pages to get started. eBay then asks you to select a theme, provide basic information, and review and subscribe.

Selecting a theme

To select a theme, simply choose a layout that you like. I chose the Classic Left. Next, choose a color. I chose Sapphire Blue.

You can change these selections at any time—and it is fun to mess around with themes; however, when first setting up, choose quickly so that you can get your store up and running.

Providing basic information

The next page asks you to provide basic information. In Figure 17.2, you see the information I used to open my store.

Store name

First, choose a name: you get 30 characters for this. Choose something that reflects what you will be selling, or choose something close to your user ID to brand yourself even more. I chose The Queen of Auctions—All AboardInc, because I'm trying to brand myself as The Queen of Auctions.

Store description

Next is a very important section. You get 300 characters to describe what you sell and what buyers may find in your store. An eBay employee worked with me on this and told me to include all my important keywords, because eBay ranks really high on all search engines (such as Yahoo! and Google). This means that through your store's description alone, someone searching on the Internet can pull up your store by typing certain keywords. I made sure that I had "auction tracking," "how to sell on eBay," "dinnerware," "flatware," "antiques," and "collectibles" in my description.

Logo

Finally, you can use a pre-designed logo that will be displayed in all of your listings, but I highly recommend designing one of your own. It is a great selling tool, and I love how my logo looks in all my listings. Make your logo personable and friendly, and it will help buyers to feel comfortable buying from you. I use a picture of myself with a caption that reads, "The Queen of Auctions." I also show one of my books. I think it really helps buyers feel comfortable buying from a friendly face. I paid a graphics person (who happens to be my brother) about $50 to design this for me. It was so worth it!

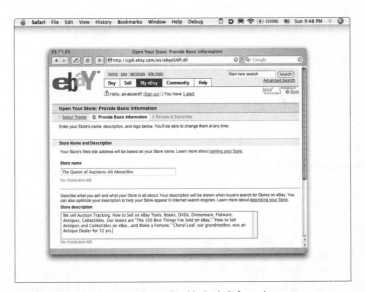

Figure 17.2. The Open Your Store: Provide Basic Information screen page from eBay, filled out with my information.

Reviewing and subscribing

Before setting up your store, eBay asks you to review and subscribe. Choose the level of store that you want (basic is what I recommend to start); then eBay asks you how you heard about its stores. (It would be great if you could click a button that says **Lynn Dralle,** but, alas, not yet.) Finally, just click **Subscribe,** and you have an eBay store.

Customizing your store

After you have subscribed and opened your eBay store, take the time to customize it. There are many ways to do this, and they go beyond this book's scope. So, here, I discuss the most important feature: creating and editing categories. I recommend, however, that you spend some time playing with all the available options.

Choosing categories

Categories are important for two reasons:

- They allow your buyers to search your auctions and store by category.

- At the bottom of every one of your auction listings, eBay shows four items from your store that are in the same category as your listing. This is a great cross-selling feature. See Figure 17.3 to see what it looks like.

☼ **Bright Idea**

eBay has another great feature for eBay store owners (the perks never stop). They actually have a toll-free phone number (866-322-9103) that is answered from 6 a.m. to 6 p.m. Pacific time, every day, by a real, live person who answers pretty quickly. I use this a lot! If you have questions about the customized options, give them a call. Don't waste any of your precious time trying to figure something out when expert help is just a minute away.

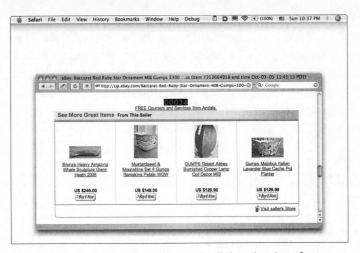

Figure 17.3. The bottom of one of my auction listings that shows four different items for my buyer to check out. These are from the same internal store category as my listing.

eBay recommends choosing categories that reflect the variety of merchandise you plan on carrying, so you're allowed to name up to 20 different categories. It also recommends having a category called "On Sale" or "50% off" to drive traffic to sale items. To give you an idea of category options, here are the ones I use:

> Royal Copenhagen, Bing & Grondahl, Auction Tools—
> Books & Videos, Books/Catalogs/Paper Items, Jewelry,
> Antiques, Collector's Plates, Trade Beads & Loose Gems,
> Lamps & Lighting, Collectibles, New Gift Items, Flatware,
> Dinnerware, Furniture, Clothing, Christmas Items,
> Pottery, Vintage Games/Toys, and Other Items.

Modifying your store

Any time you need to modify items in your eBay store, click on the little red door logo that appears next to your user ID. Your user ID, feedback number, colored star, PowerSeller logo (if you are one), and the red door logo show up on all of your auction pages and on your My eBay page. Clicking on the red door logo takes you to your eBay store page. At the very bottom, on the right-hand side is a button that says **Seller Manage Your Store.** (You can also get to this screen from the My eBay page, where the same button is on the left-hand side under My Subscriptions.) Clicking on it takes you to a Manage Store page. To modify your categories, look to the left, and you see a setting that says Store Design. Under this is a button that says **Store Categories,** which takes you to the page where you can input category changes.

Changing from an auction to a store listing

The last thing you need to know is how to take a listing that doesn't sell at online auction and move it into your store without having to reinput all the information. Here's how:

1. Pull up the item by using the eBay item number in any search box. Once it comes up, the front page will say **Relist** in the big button; down lower it will say To List Another One Like It Use the Sell Similar Option.

2. Click the **Sell Similar** button. Do not click the **Relist** button (you want to change the selling format and **Relist** doesn't give you that option).

3. When the next page comes up, scroll down and click on the button that says **Selling Format.** Please see Figure 17.4 to see what this page looks like.

4. Click the button by the option that says **Sell in Store Inventory**.

5. Click **Continue.**

   When you use the Sell Similar feature, you have to go through every single eBay screen (unlike Relist, where you can just go to the pages you need). This is kind of a time-waster. However, if you click **Continue** when Category comes up, and click **Continue** when the Title & Description page comes up, the only changes you need to make are on the third page, Pictures and Details. On this page, change your price to a fixed price.

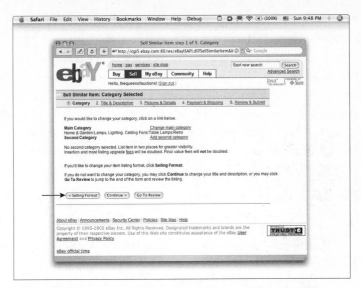

Figure 17.4. The eBay Sell Similar screen, where you click on the **Selling Format** button to move your item into your eBay store.

I price items in my store anywhere from $4.99 to $199. Sometimes, I even price the item higher than it ever was at auction. I have done this with dinnerware, raising the price from $9.99 to $14.99, $19.99, or even $24.99, and stuff still sells!

After you change the price, make sure the duration is what you want. I always use GUC (Good until Cancelled), take out any extra photos (15¢ each), and finally, make sure that the gallery has been added back in (only 1¢). Then click **Review** and review until you get to submit. Click **Submit,** and you have an item in your eBay store. Just like that!

Donating to charity, selling on consignment, or holding a garage sale

Holding a garage sale probably isn't your idea of a good time, but it is an option to get rid of some stuff that hasn't sold in your store after a year or two. I leave my items in my eBay store for one to two years, depending upon how saleable I believe they are. The listing costs only 3¢ a month, so a 36¢ investment to sell a $10 item isn't bad.

For non-selling items after 1–2 years, I have three options. I can take them to the local thrift store and get a receipt for a charitable deduction on my income taxes, I can take them to a consignment store, or I can have a garage sale.

I take only large, big-ticket items to my local consignment store. For example, I have a piano-type antique organ that I bought for $75 that didn't sell after six months in my eBay store for $199. So, I am taking it to my local consignment shop, because I must get it out of my house! My consigners will take 35 percent, and I feel that's fair.

The only type of garage sale that I have anymore is a $1 garage sale. It's easy to prepare for, because everything is $1 each. There's no pricing involved, and you can sell hundreds if not thousands of items this way. My family and I did this at the very end of liquidating my grandmother's estate, and it was a tremendous success. We sold about 4,000 items at $1 each over a three-day period. The customers loved it! And you've already tried selling your items on eBay, so you know that you aren't giving anything away. I encourage you to give it a shot.

Just the facts

- Always relist an item a second time at auction if it doesn't sell the first time.

- Try lowering the price or changing your title and description to encourage bids the second time around.

- If an item doesn't sell the second time at auction, list it in your eBay store.

- Customize your store and pick categories that make sense for you.

- If an item has not sold out of your store after a year or two, consider donating it or taking it to consignment.

PART V

The Future of Your Business and eBay

GET THE SCOOP ON...
Keeping loyal customers ▪ Marketing your eBay
store ▪ Building a platform

The Future of Your Business on eBay

You've been listing and listing and selling and selling, and you finally have a great presence on eBay. That's fantastic. Now you may be asking, how do I take this to the next level? Because about 20 percent of my sales are to returning customers, in this chapter, I talk about how to make and keep loyal customers. I also discuss how you can drive traffic to your auctions, and how you can market your eBay store.

Making (and keeping) loyal customers

Buyers who have had a successful transaction with you in the past are the easiest to market to. Here are some ideas to keep in mind when providing excellent customer service—note that most of these are based on reacting quickly and staying on top of your business:

- Answer all questions and e-mails quickly.
- Post questions and answers that will benefit others on the auction item page.

337

> ☼ **Bright Idea**
>
> Mention in your listing what similar items you might have up for sale during
> that same week. If I list an entire china set but have broken it out into many
> small auctions, I always say, "We have more of this wonderful pattern up for
> sale this week. Save on shipping with multiple purchases." Also, if I'm listing
> a lot of jewelry items, I say in my listing, "We are listing a lot of interesting
> jewelry and beads this week from my grandmother's personal collection. Please
> check out our other listings and save on shipping with multiple purchases."

- Offer a savings on shipping with multiple purchases.

- Ship as quickly as possible.

- Let your customer know that his or her item has shipped.

- Leave feedback (automatically) as soon as you are paid
  (see Chapter 15).

- Ask your customers to sign up for your e-mail list, so that
  you can let them know about special offers.

- Deal with problems as quickly and professionally as you can.

- Don't be afraid to offer partial or even full refunds. It will
  pay off in the long run and keep your customers happy.

Driving traffic to your eBay auctions

You can drive traffic to your auction in a number of ways, as
shown in the sections that follow.

Make the most of business cards

First, always put some type of thank-you card, business card, or
promotional flyer in every box you ship out. (I talk about promotional flyers in the "Marketing your eBay store" section,
because eBay has a fun program to help you make them.)

Also get business cards made to hand out to everyone you
meet, because you never know who could be a potential customer. My grandmother always gave a business card to every person she met; it was as natural to her as shaking someone's hand.
As soon as she was introduced, I saw her go for her purse, and I

can still see her pulling off the top business card to hand over. She was an amazing salesperson. You can be a great salesperson, too, by just remembering that you are your own best advertising.

Help customers hunt down special items

At least twice a week, people e-mail me looking for a special item, and I try to help them find what they need. Start wanted lists. A wanted list is just the item the person is looking for (like Noritake Princess Gravy Boat) and the person's name and e-mail. Keep track on a computer spreadsheet or database. You just never know what you may come across, and customers appreciate that extra touch. You can also send out an e-mail every so often to these people saying, "Just wanted to let you know that we are still looking for the _____ you requested. Please let us know if you would like us to continue our hunt or if you have already found this." At the end of the e-mail, of course, list your eBay store's Web address, note your eBay user ID, and include a request to sign up for your e-mail list. By showing that you care about your customers' special requests, you can help drive traffic to your auctions and your store.

Include the right keywords

One of the best ways to drive traffic to your eBay auctions is to make sure you have the correct keywords in your titles. I specialize in antiques and collectibles, so I make sure that my listings use "antique," "collectible," "old," "vintage," and "rare" in the title. If you specialize in books, make sure you use "book," "books," "fiction," "nonfiction," "antique," "rare," "first edition," and so on in the majority of your listing titles.

Collect e-mail addresses and build a platform

In addition to collecting e-mail addresses through your eBay store (discussed in the "Manage your listing header" section of this chapter), build your own mailing list. In every e-mail you send out, include a link to your eBay store and auctions, along with a button customers can click to sign up for your mailing

---

Watch Out!

Be careful with the e-mail addresses of your eBay customers. eBay is very protective of these and has specific rules about mass e-mails. You may send e-mails to customers offering them something similar to an item that they have already purchased from you through eBay on a case-by-case basis. To send an e-mail announcement to a batch of e-mail addresses, you need to ask these customers to sign up for your e-mail service. You must also give customers a chance to opt out at the bottom of each e-mail. This can get tricky, so I recommend using an e-mail list program to keep track of the names and addresses. These programs are called auto-responders, and most Web hosts offer them. Check with your Web host. I use Kick Start Cart as the host of my Web page and shopping cart, but there are many options.

---

list. Use this mailing list to let your customers know about great new items that have just come in, or to advertise a special sale.

E-mail your customers on a regular basis and build a platform or following. Make your e-mails personable and interesting. This will help to build a loyal following of repeat customers.

Link from other Web sites

If you have your own Web site (apart from eBay), definitely place a link or button on your home page that asks viewers to "Click Here" to see your eBay store and auction items. This is a great way to target customers who are already familiar with you and your Web site.

Linking from other Web sites is also a great way to drive traffic to your auctions. You can pay for placement on similar Web sites, but to get the most for your money, do your research and stay within a set budget.

Use Google, Yahoo!, or Alexa and find the names of similar or complementary sites that sound interesting. Next, contact those sites to see what they charge. Most of them charge by click, though. As an example, www.tias.com (a large online antiques and collectibles Web site) charges 30¢ per click for a banner ad, which is something I'd like to try. I already use the free publicity service offered on the Tias site. I can post press releases with photos for free, so I try to post a new press release every month. For more information on posting free press releases on the Tias.com site go to login.news-antique.com.

Network with similar sellers

You may be wondering why someone else who is selling similar items would want to network with me. Aren't we all competitors? No, we aren't. I learned this fact years ago from my grandmother, who taught me that the majority of antiques dealers are a super bunch of people. They are not mean spirited and are more than willing to help their cohorts in any way they can. This is the same with eBay. After exhibiting at eBay Live (2005) I have to say that I have never met a more helpful, gracious, and fun group of people. We were all happy and willing to trade tips, tricks, and secrets. It was a marvelous experience!

Other ways to network include attending trade shows and events, spending time in chat rooms, and joining clubs on the Internet. Once you have met some friends who are selling similar items, trade links on your Web sites or set up a referral system. You may also find chat rooms and category-specific areas on eBay to exchange information. I highly recommend spending some time researching how you can network with others, as it will certainly pay off for you.

☼ Bright Idea

I highly recommend that you attend eBay Live—a gathering of eBay executives, employees, and buyers and sellers—on an annual basis; it's held in a different city each year. There are exhibitor's booths, classes, special events, and basically three days of fun!

Marketing your eBay store

How do you market your eBay store? What can you do to make it more visible? There are six ways that eBay lists on the Manage My Store page (see Figure 18.1) under Store Marketing:

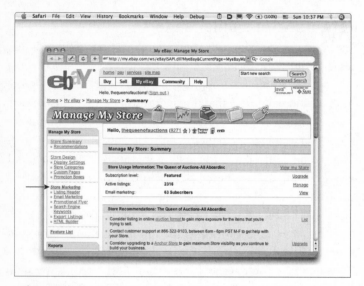

Figure 18.1. The Manage My Store page that shows the six marketing options on the left-hand side.

- Listing header
- E-mail marketing
- Promotional flyer
- Search engine keywords
- Export listings
- HTML builder

I take a quick look at each one in the following sections.

Manage your listing header

The listing header is basically the logo banner that I discuss in Chapter 17. See Figure 18.2 for an updated banner. Use a banner to build your brand and drive traffic to your store by including it in all of your eBay listings. When you click on the **Listing header** button, you also have the option of including a store search box in each of your listings. eBay recommends this only if you have a large number of active listings. I do, so I check this box. I also check the boxes that say **Include a link to Add to Favorite Stores** and **Include a link to Sign up for Store Newsletter.** This way, buyers can easily put my store in their favorites and easily sign up for my store newsletter.

Figure 18.2. My listing header shows up in all of my auctions and all my store listings. Note the store search box and the buttons to sign up for my e-mail list and to add me to your favorite sellers.

The last thing you can do on this page is to choose five categories to show up next to your store logo. This helps buyers see other items in a category; for example, if a buyer is interested in dinnerware, he or she can click on my **dinnerware** button and will be shown the 964 items that I have listed in that category.

Market through e-mail

The **e-mail marketing** option button takes you to a page where you can create e-mails and send them to anyone who has signed up to be on your e-mail list (see Figure 18.3). I just today added the button that includes a link from all my auctions to the **Sign up for Store Newsletter** button. I think this will bulk up the

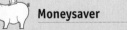

Moneysaver

As a Basic Store owner (see Chapter 17), you can send out 100 free e-mails each month. As a Featured Store owner (the level I've chosen), I can send out 1,000 free e-mails each month. After this number, each e-mail costs one cent. This is an inexpensive way to e-mail marketing promotions to completely targeted customers. Use this feature!

e-mail list I've already started on eBay. I currently have 58 sub-scribers, and I bet that number will increase quickly.

eBay allows you to send e-mails out only every two weeks, so get in a good routine and use this option. I sent one out in early May when I was having a special promotion. Then I sent one out in late May telling these customers about all the great new gift items at super prices that I have listed. It is a neat feature, because you can show photos of up to 20 of your items in the e-mail.

Figure 18.3. The marketing e-mail I sent out today through my eBay Store. I am sure that this will generate some interest!

Create a promotional flyer

eBay has another neat feature for eBay store owners: you can create and print out promotional flyers to include in all of your shipments to your buyers. You can choose different borders, fea-ture items from your store, and change the flyer as often as you like. You may want to feature books one month, and then feature kids clothing for back to school.

To make one of these flyers, click on the **Promotional Flyer** button on the Manage My Store page (see Figure 18.4)

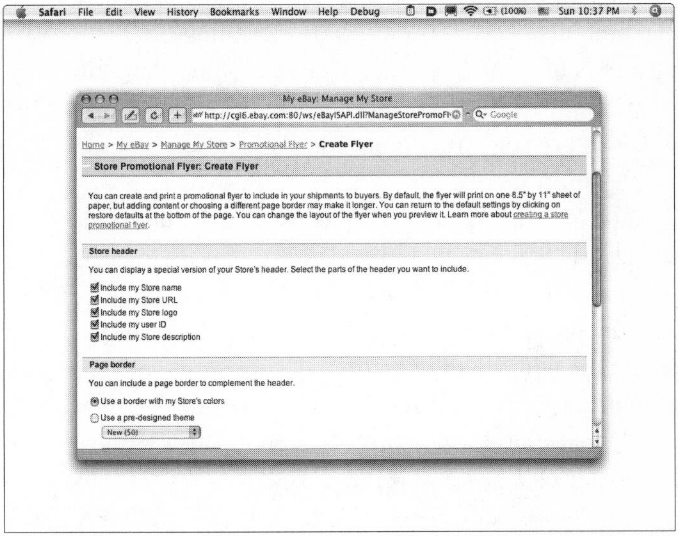

Figure 18.4. The Promotional Flyer set-up page. Notice how easy it is to use—even a computer-challenged person like me can make one!

You're asked whether you want to include your store name, store logo, Web address, user ID, and store description. I choose to include all of these.

Then you can pick a page border or not, and you have a lot to choose from. If, for example, you're going to be doing a back-to-school promotion, you could use books as a border.

You then have the option of entering a custom message. Just as with e-mail marketing, you can showcase items (but only four on the flyer) and also list up to six more items. Be careful, because if you choose too many, the text and photos will run over the size of one 8½ by 11 page, and you want to stick to that size so that you can easily print the flyers. You can change your flyers as often as you want and print them out on an as-needed basis. I highly recommend trying these!

Use search engine keywords

eBay automatically takes keywords from your store's front page and your 20 chosen categories and uses them to create page titles and meta tags, technical terms for things that help search engines better understand and present your eBay store pages. In this way, you increase your chances of potential buyers finding your store pages when they use big search engines like MSN, Google, and Yahoo!.

Click on the **Search Engine Keywords** button on your Manage My Store page and make sure that the ones that eBay has chosen for you are correct. As an example, when I checked the primary and secondary keywords on my store front, they weren't the best choices. My primary keywords were "The Queen of Auctions All Aboard Inc.," and my secondary were "dinnerware," "collectibles," "flatware," "antiques," "new gift items," and "jewelry." I changed my primary keywords to "The Queen of Auctions How to Sell on eBay Tips Tools Tricks," and I changed my secondary to "dinnerware," "flatware," "antiques," "collectibles," "royal Copenhagen" and "bing & grondahl." This is much more indicative of what I am selling. Check to see how eBay has listed your keywords and correct them, as needed.

Export listings

eBay makes available a file of all your store inventory listings. Once this has been exported, you can use it to expose all your listings to third-party search engines and product comparison sites. You need to make arrangements with these third-party partners to download the file. It will most likely cost money, and some of the third-party partners would be product search engines like Froogle, Yahoo!, and MSN.

I signed up for Froogle (an offshoot of Google) and found that it is free to download all of my listings. I had no problem following the links and signing up, but it got confusing when it was time to actually download the listings. eBay uploads all the

> ### ☼ Bright Idea
>
> Don't forget about the eBay store hotline, which is open 6 a.m. to 6 p.m. Pacific time, Monday through Friday, at 866-322-9105. Don't waste any of your time figuring out something when you can have an eBay store representative on the line within minutes. You may have to wait on hold, but it's still a lifesaver.

items in XML (extensible markup language—but you don't need to know that!), and Froogle wants you to download the items in a different format. This can be tricky, and I have hired my computer expert (my brother) to figure it out for me. It may not be possible to use Froogle, so here are some other options from my research: BizRate, Shopping.com, DealTime, MSN Shopping, mySimon, NexTag, Kelkoo, and PriceGrabber.com. These work but may cost you money.

Use the HTML builder

The last of the six marketing options listed on the Manage My Store page is the HTML builder. HTML stands for hypertext markup language, and it's used to build Web pages and links. eBay offers three really neat tools to create graphical and text links for your eBay store, eBay listings, or off-eBay Web site.

First, eBay offers a Simple Link Builder, which creates simple text or picture links to your listings, store pages, or store searches. Second, eBay also offers an Advanced Link Builder, which allows you to create a layout with multiple links to your listings, store pages, or store searches. Third, eBay has an Off-eBay Item Link Builder that creates dynamically updated links to your current store listings. This is really helpful, because it automatically updates as your listings change.

eBay has made these tools so easy that even though I'm computer illiterate, I didn't have to call my computer expert brother to build a link. Cool! I used the Advanced Link Builder for my off-eBay site, and now all I have to do is get the HTML link to my Webmaster (again, my brother). And it's worth having this link from my off-eBay site, because if a buyer gets to your eBay store from an off-eBay link, and that buyer purchases, you can get up to 75% of the store listing fees back as a referral credit. Now that is awesome!

Just the facts

- Do your best to keep and make loyal customers.
- Collect customer e-mails and use them to market to your customers on a timely basis with special offers.
- Network with other eBayers and similar sellers.
- Market your eBay store using the six free options on the eBay site.
- Your eBay store can be your biggest profit center. Spend time working on it.

GET THE SCOOP ON...
Reviewing eBay's predictions ■ Putting
eBay's growth to work for you ■ Understanding
phishing and fraud

The Future of eBay and Online Auctions

Chapter 19

The future for eBay and all online auctions looks really promising. eBay predicts more record growth, and I believe that more and more consumers will continue to embrace this marketplace. In my opinion, eBay will grow more into fixed pricing, while still retaining the auction flavor that made it so successful. As eBay grows and changes, sellers must grow and change with it. We must stay current, educate ourselves, and keep up with eBay. By doing this, we can use eBay's growth to our advantage.

One element that stands to hamper eBay's growth is phishing (phony, fraudulent e-mails), so this chapter addresses phishing, too.

Looking at eBay's predictions

eBay expects its record growth in both U.S. and international net revenue to continue. In fact, its international business will probably eventually outpace U.S. sales.

eBay also predicts increasing gross profits. To do this, you can bet that eBay will raise prices on a consistent basis over the years. Recent fee increases have really hurt small sellers, so we can only hope that eBay will hold off on raising fees for a few more years or find ways to increase gross profits without hitting the small mom-and-pop operators (like us).

Focus on store business

It appears that eBay is focusing on its eBay store business as opposed to its eBay online auction business, which is good news. I believe that eBay will work hard to grow this sales channel, especially because its back-end final value fees are so much higher than at online auction (see Chapter 17 about eBay store fees).

Buy up the competition

eBay will also need to stay ahead of its competition, because Google, Yahoo!, Amazon, and other companies are attempting to gain market share away from eBay. In response, eBay will continue to snap up its competition, like the purchase of PayPal and part of Craig's List (an online classified ad company) in the past few years. eBay has plans to purchase Shopping.com, and I have no doubt that this will continue to be a trend. If you can't beat them, buy them!

A trend toward high-volume sellers

eBay is also trying to woo large corporations like Disney, Sears, and Sony to sell on its site. Whether these large companies sell lots of overstocks, returns, or damaged goods in quantity or individually with fixed pricing, eBay wants to own Internet commerce—and to accomplish this, eBay is targeting those big companies for its site. This means that eBay is moving away from the mom-and-pop eBayers, so you want to watch carefully to see where this trend is headed.

I believe eBay will continue to promote a site of camaraderie and community, but what I noticed this year at eBay Live was that most of the exhibitors were larger companies. The tone of the event was that although all of the small sellers are endearing, eBay is going after the Titanium Power Sellers ($250,000 in sales each month), not the Gold ($10,000), Silver ($3,000) and Bronze ($1,000) folks like us.

Using eBay's growth to your advantage

We can all leverage eBay's growth and changes to our advantage. We must watch what is happening and always be cognizant of the new changes. eBay is an amoeba that is fluid and moving. Be smart and take the time to be on the site every day (if you are a serious seller), otherwise you will miss something important. During the six-month process of writing this book, eBay has probably made minor changes to 1,000 different pages. Be smart and know what is going on. In this section we will talk about two important areas for you to have an advantage.

The need to go international

The first area to focus on is eBay's international growth in revenues. eBay is looking to foreign buyers to help continue its impressive sales numbers, which means that as a seller, you must also look internationally. If you aren't currently able to ship to every country in the world, you need to figure out why not and see how you can make this a reality. The international marketplace will continue to help increase your sales, so you must make it easier for buyers from other countries to shop from you. Whether this means quoting international shipping rates right in the listing or immediately answering e-mails that request shipping quotes, be sure to address this opportunity. Stay on top of this trend and bend over backward to make each international customer's shopping experience with you a delightful one. Just as eBay has, you want to become more foreign in your mindset.

Adjust your business to thwart price increases

The best way to combat eBay's potential price increases is to shift your business to the areas where eBay's fees make sense. Here's an example: eBay charges only $80 to sell and list an

$8,000 car at auction (that's 1.0%), but charges $1.22 to sell and list a $10 vase at auction (12.2%) and $6.12 to sell and list a $100 coat at auction (6.12%). With price differentials like this, consider moving some of your business to areas where the selling and listing fees are a smaller percentage of your sales.

The bottom line is this: The higher your average ticket or selling price, the lower a percentage you will be paying in selling and listing fees. This tells you that eBay wants the higher ticket items listed and sold on its site. eBay wants the mom-and-pop stores to be doing big volumes. This can be you. Remember that it's just as easy to sell a $50 ticket item as it is to sell a $9.99 item. The time involved is literally the same.

The good news is that there will always be a robust online auction industry, on eBay and elsewhere. The online auction concept has won over many skeptics, and it will continue to thrive. There will also always be a market leader in this industry, and it is on the market leader's Web site that you want to list and sell your items. Right now, the market leader is eBay, and I believe it will stay there for many years to come. However, more competition can be a great thing for small sellers. As more and more companies attempt to steal market share, eBay will be forced to work harder to keep its sellers and buyers happy. This can only be positive for us. There are a lot of free auction sites out there right now trying to build market share and recognition. It can't hurt you to try some of them out. They are free!

More good news is that eBay is actively its eBay online store business (and I don't mean those pesky drop-off stores). My eBay store business is thriving, and I find that some days, I sell five to ten items out of it. It is really a neat way to supplement my income and sell items that I wasn't sure were saleable. Please build up your eBay store business (advice is in Chapter 17). It is a huge opportunity.

Avoiding fraudulent phishing e-mails

One issue that needs to be carefully monitored by eBay and sellers alike is the phishing problem. It is threatening the security of the eBay marketplace, so be sure to stay up-to-date on this important issue.

Phishing, also known as spoof e-mails, is when a third party sends you an e-mail that looks like it comes from eBay, PayPal, or any type of banking institution. The e-mail asks you to follow a link to update your account or to give sensitive financial information, in an attempt to defraud you.

Note: eBay and PayPal will never send an e-mail asking you to follow a link to input financial information.

Knowing this is the number one way to protect yourself. Always access eBay pages by going to the home page and finding the links from there.

I get about ten spoof e-mails every day (see Figure 19.1). Even though I know about phishing, I almost answered one this week and gave out my eBay user ID and password. It looked so real coming from an eBay member that said, "Where is my item? If I don't hear from you in two days, I am filing negative feedback." That got my attention, and I immediately clicked on the link to take me to the eBay item number. eBay then asked me to sign in, and I went ahead and inputted my information. Luckily, my computer expert had installed a firewall, which popped up and said, "Do you really want to send this information to skeleton88?" It was not sending my information to eBay but to a scammer. The sender on this was eBay Safe Harbour aw-confirm@eBay.com, and the subject line was "eBay Account—Suspicious Activity."

eBay says that if it sends you an e-mail asking for pertinent personal information, the request will also show up in your My eBay

 Watch Out!

Notice how real the fake e-mail in Figure 19-1 looks. The e-mail address looks real, too. But no matter how real it looks, never, ever follow a link from an e-mail when it asks you to update your information. Always go in through the home page, and then find the area where you need to input information. Almost 100 percent of the time, these e-mails with links are phony. If eBay asks you to update information, it will ask you to do it through its home page.

page under My Messages (on the left-hand side of the page). *Always, always access these messages through the eBay home page.*

The issue of phishing e-mails and fraud on eBay and PayPal must be addressed. eBay has been working diligently to combat this problem, but it's still out of control. It is my hope that eBay can wipe out phishing fraud in the near future.

Dear valued PayPal member,

Due to concerns, for the safety and integrity of your PayPal account we have issued this warning message. It has come to our attention that your account information needs to be restored due to following:

- inactive members
- frauds and spoof reports
- different IP logins to your account

If you could please take 5-10 minutes out of your online experience and renew your records and you will not run into any future problems with our online service. However, failure to update your records will result in temporaly limited account access and suspension.

Once you have updated your account records, your PayPal account service will not be interrupted and will continue as normal. Please follow the link below, login to your account and renew your account information:

➤ http://www.paypal.com/cgi-bin/webscr?cmd= login-run
            or the link below and select login.

➤ https://www.paypal.com

Sincerely,
PayPal Department

Figure 19.1. Sample phishing e-mail; it looks real, but isn't.

Just the facts

- Stay ahead of the curve and watch what eBay is doing.

- Shift your business to where eBay is shifting its business.

- Make international shipping a big focus.

- Never answer a phishing e-mail and always access important information through a Web site.

- Forward all phishing e-mails to eBay so that it can help wipe out this problem.

Auction House: _____ **Item #:** _____

Item: _____

ACTUAL LISTING

Category: _____

Description: _____

_____

_____

_____

_____

_____

_____

_____

_____

_____

_____

_____

**#
of days**

Listed: ___/___/___ ___:___ _____
      Date Month/Day/Year   Time   am or pm   Day of Week

Ends: ___/___/___ ___:___ _____
      Date Month/Day/Year   Time   am or pm   Day of Week

PAYMENT METHODS ACCEPTED

☐ Money Order ☐ Cashier's Check ☐ Personal Check
☐ Visa ☐ MC ☐ Amex ☐ Discover ☐ Escrow ☐ _____

PRICE

Minimum Bid: $ _____ **Reserve:** ☐ No ☐ Yes: $ _____
☐ **Actual Shipping** ☐ **Fixed Shipping: $** _____

Auction Comparisons	Sold at: $ _____
	No bids at: $ _____
	Reserve unmet at: $ _____

My Maximum Bid: $ _____ **Market Value: $** _____

BIDDING HISTORY/STRATEGY

_____

_____

_____

_____

_____

I WANT THIS ITEM....

0----1----2----3----4----5----6----7----8----9----10

Not very much   Medium   Very Much

Figure A.1. Front of I Buy sheet.

Auction House: _____ Item #: _____

Item: _____

SELLER INFO

Date Ended: __/__/__ # of Bids: _____ Winning Bid: $_____

User ID: _____

Email Address: _____

Name: _____ Phone:( ) _____

Address: _____

_____

City: _____ State: _____ Zip: _____

_____ Email: __/__/__ Reply: __/__/__

_____ Email: __/__/__ Reply: __/__/__

PAYMENT METHOD

$ Amount for Item: $ _____

$ Amount for Shipping: $ _____

$ Amount for Insurance: $ _____

TOTAL PAID-Date Sent __/__/__ $ _____

  Date Seller Received __/__/__ How Paid: _____

SHIPPING INFO

How Shipped: ☐UPS ☐USPS ☐FEDEX ☐_____

Tracking #: _____

Date Shipped: __/__/__ ☐Ground ☐Air ☐_____

Date Received:__/__/__ Notes: _____

FEEDBACK	Date	Positive	Negative	Neutral
I Sent:	__/__/__	☐	☐	☐
I Received:	__/__/__	☐	☐	☐

Picture of item or Payment Receipt

Copyright LA Dralle 1999

Figure A.2. Back of I Buy sheet.

Auction House: _____ Item #: _____

Item: _____

NOTES

Size: _____

Brand/Artist/Co.: _____

Markings: _____

Color: _____

Condition: _____

Age or History: _____ Quantity: _____

Photo Info: _____

ACTUAL LISTING

Title: _____

Category: _____

Description: _____

_____

_____

_____

_____

_____

_____

# of days

_____

_____

Listed: ____/____/____   ____:____ _____
       Date Month/Day/Year   Time   am or pm   Day of Week

Ends: ____/____/____   ____:____ _____
      Date Month/Day/Year   Time   am or pm   Day of Week

PRICE

Sold at: $ _____

Auction   No bids at: $ _____
Comparisons
          Reserve unmet at: $ _____

Market Value: $ _____

Date Purchased _____ Price Paid: $_____

From: _____

Minimum Bid: $_____ Reserve: ☐No ☐Yes: $____

☐Actual Shipping ☐Fixed Shipping: $ _____

ADDITIONAL NOTES: _____

_____

_____

Figure A.3. Front of I Sell sheet.

Auction House: _____ Item #: _____

Item: _____

BUYER INFO

Date Ended: ___/___/___ #of Bids: _____ Winning Bid $ _____

User ID: _____

Email Address: _____

Name: _____ Phone:(   ) _____

Address: _____

_____

City: _____ State: _____ Zip: _____

_____ Email: ___/___/___ Reply: ___/___/___

_____ Email: ___/___/___ Reply: ___/___/___

SHIPPING INFO

Package Weight: _____ ☐Ground ☐Air ☐ _____

Shipping Charges: $ _____ Date Shipped: __/__/__

How Shipped: ☐UPS ☐USPS ☐FEDEX ☐ _____

Tracking #: _____

_____ Email: ___/___/___ Reply: ___/___/___

PAYMENT METHOD

☐Money Order ☐Cashier's Check ☐Personal Check

☐Visa ☐MC ☐Amex ☐Discover ☐Escrow ☐ _____

Credit Card #:_____ Exp.___/___

$ Amount for Item:	$ _____	Sales Tax
$ Amount for Shipping:	$ _____	
$ Amount for Insurance:	$ _____	
TOTAL RECEIVED-Date __/__/__	$ _____	$_____

PROFIT/LOSS   LESS:

Listing Fee: $ _____

___% × ___ + ___% × ___ Selling Fee: $ _____

Additional _____ Fees: $ _____

Credit Card Fee ___%: $ _____

Actual Shipping Charges: $ _____

Cost of Item: $ _____

TOTAL PAID OUT: $ _____

Profit/(Loss): $ _____

FEEDBACK	Date	Positive	Negative	Neutral
I Sent:	__/__/__	☐	☐	☐
I Received:	__/__/__	☐	☐	☐

Copyright LA Dralle 1999

Figure A.4. Back of I Sell sheet.